GALILEE, JESUS AND THE GOSPELS
Literary Approaches and Historical Investigations

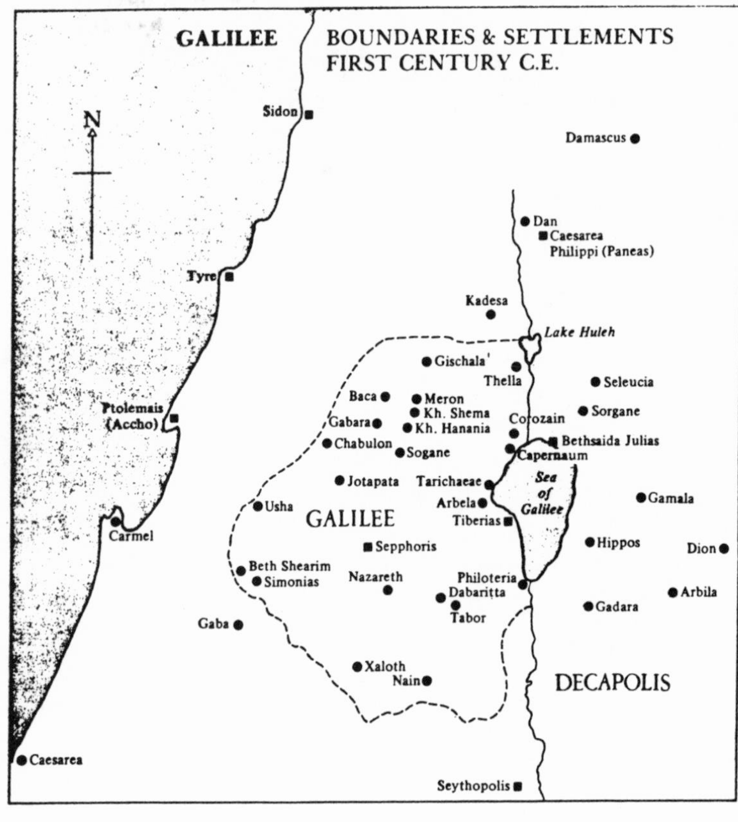
GALILEE
BOUNDARIES & SETTLEMENTS
FIRST CENTURY C.E.
N
Sidon
Damascus
Dan
Caesarea
Philippi (Paneas)
Tyre
Kadesa
Lake Huleh
Gischala'
Thella
Seleucia
Baca
Meron
Kh. Shema
Kh. Hanania
Corozain
Sorgane
Ptolemais
(Accho)
Gabara
Chabulon
Sogane
Bethsaida Julias
Capernaum
Jotapata
Tarichaeae
Sea
of
Galilee
Gamala
Usha
GALILEE
Arbela
Tiberias
Carmel
Sepphoris
Hippos
Dion
Beth Shearim
Simonias
Nazareth
Philoteria
Dabaritta
Arbila
Tabor
Gadara
Gaba
Xaloth
Nain
DECAPOLIS
Caesarea
Seythopolis

SEAN FREYNE

Galilee, Jesus and the Gospels

LITERARY APPROACHES AND HISTORICAL INVESTIGATIONS

FORTRESS PRESS
PHILADELPHIA

Indexes by Helen Litton

First Fortress Press edition 1988

Library of Congress Cataloging-in-Publication

Freyne, Sean
Galilee, Jesus, and the Gospels.
Bibliography: p.
Includes index.
1. Galilee in the New Testament. 2. Galilee (Israel)—History. 3. Jesus Christ—Person and offices. 4. Bible. N.T. Gospels—Criticism, interpretation, etc. 5. Jews—History—168 B.C.–135 A.D. 6. Judaism—History—Post-exilic period, 586 B.C.–210 A.D.
I. Title.
BS2545. G34F74 1988 226'.067 87–45890
ISBN 0–8006–2089–5

Manufactured in the U.S.A. 1-2089

94 93 92 91 90 2 3 4 5 6 7 8 9 10

Contents

ABBREVIATIONS

Standard abbreviations are used for the biblical books, apocrypha pseudepigrapha, Dead Sea Scrolls, tractates of the Mishnah, Tosepta and Talmuds. The Loeb translation of Josephus is used.

AASOR	*Annual of the American School of Oriental Research*
AGFU	*Arbeiten zur Geschichte des Frühjudentums und Urchristentums*
ANRW	*Aufstieg und Niedergang der Römischen Welt. Geschichte und Kultur Roms im Spiegel der neueren Forschung*, ed. H. Temporini and W. Haase, Berlin—New York: de Gruyter, 1972—
b	Babylonian Talmud
BA	*Biblical Archaelogist*
BAR	*Biblical Archaeology Review*
BASOR	*Bulletin of the American School of Oriental Research*
BJRL	*Bulletin of the John Rylands Library*
BZ	*Biblische Zeitschrift*
CBQ	*Catholic Biblical Quarterly*
CBQMS	*Catholic Biblical Quarterly Monograph Series*
Compendia	*Compendia Rerum Judaicarum ad Novum Testamentum*
ET	*Expository Times*
E.T.	English translation
ETL	*Ephemerides Theologicae Lovanienses*
FRLANT	*Forschungen zur Religion und Literatur des Alten und Neuen Testaments*
HR	*History of Religions*
HTR	*Harvard Theological Review*
HUCA	*Hebrew Union College Annual*
IDB	*Interpreter's Dictionary of the Bible*
IEJ	*Israel Exploration Journal*
J.A.	*Jewish Antiquities*
J.W.	*Jewish War*
JAAR	*Journal of the American Academy of Religion*
JBL	*Journal of Biblical Literature*
JJS	*Journal of Jewish Studies*
JPS	*Journal of Peasant Studies*
JQR	*Jewish Quarterly Review*
JR	*Journal of Religion*
JRS	*Journal of Roman Studies*
JSJ	*Journal for the Study of Judaism*
JSNT	*Journal for the Study of the New Testament*
JSOT	*Journal for the Study of the Old Testament*
JSSR	*Journal for the Scientific Study of Religion*
JTS	*Journal of Theological Studies*
M	Mishnah
NT	*Novum Testamentum*
NTS	*New Testament Studies*
y	***Yerushalmi*** (Palestinian Talmud)
PEQ	*Palestinian Exploration Quarterly*
PIBA	*Proceedings of the Irish Biblical Association*
RB	*Revue Biblique*
RQ	*Revue Qumran*

RScR	*Recherches de Sciences Religieuses*
RSR	*Religious Studies Review*
SANT	*Studien zum Alten und Neuen Testaments*
SBL	Society of Biblical Literature
SJOT	Scandinavian Journal of Old Testament
SJT	Scottish Journal of Theology
T	Tosefta
TDNT	*Theological Dictionary of the New Testament,* E.T. 10 vols. ed. G. Kittel and G. Friedrich, Grand Rapids: Eerdmans. 1968—
TZ	*Theologische Zeitschrift*
YCS	*Yale Classical Studies*
ZDPV	*Zeitschrift des Deutschen Palästina-Verein*
ZNW	*Zeitschrift für die Neutestamentliche Wissenschaft*
ZTK	*Zeitschrift für Theologie und Kirche*

INTRODUCTION

IT is surely significant that the only occasion on which the adjective Γαλιλαῖος, 'Galilean', is used in the gospels to describe Jesus is during his trial (Mt 26:69), and then by a maid-servant of the high priest, residing in Jerusalem. One detects a mild note of disparagement in her comment to Peter on the same occasion: 'You are one of them surely, for you are a Galilean' (Mk 14:70; cf. Lk 22:59), with a reference to their Galilean accent in Matthew's version of the exchange (Mt 26:73).

It is not that the evangelists seek to disguise the Galilean origins and career of Jesus; quite the contrary in fact, with over sixty references to the region in the gospel narratives about him. Josephus could extol the natural fertility of Galilee, the province which he himself was to govern briefly at the beginning of the first revolt. Yet, to call somebody 'Galilean' had definite pejorative overtones, at least from the point of view of first-century Jerusalem orthodoxy, it seems. Nowhere is this better illustrated than in the Fourth Gospel, when the Jerusalem Pharisees seek to discredit one of their own number, Nicodemus, who sought a fair trial for Jesus, with the taunt: 'Are you also a Galilean?' In the context this is equivalent to being 'ignorant of the law and accursed' (Jn 7:45–52), or to what was equally disparaging, being a Samaritan (Jn 8:48).

Josephus extols not merely the countryside, but also the courageous and unselfish character of its inhabitants, as he is about to take over command of the province, yet he cannot disguise entirely his true feelings about Galileans—feelings that are shared by his fellow Jerusalemites of the priestly and aristocratic classes. In his *Jewish War* he reports the advice given to the masses by the Jerusalem leaders as they were about to avenge a Galilean pilgrim who had been killed by Samaritans on his way to a Jerusalem feast: 'Take pity on your country and sanctuary, as well as your wives and children,' they urged. 'All these were threatened with destruction for the purpose of acquiring justice for a single Galilean' (*J.W.* 2:237).

The rabbinic sources are no more flattering, though of later composition and with their own axe to grind against Galileans in general, as the scribal schools were pushed northwards, especially after the Bar Cochba revolt in the second century. Galileans are quarrelsome, dubious in their knowledge and observance of halachah, and generally not very trustworthy. Not that Galileans are thought of as non-Jews, and the epithet 'Galilee of the gentiles' is never used to explain their inferiority, as perceived from the perspectives of the temple aristocracy or the scribal schools and their adherents.

One wonders if the stigma attached to the description 'Galilean' as it is encountered in the sources from the Second Temple period can explain the fact that Galilee plays such a small part in the vast amount of writing about Jesus, both ancient and modern. There has been little attempt to examine seriously the Galilean context of Jesus' life, and even less attention has been paid to the kind of Jewish faith and practice one was likely to encounter there. In modern times Emil Schürer's influence on subsequent treatments is easily documented. Since, according to him, Galilee had been judaised by the Hasmoneans as late as 100 BCE, one could not expect to find there a genuinely Jewish ethos, but rather a mixed population with a syncretisic religious mentality, as Walter Bauer wrote in 1926. Thus the ground had been prepared for Walter Grundmann's book, *Jesus der Galiläer und das Judentum*, (Leipzig, 1941), in which he argued that as a Galilean, Jesus was not a Jew!

If historians of Jesus have made little serious effort to explore the Galilean roots of his career, Christologians also have paid little attention to this dimension, even in their quest for the historical Jesus. As long as the high, Chalcedonian Christology remained unchallenged, there was little interest in the social and cultural context of Jesus' earthly ministry. True to the spirit of the age, the nineteenth-century liberal quest tended to romanticise the Galilean setting of Jesus' ministry, as well as the simple, unspoiled character of his Galilean fisher friends. Bultmann's lack of interest in the historical Jesus and the Jewish roots of early Christianity created a climate of scepticism in New Testament studies in which questions about Galilee and Galileans were quite unfashionable, and this state of affairs was naturally reflected in Christology also. The so-called new quest for the historical Jesus, inaugurated by Bultmann's pupils, did not rectify this situation with its desire to show the continuities between his kerygma and that of the early church in rather abstract categories.

It is against the background of this neglect of Galilee by both historians and theologians in their discussions of Jesus that the present study attempts to integrate questions of social identity and theological reflection. We shall be attempting as full a description as possible of the social and religious world of first-century Galilee, as well as Jesus' role in that setting, and investigating how such a picture coheres with his identity as this emerges within the narrative accounts about his life within the New Testament. The suggestion is that the particularity of Jesus' Galilean career is both historically important and theologically relevant. The approach will be both literary and historical. Insights and methods from various disciplines are increasingly brought to bear on the New Testament writings, since today, with a heightened hermeneutical awareness, many scholars have come to recognise that no one perspective can exhaust the possibilities of our texts, or adequately uncover their varied fields of reference. Such a pluralism of approaches has, of course, its own dangers. Keeping up with the latest trends can easily lead to anarchy, and some controls are called for. This remark may help to explain at the outset the decision to allow a literary approach to the gospels (Part One) to take precedence over the more usual historical investigation (Part Two), as the first step. Hopefully, a critical reading of the gospels may set a more realistic historical agenda than might otherwise be achieved.

I am indebted to many people for assistance of various kinds throughout the period of research and writing of this book. Critics of my previous study of Galilee as well as colleagues at Trinity College and elsewhere, with whom I have been able to discuss certain aspects and issues, will recognise their contribution to the discussion at various points. The Alexander von Humboldt Stiftung financed a study leave in Tübingen, during which I had many helpful conversations with Professor Martin Hengel. A generous grant from the Arts and Economic and Social Sciences Research Fund of Trinity College made a visit to Israel possible. On that trip I received invaluable assistance from Professor Gideon Foerster of the Department of Antiquities, and from his field staff in Galilee, as well as from Dr Dan Urman of Beersheba University. A two-month visiting Professorship in the chair of Judeo-Christian studies at Tulane University, New Orleans, afforded freedom from normal departmental chores and made possible the completion of the first draft. A complete second draft was achieved while enjoying the hospitality of my parents-in law, Joan and Ron Todd, on the Gold Coast in Queensland, Australia. However, as the work draws to a close, I am most deeply conscious of the invaluable support, encouragement and helpful criticism I have received from my immediate family—Gail, my wife, and my daughters Bridget and Sarah. I trust that by dedicating my efforts to them they will have some inkling of how much they mean to me in my work and in my life.

CHAPTER ONE

Jesus the Galilean: Problems and Prospects

JUST over a decade ago I began research on what for me was a very new field of enquiry, namely, the study of Jewish faith and life as these are expressed in a particular region, Galilee, during the Second Temple period. The suggestion was Martin Hengel's that there was need for a monograph which would collect the literary and archaeological evidence from antiquity for a region which at different times and in different ways had been the home of both the Gospel and the Mishnah. His magisterial study, *Judentum und Hellenismus* (Tübingen, 1973), provided a broad framework for understanding and interpreting social realities, cultural affiliations and religious beliefs and practices. In first-century Galilee, as indeed in all of Palestinian Judaism of the Second Temple period, these aspects of life were inextricably bound together.

Previous discussions of Galilean life had dealt with such issues mainly in the context of studies of Jesus and his movement and a number of stereotypes were repeated—Galilee as the hotbed of Zealotism; Galilee as a province seething with social and economic unrest due to exploitation; Galileans as lax in the matter of Torah observance and given to an apocalyptic outlook. Ernst Lohmeyer's study, *Galiläa und Jerusalem* (Göttingen, 1936), may be taken as both typical and influential in this regard. On reflection it was not difficult to recognise the source of some at least of these positions so securely held. An apologetic Christology, especially one imbued with liberal values, required a setting for Jesus' life that was the polar opposite of all that Jesus was held to have affirmed, since discontinuity with his environment was seen as support for his claims to uniqueness. A view of the religion of Second Temple Judaism as debased and sterile was also an essential ingredient of the picture. When these biases in the scholarly portrait of Galilee were recognised, it seemed to me that the evidence was capable of a rather different interpretation.

Yet the question of how to depict Jesus and his movement from an inner-Galilean perspective remained a live one. In my previous study, *Galilee from Alexander the Great to Hadrian. A Study of Second Temple Judaism* (Wilmington/Notre Dame, 1980), the gospels were used as one set of evidence among others for documenting the situation. Indeed when viewed from the point of view of the objectives of that larger project it was apparent that they gave us a very limited picture of Galilean life, even though the story is firmly anchored to the region. Despite this awareness of how thinly the gospels describe Galilee, the project of focusing on their portrayal of Jesus and his movement in that setting seemed a worthwhile one for several reasons. In the first place it afforded the opportunity to test again some of the conclusions of my previous study, taking account of new evidence, mainly archaeological, as well as the criticisms and suggestions of scholars interested in the field. Besides, such an enterprise posed wide-ranging questions of methodology concerning the nature of the gospels and the hermeneutical concerns of those interested in the history of Jesus. By explicitly raising these issues at the outset it is hoped that my own presuppositions will be made clear and that some definition may be given to the most adequate way to conduct a study of Jesus in Galilee.

1. Current Trends in Gospel Studies

It is impossible not to be struck by the variety of approaches that are current in New Testament studies today, particularly in regard to the gospels. Even if we ignore the structuralist stance which for the present at least seems to be somewhat on the wane, one can readily recognise two very different trends in the recent past, each to some extent building on the older approaches of form and redaction criticism. On the one hand there are the social world approaches that can be seen as a development of the interest in *Sitz im Leben* of classical form criticism. These now range from the descriptions of the total life-situation to the more theoretical application of various social-scientific models to that world. On the other hand, modern literary approaches to the gospels may be viewed as the extension of the better insights of redaction criticism, with its focus on authorial intention and the unity of the completed work. Again the range of approach is quite varied—from the more conventional analysis of plot, character and situation, to full-blown reader-response criticism as employed by such critics as Wayne Booth, Seymour Chatman and Stanley Fish. Initially at least, the insights of both approaches seem to be so divergent that no reconciliation would appear possible between them. The former is concerned with the extra-textual referent, whereas the latter concentrates totally on the intra-textual, fictional world. So different in fact are the concerns of each approach that the practitioners of the one often seem unaware of the aims of the other. In truth, however, both approaches have their strengths and their limitations, a brief consideration of which is the necessary first step in clarifying the stance of the present study.

Writing in 1975, Jonathan Z. Smith outlined four related but quite separate activities in the social description of early Christianity.[1] These were: i) a description of the social facts given in early Christian materials; ii) the achievement of a social history of some phase of early Christianity; iii) an analysis of the social organisation of early Christianity in terms of the social forces that led to its rise and organisation, and iv) an interpretation of early Christianity as a social world—that is, as a world of meaning that provided a plausible structure for those who chose to inhabit it. To these levels of social analysis John Elliot has added a further one—sociological exegesis—in which the methods and modes of analysis proper to sociology are brought to bear on a specific text.[2] In this way he proposes an eventual construction of the total social world of early Christianity, with the social worlds of each of the New Testament writings providing the building

1. See 'The Social Description of Early Christianity', *Religious Studies Review*, 1(1975) 19–25.

2. See *Home for the Homeless. A Sociological Exegesis of 1 Peter. Its Situation and Strategy*, Philadelphia: Fortress, 1981, 7–13.

blocks for such a construction. Elliot is particularly concerned about the explicit use of theoretical models in this task, either in exploring social worlds descriptively or in testing a particular hypothesis against the given data. It is only by aiming at such a level of methodological sophistication, he maintains, that various conceptual models can be tested against the available data and real advances take place by the choice of the most suitable one for analysing the data to be explained.[3]

In general it must be said that social world approaches have made us much more aware of the fact that early Christianity was not just a movement of ideas, but rather one in which new social configurations were to emerge with implications that were economic, social and political as well as religious and theological. Sociological theory does not have to be explicit in order to make it possible to do social history, yet, as Elliot points out, the very selection and organisation of various phenomena implies some conceptual model, and the effort to make this explicit does help towards an awareness of the perspectives one is in fact highlighting and enables a critical examination of these. Besides, a conscious use of models will help as a heuristic device in framing new questions that can assist in uncovering obscure or hitherto unnoticed aspects of our texts and the movements that gave rise to them, and to which they in turn contributed. Rigid adherence to theory has its own pitfalls, however, since it can lead to a desire to force the evidence into a mould for which it is not entirely suited and the consequent distortion of the evidence. A flexible approach seems called for therefore, given the nature of our sources, their distance in time from us and the partial evidence they provide about life in the ancient world. There must be a constant interplay between theory and evidence, and a readiness to abandon a particular theoretical model if it does not fit the evidence we do have. As a result it would seem that most sociological approaches to the New Testament will be descriptive rather than hypothesis-testing.

3. For his most recent discussion see 'Social-Scientific Criticism of the New Testament. More on Methods and Models', *Semeia* 32(1986) 1–33, especially 3–9.

Sociological exegesis as described by Elliot and others is concerned with individual texts. Yet its perspective is different from that which operates in literary and hermeneutical studies of the New Testament. In social world/historical studies texts are treated as windows, through which, by means of inference from their semantic, structural and paradigmatic aspects and by means of comparison with social structures and modes of interaction similar to those which they exhibit, a picture emerges of the social world they are intended to address.[4] Literary approaches, on the other hand, stress the creative moment of a text's production. In narrative texts a fictional world is created that functions as a mirror in which we encounter our own world-view, irrespective of whether or not the world of the text refers to a real world or not. Inevitably, the stress is on the author's creativity rather than on the referent of the text in the real world.

This tension between real and fictional social worlds is not the only one existing between the two approaches to the New Testament. As previously mentioned, there is quite a range of approaches to be found as we move full circle from a detailed consideration of the author, through preoccupation with the text, to a concern, finally, with the reader's creative role in the production of the text. At this point we would seem to be at the opposite pole to social world/historical approaches with their emphasis on the real author's intentions and the referential nature of the text.[5]

Among reader-oriented approaches to the New Testament reader-response criticism is the one currently most in favour.[6] This approach has applied to the phenomenon of the act of reading a basic insight in Paul Ricoeur's seminal article, 'What

4. See Elliot, *Home for the Homeless*, 11.

5. For a general discussion of the issues involved see my article, 'Our Preoccupation with History. Problems and Prospects', *Proceedings of The Irish Biblical Association*, 9(1985) 1–19.

6. This is apparent from the emergence of a special seminar dealing with reader-response criticism in S.N.T.S. the most influential society for the study of the New Testament. For a general orientation see E.V. McKnight, *The Reader and the Bible*, Philadelphia: Fortress, 1986; R. Fowler, 'Who is the Reader in Reader-Response Criticism?', *Semeia* 31(1985) 5–26. S. Moore's as yet unpublished doctoral dissertation, 'Narrative Homiletics: Lucan Rhetoric and the Making of the Reader', Trinity College Dublin, 1985, is in my opinion the most sophisticated application of the method to an individual gospel, as well as being a highly impressive discussion of the theoretic basis for the approach.

is a Text? Explanation and Understanding',[7] namely, that texts are not oral discourse that happens to have been written down. Ricoeur draws our attention to the 'benign deceit' of texts which lure us into thinking that we are listening to a recorded dialogue between a real author and a real reader. Yet, as he reminds us, the one (the author) is absent to the other (the reader) in the act of reading, and the same applies in the act of writing. The situation, therefore, is much more complex than we often suspect, and reader-response criticism provides us with a number of helpful constructs in order to better comprehend the phenomenon.[8] Thus on the text-production side the implied author and narrator, as distinct from the real author, emphasise the fact that the latter can distance his/her own personal characteristics from the narrative work being produced, thus underlining its fictional character as a telling rather than a showing. On the text-reception end the narratee and ideal reader constructs again help to emphasise the distance between the real reader and the real author and the need for the active involvement of the reader with the text in the act of reading, in order to capture all the instructions, hints and other guides to reading that are to be found within the text and addressed to an ideal reader. Thus the essential contrast between textuality and orality is highlighted. One feature of narrative texts in particular is the ubiquitous and omniscient narrator's presence and privileged insights into character, motivation and plot outcome. These are shared with the ideal reader in subtle ways, thereby highlighting the creative and fictional dimensions of such texts, no matter how 'historical' we deem them to be.

Many will question the advisability of using techniques that were developed in the context of the modern novel and its criticism for the study of ancient texts. This is particularly true because, as R. Scholes and R. Kellogg have pointed out in their influential study, *The Nature of Narrative* (New

7. Reprinted in *Hermeneutics and the Human Sciences*, ed. J. Thompson, Cambridge: Univ. Press, 1981, 145–65. See further my colleague, W. Jeanrond's important study, *Text and Interpretation as Categories of Theological Thinking*, E.T. Dublin, Gill and Macmillan, 1988.

8. For a succinct but useful recent treatment see S. Rimmon-Kenan, *Narrative Fiction: Contemporary Poetics*, London and New York: Methuen, 1983; also W. Booth *The Rhetoric of Fiction*, Chicago, Univ. Press, 1961.

York, 1966), there has been a remarkable development over the last few centuries in the management of point of view in narrative because of the opportunities that that genre affords narrative artists in combining empirical and fictional techniques of narration. At the same time these critics maintain that the modern novel should be seen as one stage of a much larger history of narrative, reaching back to earliest mythological narration.[9] As ancient narrative texts, our gospels can be seen as part of that history, indeed representative of an important and creative stage of its development within the Graeco-Roman world. In different degrees all the gospels can be shown to have combined both the empirical (in the sense of the historical and mimetic) and the fictional (in the sense of the didactic and romantic) aspects of ancient narratives, before these had become separated into discrete forms.[10] There is, therefore, both a historical and a didactic dimension to all four, even though it is the empirical perspective that dominates. Thus, Luke consciously veers towards the historical, differentiating between the past of Jesus and the present of his own day as is clear from the prologues to both his works, whereas Matthew, with his treatment of the main character as both model and teacher of the community, even in the present, is more concerned with the mimetic and didactic dimensions of narrative. Yet neither dimension is entirely lacking from any of the gospels. The modern novel has attempted to recapture some of these dimensions of ancient narrative before they became entirely discrete forms in terms of history and romance. The techniques that have been developed to uncover its sophisticated form may, therefore, not prove unhelpful in gospel studies also, provided they do not exclude any of the various dimensions and perspectives of our texts as unworthy of further investigation.

That is not to suggest that one can uncritically adopt the social world of the text as the real social world of the historical characters that are portrayed within the narratives. To do so would be naïve historicism in the light of our modern historical consciousness and our awareness of the

9. See *The Nature of Narrative*, 241f.
10. Ibid., 12–14.

nature of the sources.[11] Yet, equally, we cannot a priori exclude the possibility that some realistic features of the narrative dimension of our texts may have a genuine contribution to make in recovering the presumed actual world behind those texts. This contribution may not be the result of first-hand knowledge of the actual situation based on information, either personal or received. Yet it must be recognised that an accepted convention of all realistic narrative writing is the attempt at verisimilitude, which arises from the desire to be as convincing as possible, admittedly from a particular point of view, to an ideal reader. This striving for verisimilitude is not the same as reporting facts, but it will be based on the author's own life experience and the probabilities inherent in the situation being described, as these can be presumed to be shared by an ideal reader.[12]

Faced with the issues of fact and fact-likeness, modern studies, based on form and redaction criticism, have for the most part approached the gospels as stratified layers of tradition that can, through the use of proper criteria, be stripped off and dated after the manner of an archaeological dig, until eventually bed-rock Jesus tradition is arrived at. However, this approach labours under the increasing doubts about what constitute adequate dating criteria, especially the one of cultural dissimilarity.[13] In addition, such an approach has a deliberate bias against the editorial seams which are presumed to be worthless in terms of historical reconstruction, for anything but the final redactional level. Yet in the perspective of narrative criticism these very seams, which are usually utterances of the narrator, give reliable commentary for the ideal reader as the narrative progresses. It must be assumed, therefore, that such transitional passages are highly significant for the author/narrator and that careful attention will have been given to all aspects of their constructon. Foremost among these narratorial markers are the geographi-

11. See N. Petersen, *Literary Criticism for New Testament Critics*, Philadelphia: Fortress, 1978.

12. For a suggestive discussion of verisimilitude in narrative and the motivation of the author see S. Chatman,*Story and Discourse. Narrative Structure in Fiction and Film*, Ithaca and London: Cornell Univ. Press, 1978, 48–53.

13. See M. Hooker, in 'Christology and Methodology', *NTS* 17(1971) 480–88; she has pointed out the inherent weaknesses of the dissimilarity criterion.

cal and other topographical references in the text, and, on the assumption of a far greater degree of conscious verisimilitude than is currently regarded as likely, these passages become significant pointers for testing our hypothesis about the historical value of some, at least, of the realistic features of our gospel narratives.

2. The Galilean Perspective of the Gospels and Studies of the Historical Jesus

As mentioned in the Introduction, attention to the fact that Jesus was a Galilean does not feature very prominently in the various studies about him, either theological or historical. Some consideration of this curious omission in a representative selection of both approaches may help to clarify the aims and methods of the present study further.

Though the necessity and possibility of the quest for the historical Jesus continues to be at the centre of Christological discussion, it is obvious that the shadow of Bultmann's scepticism still lingers on. Consequently, it is the fact of Jesus' life, not the 'how' or the 'why' that is considered important. When those whom Schubert Ogden, in his important study, *The Point of Christology* (London, 1982), calls 'revisionist Christologians' have ventured further it has usually been to explore the inner life of Jesus and his relationship with God. Consequently, there has been little concern with the social and religious implications of his movement, insofar as these have manifested themselves publicly in a specific cultural setting.

Ogden has exposed the weaknesses of such an approach, both historically and philosophically, insisting that the real point of Christology has to do with the meaning of ultimate reality that Jesus disclosed and the consequent different understanding of human existence that was implied, both individually and politically. Yet Ogden and others, e.g. David Tracy[14] believe that because our documents are already the product of early Christian faith in Jesus, their earliest recoverable layers give us access only to the first Christians' existential-historical understanding of Jesus and not to the

14. See his *The Analogical Imagination. Christian Theology and the Culture of Pluralism*, London: SCM, 1981, 233–41 and 259–65.

empirical historical facts, which in their view can never be recovered. Once Ogden's philosophical categories are translated into those of a religious system, what he is calling for is an approach to Christian faith that examines the way in which the Jesus movement has reinterpreted the central symbols of Judaism and the consequent new way of life that emerged. Unfortunately, Ogden relies on the exegetical work of Willi Marxsen, who represents the post-Bultmannian position that even our earliest witnesses to Jesus are faith-inspired, and are therefore inadmissible for historical investigation of Jesus. However, a broader social world approach, such as that adopted by Gerd Theissen and others, moves beyond the historical scepticism resulting from a narrow form critical approach by focusing on the symbolic patterns and their functioning in a particular social milieu. Continuities and discontinuities of symbolic expression and behavioural attitudes are detected much more easily against the backdrop of that wider pattern of social change, and the proper historical inferences, both for Jesus and the movement that continued a certain way of life in his name, can be drawn with greater security.[15] In short, Ogden's statement about the point of Christology, once it is translated into the language of symbolic systems, can serve usefully to frame our question also, except that we now wish to include a particular place—Galilee—and a particular time-span—the public career of Jesus of Nazareth—in attempting to describe the specific expression of ultimate reality that Jesus' career manifested in that setting and the concrete implications for living that were involved for those who experienced him.

At the other end of the spectrum in terms of the Jesus-of-history debate are such liberation theologians as Leonardo Boff, Jan Sobrino and Juan Luis Segundo.[16] While sharing Ogden's political concerns, their starting point—explicit or implicit—is the concrete experience of marginality because of the oppression and poverty of many people in the third world

15. I have in mind here the work of G. Theissen in particular, *Sociology of Early Palestinian Christianity*, E.T. Philadelphia: Fortress, 1978.

16. See, respectively, *Jesus Christ Liberator. A Critical Christology for our Times*, E.T.New York: Orbis, 1978; *Christology at the Crossroads*, E.T. New York: Orbis, 1978; *The Historical Jesus of the Synoptics*, E.T.New York: Orbis, 1985.

today. They have, therefore, a genuine concern with articulating the political dimension of Jesus' career rather than with exploring the meaning of ultimate reality disclosed by him with its absolute claims on us. Consequently, these theologians operate with an overall trust in the synoptic tradition, while recognising the post-paschal point of view. In this regard the study of Segundo in particular shows a nuanced approach to the problem, and his own perspective is to look for signs of post-paschal eschatological and ecclesiological concerns retrojected back on to the accounts of Jesus' career, and to separate the one from the other. Furthermore, in assessing the historical Jesus' career one must avoid such anachronisms as imputing to Jesus a consciousness of a class-struggle or a preoccupation with religious attitudes, divorced from political, social and economic realities.

It is all the more remarkable, therefore, that no serious attention has been paid by these theologians to the distinctive features of the Galilean social and political situation, even though the synoptic accounts are their starting-point. Segundo writes: 'Jesus was a Jew, living in a Jewish milieu, and all the cultural co-ordinates of that culture passed through him' (p. 63). Yet in the subsequent treatment this insight is never adequately explored, and the political aspects of Jesus' words and deeds are often asserted rather than established in relation to an accurate assessment of the prevailing conditions in Galilee. A similar criticism can be levelled at Boff and Sobrino also. While the call to retrieve the political implications of Jesus' career is entirely praiseworthy the assessment of those implications does not always avoid the danger of allowing particular hermeneutical biases to cloud the historical judgments that have to be made in regard both to the actual situation that prevailed and to the impact of Jesus' deeds and words there.

Edward Schillebeeckx's two-volume work, *Jesus, An Experiment in Christology* (New York, 1979), and *The Christ. The Experience of Jesus as Lord* (New York, 1983), shows a greater awareness than do the liberation theologians of the hermeneutical issues involved in using the gospels for a history of Jesus, and is less sceptical of the possibilities of such an enterprise than Ogden or the post-Bultmannian exegetes whom he favours. Schillebeeckx recognises the problem of using the gospels for empirical-historical enquiry. The earthly Jesus is only recoverable from the sources insofar as the impact of his followers' encounter with him can be discerned from the various images in which the early Christians chose to express that encounter. Yet the kerygmatic statements of the New Testament, including the very earliest ones, are for, Schillebeeckx, historical in intent, and they therefore allow us to trace the career of Jesus as the anti-pole of the Christ-confessing churches, in that the figure of the historical Jesus lies directly behind the faith-inspired pictures given by the evangelists. In affirming the historical intention of the kerygma, he is not guilty of naïve historicism, since he recognises that all historical events are by their nature ambiguous, yet this fact makes historical enquiry all the more essential, since a critical Christian faith today calls for making decisions about certain historical events surrounding the life and death of Jesus that give them the character of disclosure for the believer.

It may be objected that this theological agenda already casts doubts on Schillebeeckx's findings since, unlike Ogden, he does not regard empirical-historical enquiry as having a merely negative function with regard to Christian faith by establishing that Jesus in fact existed and behaved in a certain kind of way. Yet it should be said in his defence that there is nothing improper in operating with a theological agenda, provided one continues to exercise a hermeneutic of suspicion, something that is not always obvious in the work of those who profess to be approaching the gospels in a purely objective manner. Rather, the difficulty is that Schillebeeckx does not follow through on his own hermeneutical insight that Jesus is the reflex side of the Christian kerygma. Had he done so, he would not have begun with the criteria of authenticity, of whose problematic character he is well aware, especially the one based on the dissimilarity of Jesus both to his Jewish environment and to early Christian faith in him, which inevitably distorts the continuities that were involved. The Galilean dimension of Jesus' career is of no consequence therefore, even though when dealing with the Fourth Gospel he takes seriously the fact that, according to that narrative, the Galileans were accepting of Jesus. Yet in Schillebeeckx's view this has consequences only for the post-Easter phase of early Christianity. One might have expected that his study would have begun with this dimension of the texts in the light of his earlier observations about the inaccessibility of the historical Jesus to us, except through the witness to him of the Christ-confessing churches. That starting-point, rather than one based on criteria of authenticity, would have raised the question of the importance of the Galilean dimension of Jesus' career, since it is central to all the accounts, even the early kerygmatic one of *Acts* 10:36–9.

This conversation with the hermeneutical assumptions of some of the more recent Christological writings, especially in the treatment of Galilee, has helped considerably in clarifying the goals of the present study. We were impressed by Ogden's statement about the point of Christology when translated into the language of a religious system, but were not convinced by his historical scepticism in regard to the gospels, which is somewhat dated. The liberation theologians have emphasised the strong social and political dimension of Jesus' ministry, even though they sometimes appear to lack a thoroughly critical approach in their historical reconstruction. Schillebeeckx has formulated the question of the historical Jesus in such a way as to overcome, at least in theory, the historical scepticism of Ogden e.g., yet in his execution of the task he would appear not to have carried through the necessary move from the Christ-confessing churches' portraits of Jesus to an enquiry into the historical Jesus in a Galilean setting. Indeed the absence of any concern with this aspect of Jesus' ministry confirms our initial suspicion that this is the neglected issue in contemporary discussions of Jesus. It remains to examine if this is equally true of the more historically oriented approaches to Jesus of the recent past. Our survey makes no pretence at completeness, but rather enters into a critical dialogue with some of the more significant accounts.

Several studies concentrate almost exclusively on the sayings tradition and, more particularly, on the parables of Jesus. While building on the earlier historical studies of Jülicher, Jeremias and Dodd, the more recent studies of Jesus as parabler have been greatly influenced by contemporary awareness of the rhetorical function of language. In particular, Amos Wilder's emphasis on the rhetoric of Jesus and Paul Ricoeur's theory of metaphor have been highly influential in North American parable studies.[17] Bernard Brandon Scott is the most explicit on the reasons for this concentration on the parables in the quest for Jesus: the sayings of Jesus give us direct immediacy to the intention of Jesus, unlike the deeds which are embedded in narratives that are not interested in answering our modern question about him. We can ignore for the present the fact that Scott seems so confident about knowing the actual sayings of Jesus[18] and notice instead that the alternative, namely, that we should perhaps be interested in what the narratives about Jesus do tell us, scarcely arises for him. Because studies such as those of Scott, Crossan and Funk, as well as others in the same tradition have a clear bias in favour of words over deeds, even though these too form an integral part of the tradition about Jesus from the start, one is entitled to ask whether this judgment is based on the nature of the evidence or on some more contemporary bias that finds the accounts of the deeds an embarrassment to the modern mind.[19] This is not to deny that real gains have been achieved in the recent parable research with regard to Jesus' intentions, but when other aspects of the Jesus-tradition are not, at least a priori, given equal weight, there is a real danger of distorting the picture from the outset and of modernising Jesus.

E.P. Sanders's important study, *Jesus and Judaism* (London, 1985), is virtually the direct antithesis of Scott's study, starting as it does from 'assured facts' about Jesus and moving outward from that solid foothold to less stable ground. For Sanders the sayings tradition definitely forms part of that unsure terrain that the historian of Jesus must traverse.[20]

17. See J.D. Crossan, ed., *Semeia* 4(1975), 'Paul Ricoeur on Biblical Hermeneutics'; A. Wilder, *Jesus' Parables and the War on Myths. Essays on Imagination in the Scriptures*, London: SPCK, 1982.

18. See *Jesus Symbol-Maker of the Kingdom*, Philadelphia: Fortress, 1981, 152f. Cf. his article on the historicity of the parables, 'Essaying the Rock. The Authenticity of the Jesus Parable Tradition', *Forum*, 2,1 (1986) 3–53.

19. See W. Beardslee, 'Parable Interpretation and World disclosed by Parable', *Perspectives in Religious Studies*, 3 (1976) 123–39.

20. See *Jesus and Judaism*, 13–18 and 141–50.

Indeed he is quite dismissive of Scott (and others), being critical of the failure of some modern parable-researchers to contextualise sufficiently the impact of the shocking or the strange in Jesus' parables within Palestinian Jewish culture.[21] Sanders is widely read in Jewish literature from the period, and one of the great merits of his work is that he is constantly seeking to identify the impact of certain actions (for the most part) of Jesus in their original setting. Indeed he repeatedly asks what the likely impact of one or other aspect of Jesus' career might have been in a Galilean setting, yet in the main his focus is Jewish in the broader sense without giving too much emphasis to regional differences.

However, there are other difficulties with Sanders's discussion. One may indeed be critical of studies such as that of Scott for their modernising of Jesus, yet the decision to treat the sayings tradition, or at least a major part of it, so lightly, while being confident about determining the meaning of certain deeds of Jesus, is equally open to criticism. The reason for this emphasis would seem to arise from the rigorous standards that Sanders sets himself as an historian, interested only in the unambiguous meaning of things.[22] Thus, he concentrates on facts (one is tempted to say brute facts) whose relationship with other facts can be plausibly established in terms of cause and effect. As one example among many, he quite rightly—in my view—believes that any account of Jesus and his intentions that does not explain his death and the subsequent rise of the early Christian movement, is not as cogent as one that does explain such happenings in first-century Palestine.

While there is much to be learned from Sanders's rigorous method of carefully sifting the evidence, and we shall repeatedly have him as a dialogue partner in the second part of this study, it is difficult to be wholly convinced by his dismissal of large sections of the sayings tradition. Equally, his declared views of history, which sometimes smack of positivism, appear to impede him from entering into the subject-matter

21. See *Jesus and Judaism*, 7 and 125–9.

22. For a sympathetic review that still is critical of his failure adequately to discuss the contribution of Jesus to first-century Judaism, as well as the neglect of the social, economic and political factors which bore on this, see John Riches, 'Works and Words of Jesus the Jew', *Heythrop Journal*, 17(1986) 53–62.

of his enquiry, either in terms of its religious—dare one say, its theological—intentions, or even of its social implications. This explains why his book lacks an adequate theory of the interaction between religion and society that would provide a suitable framework for interpreting the meaning of Jesus' actions and words in the Palestinian and, more particularly, the Galilean religious context. He is of course much more conscious of that setting than those who concentrate on the parable tradition seem to be, but one is repeatedly frustrated by his refusal to press further the 'hard' evidence he has so painstakingly produced, in the hope that it might yield a more coherent picture of Jesus and his movement.

Others too have taken the Jewish background seriously, in particular Geza Vermes, who has attended explicitly to the Galilean dimension. This focus calls for special hermeneutical care since so many presuppositions are lurking in the background—either for the 'Heimholung Jesu in das Judentum' or, alternatively, for the establishing of the superiority of Jesus' religious views in comparison with a legalistic and dried-up Judaism—a religion of law rather than of grace.

Vermes, it must be said, fits into the former category. In his earlier book, *Jesus the Jew* (London, 1975), Jesus emerges as a Galilean *hasîd* comparable to such figures as Hanina ben Dosa and Honi, the Circle Drawer, more concerned with the charismatic than the institutional aspect of Jewish piety, and hence not beloved of the Pharisees. Furthermore, the various titles of Jesus—e.g. Lord, Son of God, Son of Man—which in the hellenistic milieux of the gospels are charged with Christological meaning, are seen by Vermes as no more than respectful modes of address when understood in their proper linguistic setting of Galilean Aramaic, as this can be ascertained from the Palestinian Talmud in particular. In a second volume, *Jesus and the World of Judaism* (London, 1983), Vermes develops these ideas further, expounding the gospel of Jesus the Jew as having a particular emphasis on the intentions of the heart and the need to submit to God's kingly rule, understood in ethical rather than in political or apocalyptic terms. This trustful submission to God as Father meant an absence of concern with political, social and economic realities, and a natural bias towards the individual and personal rather than the collective. In a word, as a Galilean *hasîd* Jesus represents the heart and soul of Jewish piety, and his removal from the scene by other influential Jews would seem to be as unwarranted as it is unexplained in Vermes's depiction.

While Vermes repeatedly alludes to the Galilean Jesus, and in the former work has actually included a chapter on Galilean social and religious conditions, it must be said that neither the influence of that particular background of Jesus' experience of Judaism nor its impact on the scope and direction of his public ministry is ever explored. Vermes still operates with the stereotypes of Galilean life already alluded to, and hence Jesus' encounter with Judaism is as a non-observant (by Pharisaic standards) Galilean, who is rejected by the Pharisaic masters of Jewish piety. In the end Jesus is handed over to the Roman authorities by Jews responsible for law and order, not because he committed any crime, but because of irresponsible behaviour likely to lead to popular unrest.[23] Yet Vermes never specifies what this revolutionary propaganda was, and in the light of his apolitical, individualistic interpretation of Jesus' message it is difficult to imagine what it could have been.

Vermes's Galilean *hasîd* is not wholly convincing for several reasons, some of which will be examined in detail later. His failure to adequately recognise the interaction of social, political and religious aspects in first-century Palestinian life has left the Galilean background and the religious message of Jesus unconnected in his treatment, beyond such vague generalities as 'the unsophisticated religious ambiance of Galilee which was apt to produce holy men of the Hasidic type, and their success in that province was attributable to the simple spiritual demands of the Galilean nature'.[24] As well as a curiously uncritical historicism with regard to the gospels, what is really lacking in Vermes' treatment is once again any adequate theory of the social dimensions of religious belief,

23. This is in essence his response to criticisms about the apparent contradiction between his presentation of Jesus and the latter's rejection by his fellow-Jews, citing the examples of John the Baptist and Jesus son of Ananias, *Jesus and the World of Judaism*, viiif. For reasons to be discussed in our final chapter these examples are not wholly convincing as parallels to Jesus.

24. See *Jesus the Jew*, 80.

and of the way in which symbol-systems relate to other matters of culture.

John Riches has also undertaken a study of Jesus with the promising title, *Jesus and the Transformation of Judaism* (London, 1980). Here is a more sophisticated awareness of the hermeneutical challenges which confronted Jesus in re-interpreting certain received symbols within a particular social context, in order to bring about a changed understanding of God and his demands, since, in Riches's view, that is what he was about. How is it possible, for example, to speak of the kingdom of God, and avoid certain overtones that were part of the cultural assumptions about that phrase and inject a new and different vision? At what point do the continuities and discontinuities come clearly into focus? Riches's interest in the cultural conditioning of the semantic possibilities of language points him in the direction of the sayings-tradition, but he is interested in the whole range of the sayings, particularly the legal and wisdom elements, with the parables receiving a rather summary treatment in fact. However, his study differs from the parable-research already alluded to because of his much greater interest in the implications of Jesus' words in their original socio-religious setting.

Thus the Galilean context of Jesus' ministry is quite important for Riches, and it comes into play in his analysis of the impact of Jesus' deeds and words as part of his strategy to 'to make certain fairly fundamental alterations' to the general direction of his co-religionists' attitudes towards Hellenism, as these are reflected in the various detailed programmes of resistance to be found in the Pharisees, Zealots and Essenes.[25] The resultant picture of Galilee is one of economic hardship for a marginalised peasantry, leading to social anomie, and this view determines the way in which Jesus is seen as the prophet of the kingdom whose ministry inaugurates a new era, by translating into social terms a vision of the kingdom that embraced a different understanding of God, man and the world. His life represents such a radicalisation that 'his followers, if they were to be faithful to him, could not but break out on their own'.

Riches's view of Galilean life is heavily influenced by the

25. See *Jesus and the Transformation of Judaism*, 168f.

sociological study of Gerd Theissen, whose conflictual model calls for a social world in which a sense of alienation is the prevalent mood. But this is a generalised picture that does not take sufficient account of regional factors, as will emerge, hopefully, in a later chapter.[26] Insofar as such a criticism can be substantiated, Riches's study must be deemed to be flawed, therefore, even though his manner of posing the question, sensitive as it is to the linguistic and social dimensions of symbol-systems, is to be welcomed.

Two further studies of Jesus that have proved influential are Ben Meyer's *The Aims of Jesus* (London, 1977), and A.E. Harvey's *Jesus and the Constraints of History* (London,1982). These works differ considerably in their concern with method, yet they are both interested in taking the gospel portrait of Jesus seriously. According to Harvey, the criterion that 'there is a consistency and originality in the broad outlines of the portrait of Jesus as this emerges from the entire gospel tradition', has won general assent.[27] By applying his interesting idea of historical constraints, that is, the factors within a given culture which limit the potential actions of a subject, Harvey tests the reliability of the gospels' portrait of Jesus in its broad outlines, introducing external evidence, both archaeological and literary, to cast further light on the picture. The notion of historical constraints is a useful one provided it is used in a suitably critical fashion, so that the actor as well as the audience are both under the same constraints, and these are not viewed as a mere strategy on the part of Jesus. In this regard one might have expected that the social constraint of being a Galilean would have suggested itself immediately, yet it is scarcely adverted to, as more theologically inspired constraints are discussed. Besides, the notion of constraint could give rise to a rather deterministic view of history and one is also entitled to ask Harvey to elucidate the way in which the role of the innovator might be determined and profiled by his particular approach.[28]

26. This deficiency in Theissen's understanding of Jesus' ministry is only partly rectified by his highly original and imaginative (in the very best sense) study, *The Shadow of the Galilean*, London: SCM, 1986.

27. See *Jesus and the Constraints of History*, 8.

28. See the highly pertinent discussion of N.T. Wright, 'Constraints and the Jesus of History, *SJT* 39(1986) 189–210.

Meyer refuses to be controlled by 'the tyranny of the earliest stratum of the tradition' as the only gateway to the historical Jesus. Indeed, the opening half of his book is quite unusual among the historical studies we have been examining in that it shows a thorough mastery of the ideological assumptions, both philosophical and scientific, of those who since the Enlightenment have been engaged upon the quest for the historical Jesus, a quest that is indispensable in his view. As interpreters, historians must have their consciousness informed by the tradition which the to-be-interpreted has generated.[29] Thus Meyer insists on taking the gospel portrait seriously, since in his view, the gospel writers as transmitters of the kerygma include reference to the past as part of their overall intention, and so provide us with data about Jesus that needs to be critically evaluated, to be sure, by good hermeneutical practice. Trust in the tradition can be grounded in the intention of the early church to make a claim on peoples' lives on the basis of what can be said honestly and concretely about Jesus. Thus, faith and history should not be seen as competing alternatives in the quest for the historical Jesus, but as supportive of each other, provided each recognises its limits and how it can be of assistance to the other. Faith provides a coherent picture of Jesus based on the records he has generated, which make historical hypothesis possible, whereas history ensures that that picture is critically grounded by showing that faith intends past particulars, and is therefore both intellectually responsible and creatively instructive.

In applying his hermeneutical principles to the gospel portrait of Jesus, Meyer adopts the aims of Jesus, understood as both purpose and performance, as his point of entry into the Jesus tradition. Briefly, the aims of Jesus are to be understood in the light of Israel's eschatological vocation; in this light Jesus sought to rebuild the house of Israel in accordance with the remnant idea as found in the prophets. Thus, following the gospel records, Meyer distinguishes between the public performances (in deeds and words) and the private instruction of the disciples, whose vocation and mission constitute them as the true remnant.

29. See *The Aims of Jesus*, 58f.

We shall postpone a detailed discussion of this suggestion to the final chapter, when it is hoped to explore the *role* of Jesus in Galilee, a term that suggests more strongly the social dimension of his career, in contrast to the more personal and existential overtones which Meyer's term, *aims*, suggests. If there is any quibble with this admirable study it is the lack of emphasis on the social dimension. Inevitably, Gaililee does not feature in any prominent way, yet this omission is somewhat surprising in view of Meyer's earlier comments about the historical intentions of the early Christian portraits of Jesus, in which Galilee features prominently. Apart from the more obvious explanation for this omission, namely that Meyer's concerns are primarily theological, there is also the fact that he is still operating within a form-critical framework that pre-dates recent interest in the gospels as narratives and a broader understanding of the social worlds they reveal. Whatever the reason, it would seem that an exploration of the symbolic value of the remnant, particularly when linked with the symbol of the Twelve, with special reference to Galilee, could well prove to be a worthwhile exercise, expecially in view of the experience of Galilean Jews as a marginalised sector of society within the land of Israel.

3. Outlining an Approach

It now remains to gather the various insights that have been gleaned from the discussion up to this point, clarifying and as far as possible justifying the mode of procedure to be adopted in the present study.

It must be acknowledged that the whole emphasis in gospel studies has been on their historical rather than their literary character. Consequently, an approach that adopts a self-consciously literary stance is open to the objection of being unnecessarily reactionary, and of thereby ignoring the real gains of historical method as applied to the gospels. Yet our survey of the historical studies of Jesus has shown how particular judgments have come into play in deciding what is and is not to be regarded as valid evidence, especially in choosing between the deeds and words of Jesus. It is difficult not to recognise various biases operative in such choices. Indeed it would seem impossible to avoid such preferences coming into play if *our* interests rather than those suggested by *the texts* are allowed to dictate from the outset the agenda for the historical investigation. Even when the texts are made the starting-point for the enquiry, one is faced with choices that will call for justification, but hopefully these will be based on the available data, rather than on the interests of the individual researchers. It would appear, therefore, that there is good reason for starting with the texts that tell the story of Jesus the Galilean, and that not out of deference to the new trends, but in order to establish the proper set of questions for the subsequent historical investigation.

The claims of Schillebeeckx and Meyer concerning the historical intention of the kerygma about Jesus support this mode of procedure. In addition, the hypothesis formulated earlier, namely that historical and literary approaches to narrative may not be as mutually exclusive of each other in the study of the gospels, as is sometimes assumed, is a further encouragement to such an approach. The starting-point therefore must be the gospel narratives, and in order to highlight all the facets represented in the different tellings of the story, a reader-oriented approach to narrative would seem to be a worthwhile experiment.

In the past, literary approaches such as redaction criticism were often employed to satisfy purely historical aims, namely to uncover from later redaction the earlier strata of the tradition with a view to eventually arriving at bed-rock. Approaches to the texts which are prepared to recognise their fictional quality as narratives correctly stress their freedom from such concerns, since they aim at generating an appreciation of the work as a complete and independent creation. In the first part of our study, therefore, it is proposed to play the game of the text—to borrow Hans Georg Gadamer's expression— guided by an approach that will pay attention to the constructs of implied author, narrator, narratee and ideal reader, not in order to achieve a full reader-response performance of the gospel texts, but as a way of consciously reminding oneself that, as narratives, they are tellings rather than showings. At the end of such a reading of the gospels it appears that certain questions are likely to arise that are historical as well as literary in character, namely those of the relationship between the various accounts and their possible extra-textual referents.

However, the discussion of the various studies, both Christological and historical, indicates that the historical question regarding Jesus will not readily go away, however diverse the approaches and answers. A purely literary approach to Jesus the Galilean as he emerges in the various gospel portraits would not be adequate, because it would lack a critical awareness in the light of our modern historical self-consciousness, namely that as historical beings we make history, and cannot therefore ignore such issues in evaluating our foundational texts and their extra-textual referent.[30] Certain historical questions about Jesus the Galilean arise and call for further exploration, not because it is hoped to find evidence that will be so unambiguous that faith in Jesus will be fully vindicated, but because his life and ministry must be shown to be open to the interpretations with which they were subsequently invested by those who narrated them for us. If the opinions of those ancients and moderns who claim that Jesus was a magician or a charlatan, for example, were to be sustained, then Christian faith would be based on a serious distortion. But apart from this understanding of the contribution of historical enquiry towards a critically-grounded Christian faith, it has also the role of showing the continuities between Jesus and the first Christians in terms of intention and vision, despite the changed social and linguistic milieu.

Sanders rightly claims that any account of Jesus which explains the rise of the Christian movement would be more plausible than one which left this phenomenon unexplained. Yet he does not seem to recognise that such an explanation must necessarily involve real continuities between Jesus and his movement, something which Vermes in particular seeks to challenge. It is in exploring this issue that, as previously mentioned, a social world approach can transcend the apparent impasse regarding empirical historical evidence of the so-called objective kind. Social worlds, in the sense of shared values, attitudes and assumptions about life, demand certain

30. Cf. the reflections of Paul Ricoeur on the shared horizons of history and fiction in terms of the historicity of human experience in 'The Narrative Function' in *Hermeneutics and the Human Sciences*, 274–97.

symbolic expressions about the meaning of life, and hence it becomes possible to decipher the continuities between Jesus and his movement in terms of the continuing validity of key symbolic expressions, or, alternatively, the need for new ones, from one phase of the community's life to another. Thus a purely historical approach to Jesus needs to go beyond the bare facts to a more coherent view of his ministry in its social setting, especially in regard to the ongoing significance of certain shared symbols—those of torah, temple and land in particular—and to his re-interpretation of these within the new movement.

This brings us back to the question already raised about the proper methodology for a sociology of the Jesus movement within the context of a historical enquiry. John Riches, we saw, has drawn on the work of Gerd Theissen which is based on a conflictual model of social interaction. John Elliot's multivariate or matrix model is even more elaborate, including all the various factors of the infra- and supra-structure operative in Palestinian society that are considered to have been alienating for many people in that context. However, the use of such models assumes that Galilean social life was in such a state of anomie as the result of intense social and economic pressures that gave rise to an impoverished peasantry. If, however, one were to postulate a different view of Galilean social life, namely one in which a land-owning class with small but stable holdings was the dominant social strand in the province, then a rather different sociological model would seem called for. This is in fact the view of land-owning patterns that my previous study of Galilee has proposed, and accordingly we shall have to re-examine the situation in greater detail in a later chapter.[31] The point to be underlined here is that, implicit in any sociological theory is a certain pre-judgment of the social situation to be investigated, and there is need for a hermeneutic of suspicion through a constant dialectic between theory and facts. It is for this reason that a more eclectic approach to sociological models

31. See *Galilee*, 155–208.

was espoused earlier, despite the strictures of Elliot and others.[32]

The gospels may not spell out all the elements of a complete social system in the way that Elliot's multivariate model calls for, yet they do present a coherent social world, however selective each writer may have been. By allowing these narratives to set the agenda for the second part of the present study, we are not necessarily ignoring other aspects of life that are not explicitly present in the various tellings. We shall have to decide the relevance of the gospels' silence on various dimensions of life, as well as evaluate the significance—historical as well as theological—of those which do surface in the various narratives. In choosing as the starting-point the gospels, rather than a model constructed in the light of a modern sociological analysis, there is the undoubted benefit of avoiding the temptation to stretch the available evidence too far. At the same time it must be recognised that the selectivity of the gospels' presentation has its own inherent dangers for anyone attempting a critical assessment of Jesus, in that their selectivity is based on propagandistic and kerygmatic interests. It is our judgment that, despite such features, there is also a genuine 'historical' intention, part of which is to affirm the Galilean setting for Jesus' career and ministry. The challenge will be to recognise such intentions, and even allow for the possibility that the negative evaluation of Jesus by some 'outsiders' in antiquity may also have something important to tell us.

We cannot then, entirely avoid the dangers of reading into the evidence our own prejudgments, irrespective of whether the starting-point is the gospels or a critically constructed model. There is no purely objective starting-point in historical reconstruction, even when methods from other disciplines are introduced. Our reflections on the various approaches to Jesus, historical and theological, are not intended to suggest

32. Apart from his works cited in notes 2 and 3 above, cf. Elliot's review of W. Meeks. *The First Urban Christians*, New Haven and London: Yale Univ. Press, 1985, in *Religious Studies Review*, 11(1985) 329–34, which is at once appreciative and critical in that Meeks is 'reluctant to explicate his sociological theory and models', thus making it difficult to evaluate his conclusions. Cf. also the remarks of Bruce Malina, 'Miracle or Magic', ibid 12(1986) 35–9.

that they have all chosen the wrong options, and that the present study is somehow more objective. Rather, the discussion is intended to make our own approach and its inherent dangers more explicit, thereby, hopefully, avoiding certain mistakes of fact and method that might otherwise occur. Apart from anything else, our considerations have at least underlined the neglect of Galilee as an important dimension of Jesus' career, even though this is highlighted in all the gospels, and we know enough from other ancient sources to be certain that there were genuine differences—political, cultural and religious—between life in that region and in other parts of first-century Palestine. It is this incontrovertible fact, and the way in which it has worked itself through the reports about Jesus which have come to us, that provides the distinctive point of view of the present study.

PART ONE

Literary Approaches

CHAPTER TWO

Mark and Galilee: Location, Characters and Plot

ERNST Lohmeyer's study, *Galiläa und Jerusalem*, already referred to, continues to dictate the trend of research into Mark's use of geographical locale. His conclusion about the theological opposition within early Christianity which the author makes these two locations—Galilee and Jerusalem—represent, has not won widespread acceptance. Recently, however, E. Struthers-Malbon has described the subsequent redaction critical studies of W. Marxsen and W. Kelber, both of whom have sought to develop further Lohmeyer's insight regarding the Galilee/Jerusalem tensions in Mark's account, as over-concerned with the external reference of the text, and therefore not sufficiently attuned to the internal world which the narrative seeks to create.[1]

Unburdened with such historical concerns, she proposes both a diachronic and a synchronic reading of the gospel, following a model of analysis that is based on the structuralist approach to narrative of Claude Lévi-Strauss. Her subsequent reading of the Marcan text proves to be highly illuminating in terms of the polarities which it represents and between which the narrative seeks to mediate. The Galilee/

1. See E. Struthers Malbon, 'Galilee and Jerusalem: History and Literature in Marcan Interpretation', *CBQ* 44(1982) 242–55; W. Marxsen, *Der Evangelist Markus. Studien zur Redaktionsgeschichte des Evangeliums, FRLANT* 67, Göttingen, 1956, 35–59, who regards the concentration on Galilee in the gospel as an indication of a Galilean Christian community awaiting the Parousia there; W. Kelber, *The Kingdom in Mark: A New Place and a New Time,* Philadelphia: Fortress Press, 1974, 64-5, and most recently, *The Oral and Written Gospel*, Philadelphia: Fortress Press, 1983, 97–105, who views the Galilean focus of Mark as a criticism of Jerusalem-based authority within early Christianity, represented by the failed disciples and the family of Jesus. For a detailed discussion of such interpretations of Galilee from a historical perspective cf. G. Stemberger, 'Galilee—Land of Salvation?', in W.D. Davies, *The Gospel and the Land*, Berkeley: Univ. of California Press, 1974, 409–38.

Jerusalem tension fits well into this pattern, yet it proves unsatisfactory for our present project. Structural analysis is unconcerned with the surface structure of the text and consequently ignores those aspects of Mark's story that are of particular interest for our present study, namely location, characters and roles, except insofar as these point to the deep structures which are the real interest of such an approach. It is for this reason that we must now undertake an independent reading of Mark, while taking seriously Struthers-Malbon's point that the focus must be on the intra-textual referents, at least initially.

1. Location: Mark's Depiction of the Galilean Social World

First impressions are important, and the casual introduction of Galilee in the Marcan narrative comes as some surprise, considering the momentous event that the author/narrator[2] wishes to locate there—the announcement that the time is fulfilled and that the kingdom of God is drawing near (1:14). Despite this reluctance to set the scene in detail, the importance of Galilee is underlined by a subtle use of movement from the outset. The principal character who makes the proclamation, Jesus, comes from Nazareth in Galilee to be baptised by John. This, it transpires, is a highly important event for the reader, in that we are given reliable commentary as to the real identity of the main character by means of a heavenly voice, information that is not shared with any other character within the narrative. The Spirit which Jesus receives drives him to the desert for a first confrontation with Satan, during which he is assisted by angels. It is only after 'John was delivered up', that he returns to Galilee to make his announcement, under slightly ominous circumstances, admittedly. It is subsequently emphasised twice in

2. See D. Rhoads and D. Michie, *Mark as Story. An Introduction to the Narrative of a Gospel*, Philadelphia: Fortress Press, 1982, the first full length analysis of the Gospel from a reader-oriented approach. The authors rightly point out that in Mark the point of view of the author and that of the narrator is the same, though this need not always be the case. In the subsequent discussion, therefore, the term author/narrator will be used to denote that the author frequently uses the presence of a narrator to offer reliable commentary for the ideal reader.

this opening chapter that Galilee is to be the main theatre for the action to follow. First the narrator informs us that news about Jesus spread to all the surrounding region of Galilee (1:28), and later that he visited their synagogues in all the region of Galilee (1:39). What is noteworthy in terms of the social life is the fact that when we do visit a particular synagogue it seems to function as a genuine community centre, with all the people of the particular location, Capernaum or Nazareth, gathered there.

This deliberate emphasis on Galilee together with the absence of any detailed information about the place arouses our curiosity. In this regard the absence of any description of the region is in marked contrast to Josephus, who gives a detailed account of the physical features, the boundaries and the characteristics of the inhabitants of the region, the governorship of which he is about to take over (*J.W.* 3:35–40). One is entitled to wonder if in fact the author has no interest in his setting beyond the bare necessity of having to locate it somewhere. Yet a closer reading of the text as a whole suggests that such a conclusion would be premature.

Mention of the synagogues of Galilee draws attention to the overall ethos that the author seeks to portray. Though, as we shall see, there is a distinct preference for open-air settings and the narrative moves inside a synagogue on only three occasions (1:21 and 3:1, Capernaum; 6:1, Nazareth), the narrator clearly wishes to convey the impression that Galilee is dotted with synagogues (1:39). This initial and basic impression of the Jewish ethos is further confirmed by the respect for the Sabbath shown by the people of Capernaum, who, though eager to have their sick healed, waited until after sundown before bringing them to Jesus (1:32). Jesus also is careful to show respect for Pentateuchal law, by telling the cured leper to show himself to the priest before rejoining the community, in accordance with Leviticus 14:2–32 (1:44).

Yet this is not a Jewish world that is turned in on itself in any exclusive fashion. Movement into gentile regions seems relaxed and informal (5:1–2; 6:53; 7:24,31; 8:27), as Jesus journeys into the surrounding territories that are clearly non-Jewish: the Dekapolis, Tyre and Sidon, Caesarea Philippi. This gentile environment surrounding the ministry of

Jesus is highlighted by the narrator describing the woman Jesus encountered in the region of Tyre as: 'the woman was Greek, Ἑλληνίς, a Syrophoenician by birth' (7:26).[3] Equally, non-Jews can travel in Galilee as far as the narrator is concerned, for in one of the generalising summaries that punctuate the work we are informed that as well as the Galileans who followed, a great crowd from Jerusalem, Judea, Idumea, Perea (Beyond the Jordan) as well as from Tyre and Sidon came to Jesus 'hearing what he had done' (3:7f.). This listing of Jewish and non-Jewish territories without any concern for their differences shows that as far as the author is concerned such distinctions are unimportant. The arrival of people from such outreaches corresponds to Jesus' reciprocal visitation of similar regions at a later point in the narrative. Struthers Malbon sees this as a conscious juxtaposition which has deeper significance in terms of overcoming the tension between the familiar and the strange as part of the overall purpose of the work,[4] but for our purpose its significance lies rather in the assumption of easy intercourse between Jew and non-Jew which the author takes for granted in terms of the social world of Galilee.[5]

This in turn raises the question of how we are expected to understand the political realities in Galilee, especially since the handing over of John had struck an ominous note at the outset. Herod is the only political figure to intrude on the scene, and the world that he inhabits is very different from the one that the author is seeking to create. He is portrayed in best oriental fashion as a 'king', who on the occasion of his

3. M. Hengel, in *Studies in the Gospel of Mark*, London: SCM, 1985, 29f. sees this double description, the one referring to her language and the other to her ethnic background, as another indication that the gospel was written in Rome rather than Syria, since the designation Συροφοινίκισσα would make little sense in the latter context but is attested in both Roman literature (Pliny the Elder and Juvenal) and inscriptions as a special indication of origin.

4. 'Galilee and Jerusalem', 248f., 252.

5. In this regard it is at least debatable whether the expression εἰς ὅλην τὴν περίχωρον τῆς Γαλιλαίας should not be taken as an allusion to the old expression *galîl haggoyîm* Γαλιλαία ἀλλοφύλων (Is 8:23; 1 Macc 5:15), the 'circle of the gentiles' rather than 'all the surrounding region of Galilee'. However, we do not agree with G.H. Boobyer, 'Galilee and Galileans in Mark's Gospel', *BJRL* 35(1953) 334–48, who considers that such O.T. evidence as well as the ethnic situation of first century Galilee warranted Mark in thinking of Galilee as gentile and therefore a suitable starting-point for the gentile mission.

birthday shares a banquet with his great ones (μεγιστᾶνες), his military officers (χιλίαρχοι) and the leading men of Galilee (οἱ πρῶτοι τῆς Γαλιλαίας). As he lords it over them in best gentile fashion, unlike the servant king Jesus (10:42–5), he is caricatured as being vain and licentious, ready to perform a foul deed of having a good man murdered for the sake of keeping a rash oath to a resentful woman, even though he himself was interested in John.[6] We do not meet Herod or table-companions again directly in the narrative, though the main character warns his disciples to beware of the leaven of Herod and the Pharisees (8:15). However, this display of callous power is a pointer to a world outside that of Jesus and his retinue, and they are warned that both he and they can expect little sympathy from such people (10:33f.; 13:9), particularly in view of the associations with John the Baptist that had been established since the very beginning (1:9,14; cf. 9:9–13; 11:30f.).

Herod is also depicted as having a real if superstitious interest in religious characters: he heard John willingly, the narrator tells us, even though he did not understand him and was afraid of him (6:20). Ominously in terms of the plot, he has also heard of Jesus (6:14). It does not come as a great surprise then to hear of the warning concerning Herod's and the Pharisees' leaven, however difficult it is to be sure of what precisely is in mind.[7] Secular and religious power, in terms of

6. According to B. Schwank in 'Neue Funde in Nabatäerstädten und Ihre Bedeutung für die Neutestamentliche Exegese', *NTS* 29(1983) 429–35, the discovery side by side of two triclinia, one allegedly for men and the other for women, at Machaerus supports the accuracy of Mk 6:22,24. However, as narrated, the story is certainly coloured by a number of O.T. scenes of a similar kind, and, in terms of Mark's narrative as a whole, the real interest of the narrator is to contrast Herod as king (his official title was ethnarch) and Jesus the king of the Jews. Even if Schwank's suggestion has any merit it is noteworthy that Mark seeks to link Herod explicitly with the Galileans, in order to point up the contrast with the other Galilean king, Jesus. The expression οἱ πρῶτοι τῆς Γαλιλαίας is known from Josephus also. e.g. *Life*, 220.

7. It is noteworthy that neither Matthew nor Luke are happy with the unspecified nature of this image with regard to the opponents of Jesus, and both drop the mention of the Herodians. In Mt 16:12 we hear that the leaven of the Pharisees and Sadducees is their teaching and in Lk 12:1 that the leaven of the Pharisees is hypocricy. Yet the combination of Pharisees and Herodians is intelligible in the context of Mark's gospel. As R. Fowler, says in *Loaves and Fishes. The Function of the Feeding Stories in the Gospel of Mark*, Chico: Scholars Press, 1981, writing from a reader-response perspective: 'the reader who has followed their intrigues has a reliable intuitive feeling what the leaven refers to—the reader has seen these characters in action'.

the Herodians and the Pharisees, can come together to destroy the main character, first in Galilee (3:5) and later in Jerusalem (12:13f.), when they try to trap Jesus on a political issue of paying taxes to Caesar. Thus while the political realities of Galilee are not allowed to impinge on the story, the author is keenly aware of the far-reaching effects of secular power, which he carefully delineates for the reader, especially as it is likely to affect the main character and those who choose his way.

Closely associated with the question of secular power is the issue of wealth, in view of the opulence of the Herodian court on the one hand, and on the other, the rejection by the main character of material goods for his followers, who are enjoined to trust themselves to the hospitality of others (1:14–20; 6:8–10), an injunction which they failed to observe, the author/narrator wishes us to know (cf. 6:37). Yet the very injunction presupposes possessions in the first instance. Certainly we do not meet any grinding poverty in Galilee, as Mark depicts the situation.[8] In this regard the Jerusalem widow who cast into the sacred treasury her whole living, that is two mites, the relative value of which the narrator is careful to underline for the reader by giving the Roman equivalent (12:42), is an interesting example of urban poverty in contrast with the Galilean woman who had exhausted all her possessions on doctors, before approaching the wandering healer, Jesus (5:20). In this perspective the condemnation of the Jerusalem scribes who devour the houses of widows as they claim privileged treatment in the community (12:38–40) takes on a special significance, as we shall see.[9]

The lake-shore offers a good, if special, insight into the economic situation. Zebedee runs a fishing business that can accomodate both himself and some hired workers (μισθῶτοι) 1:20), and the 'other boats' of 4:35 suggest plenty of activity in that regard. At Capernaum we meet Levi, the tax-collector, probably a local officer in charge of border duties

8. Howard Clark Kee, *Community of the New Age. Studies in Mark's Gospel*, Philadelphia: Westminster Press, 1977, especially 87–97, has an excellent discussion of the economic and social aspects of Mark as these surface in the text, but with the assumption that these reflect the actual situation of the Marcan community.

9. H. Fleddermann, 'A Warning about the Scribes (*Mk* 12:37b–40)', *CBQ* 44(1982) 52–68, especially, 61–6.

rather than a Roman collector of tribute, and apparently there were many of his type in the region (2:13,15), thus suggesting a busy commercial life, due to the natural resource of the lake and the easy crossing it apparently afforded to other regions (cf.4:36; 5:1–2; 6:53; 8:10).[10] By means of these repeated crossings, or at least movements to different points on the lake-shore where crowds of people constantly congregate, the narrator has succeeded in painting a picture of a vibrant and thriving locality, even if we are often in the dark as to the precise points of embarkation and arrival.[11]

The narrative rarely moves far from the lake-front with any great detail, yet we are given a few hints as regards the socio-economic life elsewhere. Jesus is a craftsman (τέκτων) from Nazareth (6:3), which suggests mobility in terms of life possibilities, unlike peasants or share-croppers tied to a particular place because of the needs of cultivation. The crowds that have been with Jesus for a number of days, and so in need of sustenance, can expect to buy provisions in the surrounding fields and villages, and have the necessary money to do so, in the view of the disciples (6:36), and in this at least they are reliable commentators, it seems. There are market-places (ἀγορά) in the villages also (6:56; 7:4), suggesting exchange of goods of a more advanced kind than simple barter. The images chosen by the main character for his stories have a distinctly rural colouring, two reflecting the trials and tribulations of the agricultural life and one drawn from nature itself (4:2–8, 26–29, 31f.). Even in the urban setting of Jerusalem this use of rural imagery is maintained, as we hear the story of the absentee landlord who sends his servants at harvest-time to collect the produce (12:1–9), and the appearance of the leaves on the fig-tree suggesting the advent of summer (13:28-30).

Through this emphasis on the economic concerns of farmers and fishermen as well as by the use of symbols drawn from their world as the primary images for the message of the kingdom, the author/narrator has succeeded in conveying a

10. See J.R. Donahue, 'Tax-Collectors and Sinners. An Attempt at an Identification', *CBQ* 33(1971) 39–61.

11. For a discussion of the possibilities suggested by the various notices of embarkations and crossings and their significance within the Marcan narrative cf. E. Struthers Malbon, 'The Jesus of Mark and the Sea of Galilee', *JBL* 103(1984) 363–7.

very clear picture of the rural character of Galilee. Never once do we enter any city explicitly, and the location of Herod's birthday celebration is not mentioned—Sepphoris, Tiberias, Machaerus? Yet there is a clear perception of the distinction between city and village and the relations between these two different types of settlement as known from the hellenistic world generally. We are told that Jesus visited the villages of Caesarea Philippi (8:26), thus accurately portraying the relationship between the villages of a particular territory and the city to which they belonged, even though elsewhere the rare hybrid κωμόπολις is used, thus indicating the fluidity that existed in such terminology for that period (1:38).[12] In another narratorial summary a threefold division of settlements occurs: villages, cities and fields (ἄγροι), 6:56), each with its own market-place where people congregated and where the travelling healer could be encountered.

By a varied use of terminology for human settlements the author/narrator has succeeded in painting a diverse social world for Galilee, but one that is realistic with regard to the appearance of crowds and the spreading of the news about the main character and his activity throughout the region. Because of the links that existed between villages and other rural settlements with the cities, and particularly because of the markets, important information could be disseminated quickly, it is assumed, and the healer and his travelling retinue, for their part, made a point of visiting those places where people gathered for secular as well as religious activity.[13]

Our search for the social world of Galilee has proved more rewarding than appeared likely at first. Even though little overt attention is given to the matter, the narrative contains sufficient information to enable the attentive reader to catch a realistic glimpse of a world that is Jewish, but permitting of easy contact with gentiles, where similarity of social situation can transcend possible divisions of a religious kind (cf.

12. See A.N. Sherwin-White, *Roman Society and Roman Law in the New Testament*, Oxford: Clarendon Press, 1963, especially 127–33.

13. It is interesting to compare the assumptions of Mark in this regard with those of Josephus in his *Life*. He too assumes that crowds from the country (ἐκ τῆς χώρας) can be summoned easily and that news about Josephus and other main characters is quickly disseminated, *Life* 99f., 102f., 205f., Cf. *J.W.*2:602.

7:27).[14] Though cities are mentioned, the perspective is outdoor and rural for the most part, with the lake and its environs receiving special attention, so that one receives the distinct impression that Galilean life, both economic and social, is determined by this waterway, suitably named the sea of Galilee (1:14).[15] The threatening presence of political power, though graphically illustrated in one instance, does not intrude itself into the lives of people from the point of view of the author, therefore. Movement, both for the main character and for people generally is completely uninhibited. Economically, Galilee appears to be self-sufficient, with its estates and markets, thus explaining the presence of toll collectors in numbers. Fish and bread are readily available in the markets of city and village (6:36; 8:4), produced within the region itself (cf. e.g. 1:16; 2:23). It is a picture of adequate sufficiency rather than one of great wealth and grinding poverty side by side, apart from the one brief glimpse into the court circles. The contrast between rich and poor seems to be much more typical of the Jerusalem urban situation. We must now explore the significance of this portrayal for the development of the plot's religious dimensions.

2. The Religious Situation of Galilee, an Essential Ingredient of Mark's Plot

The main character returns from his Jordan and desert experiences to his native Galilee with a religious message of great consequence. The declaration that 'the time is fulfilled' is a clear signal for the reader that the message about the advent of the kingdom of God was eagerly anticipated, though we are given very little indication throughout the narrative as to the forms that expectation took. Unlike the

14. S. Chatman in *Story and Discourse* writes: 'In verbal narratives existents and their space, if "seen" at all, are seen in the imagination, transformed from words into images'. Yet, 'verbal narratives can also depict movement through story-space even in cinematic ways....Thus discourse-space is the framed area to which the implied audience's attention is directed by the discourse, that portion of the total story-space that is "remarked" or closed in upon.... Verbal story-space then is what the reader is prompted to create in imagination on the basis of the characters' perceptions and/or the narrator's reports' (101–4).

15. The more usual name for this expanse of water was 'the lake of Gennesar(itis)' or 'the lake of Tiberias'. Of the gospel writers Luke is the only one to reflect this more general and accurate description consistently: 5:1f.; 8:22; 23:33.

Galileans, however, the reader is well prepared for Jesus to make this announcement, since he/she has accompanied the omniscient and ubiquitous narrator to the Jordan and the desert and been privy to the voice from heaven and the assistance of angels, information that is withheld from all the other actors in the drama. The mystery that will continue to envelop the plot as it unfolds does not trouble the reader subsequently, who is thereby very definitely situated on the side of the main character from the outset. Nevertheless, certain questions arise from this opening sequence of events that call for exploration by the attentive reader. Foremost among these is the question of religious loyalty in the province. The depicted social world was Jewish, we saw, but that leaves many possibilities as regards the precise nature of the Galilean religious attitudes as envisaged by the author.

The narrator does not leave us in suspense for very long. Jesus' first appearance, after the call of the disciples by the lake-front, is in the synagogue at Capernaum. We are informed that he was teaching, though we hear nothing of its content, but instead a demon was silenced and cast out. This episode is framed by two reactions from the people in which a key word 'authority' ἐξουσία occurs. The narrator reports that the audience was spellbound at Jesus' teaching, 'for (the explanatory γάρ[16] he was teaching them as one with authority and not like the scribes' (1:21f.). Lest we should have missed the implication of this comment, we are again informed of their excited reaction at the close: 'they were amazed so that they said to one another, "what is this? A new teaching with authority".' We should be in no doubt about the excitement that has been generated with this privileged insight into the state of mind of the synagogue congregation, but equally we are to recognise the clear criticism of scribal teaching, in the contrast with this new καινή that is, of a different order) teaching of Jesus. It is a contrast of the new and the old as the main character will himself declare shortly, when challenged on the religious practices of his disciples in comparison with those of the Pharisees and the disciples of John (2:18–22).

16. See Fowler, *Loaves and Fishes*, 162–4, for the significance of this feature of Mark as 'reliable commentary' in a reader-oriented approach.

In order to underline the rupture with the past we are informed that Jesus left the synagogue quickly and entered the house of his new-found disciples, Peter and Andrew, where he cured Peter's mother-in-law. Even though this healing took place in private, at sundown in order not to violate the Sabbath, the whole city was gathered ἐπισυνηγμένη at the door of the house with their sick, whom Jesus healed. House and synagogue are being ironically contrasted here, it would seem, as the private place becomes the place of meeting, even for observant Jews, because that is where Jesus is to be found. His very next move is to a desert place (ἔρημον τόπον) to pray, even though previously he had encountered Satan in the desert (1:12f.,35), and the fact that the synagogue was the recognised place of prayer for a pious Jew further suggests that the Jewish scribal authority, and its place of influence, the synagogue, could no longer contain Jesus and his movement.[17] Yet these clear signals have been given without one example so far of Jesus' teaching or their reaction, so skilfully has the author/narrator made the point by the juxtaposing of various scenes. Perhaps what is most surprising is the fact that it is Jesus' actions, designated as teaching, that underline the inadequacy of the scribal point of view for the author, and their lack of authority in the eyes of the populace. Thus, though Galilee is Jewish for Mark, and that fact is vital for his narrative, its religious loyalty is not determined by scribal influence. There is a search for another way.

The subsequent role of these opponents in the narrative confirms initial impressions, since we are told that on two occasions scribes came down from Jerusalem in order to discredit Jesus. Jerusalem is the centre of scribal authority it would seem for our author, and it is there that we find them operating independently. Though they can be portrayed as

17. In a highly suggestive article, R.H. Lightfoot, 'A Consideration of three Marcan Passages', in *In Memoriam E. Lohmeyer*, Stuttgart, 1951, 111–115, points out that in Mark Jesus prays only when there has been a breakdown in discipleship: 1:35; 6:46; 14:32-42. In the first instance Mark uses a *hapax* for the N.T., καταδιώκειν, to pursue (a wild animal), to describe the attitude of 'Simon and those who were with him', thereby indicating the very inadequate response of those who are called to follow Jesus, which is a foreboding for the reader of what lies ahead. Cf., also, E. Struthers Malbon, 'Τῇ οἰκίᾳ αὐτοῦ: Mark 2:15 in context', *NTS* 31(1985) 282–92.

involved in halachic matters (2:15f.; 7:1,5), and in these instances their point of view is the same as that of the Pharisees, their main concern seems to be doctrinal: who has the right to forgive sins? (2:7); the identity of the returning Elijah (9:11); the resurrection of the dead, the question of the greatest commandment and the Messiah's Davidic ancestry (12:28,35).[18] All of these issues are central to the claims that the author/narrator wishes to make for Jesus' authority; it comes as no surprise to find that the scribes play a central role in having Jesus removed, as Mark presents the matter. The main character, with his superior knowledge of what lies ahead at Jerusalem, is able to alert us personally to the source of the opposition that will lead to his death. Thus the scribes appear together with the chief priests and the elders in the first prediction of the passion (8:31) and with the chief priests alone in the third prediction (10:33).[19] In Jerusalem itself we find them plotting with the chief priests (11:18; 14:1) or the chief priests and the elders (11:27; 14:43,53; 15:1) against Jesus. Their presence at the foot of the cross comes as no surprise then, as they join with the chief priests mocking the dying Jesus: 'others he saved, himself he cannot save' (15:31), a taunt that is full of dark irony for the author and his ideal reader.

The opponents of Jesus are therefore clearly and consistently delineated within the narrative, yet of the stereotyped triad—elders, scribes and chief priests—it is only the scribes who can be encountered in Galilee, and their central role in the plot is thereby highlighted. Indeed their opinions about the returning Elijah, a clue in the author's view to the identity of Jesus, can be cited by his own disciples, thereby showing

18. It is one of the merits of M.J. Cook's study, *Mark's Treatment of the Jewish Leaders*, Leiden: Brill, 1978, that despite a rather dubious reconstruction of sources, he seeks to distinguish between the various Jewish leadership groups, as seen by Mark. For the distinction mentioned here, see 81f.

19. Since the scribes are identified with the chief priests and the elders in the plot to destroy Jesus on the one hand, and on the other, can be joined with the Pharisees in disputing matters of law, Cook (p. 91f.) thinks of two different types of scribe, based on two different sources, which Mark has conflated. However, this is an unnecessary and doubtful hypothesis, and the range of the scribal influence in terms of their links with various other opponents within the narrative can be explained on the basis of the internal dynamics of the narrative. At the same time important nuances are missed if the opponents are all simply conflated into one group as in Rhoads Mitchie, *Mark as Story*, 117–22.

that they have failed to grasp the significance of their revelatory experience with Jesus (9:11,15). The scribes' misunderstanding of his word on the cross in terms of a prayer for assistance to Elijah (15:36f.) is highly ironical, therefore. As mentioned previously, they journey down from Jerusalem in an attempt to discredit the main character in his homeland. On the first occasion they accuse Jesus of being in league with Beelzebul, the prince of demons (3:22). The ideal reader is in an excellent position to adjudicate on such a charge, since we have witnessed the descent of the Spirit as a dove on him at the Jordan, and consistently Jesus has rejected demonic recognition (1:25; 3:12; cf. 5:7). We are not therefore offended at the tone of utter repudiation of the charge by the main character. And in order to reassure us that this definitive rejection of the scribes is justified the narrator explains: 'because they said, "He has an unclean spirit" ' (3:30). At the same time, in view of the identification of his new teaching with his power to do mighty deeds in the Capernaum synagogue, the attentive reader will not miss the point that it is the source of Jesus' power that the scribes have sought to undermine, and not directly his teaching, even though they are the professional guardians of the great truths, as we learn particularly in the Jerusalem section.

The scribes' second appearance in Galilee is no less confrontational, except that now they are joined by Pharisees also, and the issue concerns a matter of special halachah, namely, the washing of hands before eating, which, the narrator informs us, is a practice of all Jews, though the disciples of Jesus do not observe it. By implication at least it is he who is to blame for such laxity. Once again, however, the main character lays the most fundamental charge at their door, twice repeated: by their tradition they make null and void the word of God (7:8,13). The full implication of the counter-charge will not be lost on the ideal reader who remembers that the teaching of Jesus was already recognised as being of a different order to that of the scribes, because it was given with authority. In his reply to this charge of laxity he has now indicated the source of that authority; his word is the word of God. Little wonder that at Jerusalem, and in the temple, they will formally challenge him: 'By what authority (ἐξουσία) do you do these things? Or who has given you this authority (ἐξουσία) that you should do these things?' (11:28). This is indeed the fundamental question that the Galilean ministry raised, and it is altogether fitting that it should be posed, however ironically, at the centre of Jewish belief, namely the temple, which the main character had just previously claimed as his own through a citation of Scripture (11:17). The ideal reader knows the correct answer, already given by the Capernaum-synagogue crowd, but a subtle allusion to the baptism of John in Jesus' counter question certainly refreshes the memory concerning his Jordan experience, to which only the reader was privy. For our author then, Jerusalem-based scribal authority is the real source of opposition to Jesus, whose deeds of power gave his teaching an authoritative quality as being from God in a way that the scribes could never match.

This portrayal of the main opposition to Jesus coming from the scribes makes the episode of the friendly scribe whom we encounter in Jerusalem all the more remarkable (12:28–34). We are surprised when the narrator informs us that he recognised that Jesus had answered well to the question of resurrection from the dead, a reply that was based on a citation and interpretation of an appropriate Scriptural passage (12:26f.). The scribe now wishes to know the main character's opinion as to which is the greatest commandment, but the intimation of his favourable attitude to Jesus at the outset gives us a clear signal that, unlike other instances, this is not a trick question. This initial impression is confirmed by the sequel. On hearing Jesus' reply the scribe reiterates the point that love is the supreme expression of God's will, greater than all sacrifice, basing his answer also on a variety of Scriptural citations to make the point. With the authority that belongs only to one who already has proclaimed the nearness of God's reign, Jesus reassures the scribe that he is not far from the kingdom of God.

In the light of the general characterisation of the scribes there are a number of significant features to this passage. It is noteworthy that the scribe's response to Jesus is a covert attack on the temple and its cult, not altogether surprising to the attentive reader in view of the earlier confrontation between Jesus and the religious authorities, deliberately located by the narrator in the temple. Since Jesus' authority is 'from heaven', it is he, not they, who can pronounce on the nearness of God's kingdom, and the scribe who is declared close to it has had to distance himself from his fellows in recognising that God's presence was no longer definitively linked with Jerusalem and its temple. We are now in a much better position to understand why the scribes came down from Jerusalem to discredit Jesus already in Galilee. His whole ministry there was already undermining the absolute claims of their city and the basis for its control, the temple. Little wonder that the chief priests and the elders are the constant companions of the scribes in their efforts to have him removed, once the narrative reaches their city.

Unlike the guardians of the cult and the city, whom the author/narrator leaves in Jerusalem, the scribes are not tied to the city in the same way, however much their influence is dependent on its survival. This means that the Jerusalem scribes can link up with native Galilean scribes and Pharisees. The fact that the people of Capernaum contrast the teaching of Jesus with that of the scribes on the very first day, suggests that we are to imagine that they have been previously active in Galilee also, a fact that emerges later in that the Galilean disciples know of the scribal teaching on the return of Elijah (9:11), and on the same occasion we find them disputing with the crowd (9:15). Earlier we met (native?) scribes, again in the house in Capernaum as Jesus declared the sins of the paralytic forgiven. Though they keep their thoughts of blasphemy to themselves, the omniscient narrator informs us that Jesus knew their thoughts and openly challenged their assumptions about the connections between sin and illness, at the same time making the most profound claims about his own authority (ἐξουσία) on earth to forgive sins, as the mysterious son of Man (2:6–12). The implications of this claim are not lost on the crowd, who, unlike the scribes, react enthusiastically by praising God and declaring that they had never seen the like. Thus the implied negative comparison of the earlier synagogue scene is now openly asserted in front of the scribes in the new place of meeting, the house.

We already briefly met the Pharisees as instigators of a plot to destroy Jesus that would also have involved the Herodians. Yet this condemnation by association (in view of the negative portrayal of Herod) does not explain their religious opposition, since, despite their links with the scribes, they would appear to have had their own point of view, in relation particularly to halachic matters. They also have their own scribes who are offended at Jesus' table—fellowship with tax-collectors and sinners (2:16); their disciples have ascetic practices similar to those of the Baptist's followers (2:18); they are directly concerned with Sabbath observance, only to have their charge of Jesus' disciples violating it refuted by the example of David, who entered the house of God in order to feed his hungry followers (2:23–26), a suitably apt example from Scripture it would appear, since just previously Jesus had had a meal with tax-collectors and sinners in the house, much to the disgust of the scribes and the Pharisees (2:15–17). With the authority we now have come to expect, Jesus, identifying himself for the second time with the cryptic Son of Man figure, declares that the Sabbath was made for man, not man for the Sabbath, and then proceeds to put the principle just enunciated into practice by healing a man with a withered hand—in the synagogue, on the Sabbath and in front of the Pharisees (3:1–6)! It is this episode that led the Pharisees to join forces with the Herodians to destroy Jesus. In itself the incident scarcely warrants such a violent reaction, and the narrator underlines from his point of view the tragedy of the response by telling us of the mixed emotions (anger and grief) of the main character at their hardness of heart.

The subsequent appearances of the Pharisees in the narrative show, however, that their opposition is just as final and irrevocable as that of the scribes. They are at one with the scribes on the issue of the hand-washing, which the narrator regards as their particular concern (7:3), and hear Jesus' telling criticism of their attitude to the word of God (7:1,5). But the most serious indictment comes in their request for a sign from heaven (8:11–14), to which Jesus replies with a cry of anguish about this faithless generation. The irony of the request will not be lost on the reader, since we are aware, chiefly because of the voice from heaven whose utterance at the Jordan we have heard, that all of Jesus' actions are indeed signs from heaven in that they are performed in the power of the Spirit then received. Thus, from the point of view of the author/narrator they are indeed beyond hope, just as the scribes were regarded earlier.[20]

In describing the main opposition to Jesus we have constantly sought the author's judgment of the situation.[21] Clearly, the chief concern is to convey a picture of enthusiastic popular reaction, side by side with small-minded and malicious attitudes that are tantamount to spiritual blindness on the part of the Pharisees in Galilee, but particularly on the part of the Jerusalem scribes. Their position among the people is seriously challenged from the outset by Jesus' authority, and his teaching is described as new (καινή), that is, of a different order. The word that best describes this difference for the author is ἐξουσία, authority, which manifests itself not just in his words but in his works as well. We are given incidental flashes of broader religious belief, but these are undeveloped by comparison with the opponents' point of view. Thus the Baptist has disciples with ascetical practices and deep loyalty to their master (6:29), but apart from this we hear nothing about them. A synagogue leader with a sick daughter has no qualms in approaching the wandering healer, lately returned from gentile territory where he was in contact with swine, and who, on the way to his home was touched by a woman with a continuous flux of blood (5:21,25), thereby showing scant regard for the purity laws. Twice we hear of popular reactions to Jesus as a possible saviour figure—John the Baptist *redivivus*, Elijah or the Mosaic prophet (6:14f.; 8:28)—suggesting a general atmosphere of expectation, something the author underlines by the tone of the announcement concerning the imminent arrival of the reign of God (1:14; 9:1). This does not surprise us in view of the repeated portrayal of the crowd as

20. Yet we cannot ignore their absence during the trial scene, even though we meet them in Judea and Jerusalem (10:1; 12:13). Cook explains this absence in terms of his pre-Marcan sources, and claims that they are present in effect through the scribal presence. However, this seems to be somewhat contrived in view of their hostile treatment elsewhere. It seems more likely that they are deliberately absent, since they are for Mark a Galilean phenomenon, whereas the scribes are from Jerusalem.

21. On point of view in Mark cf. N. Petersen, 'Point of View in Mark's Narrative', *Semeia* 12(1978) 97–121; Rhoads and Mitchie, *Mark as Story*, 35–44.

enthusiastic and sympathetic (1:32; 2:12f.; 3:7,9; 4:1; 5:31; 6:31, 34, 45, 55; 8:1), even if their discernment does not always win the approval of the author/narrator. In such a climate the scribal rejection of Jesus is all the more ironic, since, as we have seen, they are guardians of such doctrines about Israel's future as the coming of Elijah (9:11) and the Messiah's relation to David (12:15). The final comment of the author on their attitude is left to the main character who, seated opposite the temple treasury, roundly condemns their posturing in public and private life and the greed that discredits their religious practices (12:38–40).

It is not difficult to see how this picture corresponds to the social world that has been depicted for us. The most striking feature of Mark's presentation is the fact that, though Jewish in its overall ethos, it allowed for easy contact with the surrounding regions.[22] Rigorist religious attitudes did not impede this situation as far as the main character and the crowds who were attracted to him were concerned, who appear to have had scant regard for the concerns of either the scribes or the Pharisees, the one doctrinal, the other halachic. The main character operates with a sense of his own authority as God's spokesperson for his coming kingdom, and in that role he shows little concern for the boundary-setting rules, such as hand-washing and Sabbath, that are the main pre-occupation of the local Pharisees. However, it is the arrival of the Jerusalem-based scribes that sets up the real tension of the plot, pointing forward to its eventual, if ironic, resolution in Jerusalem. It was there that we encountered the sympathetic scribe whose attitude, we suggested, was the key to the whole plot, in that he had distanced himself from his fellows who had gone to Galilee in order to destroy Jesus, and whose views on the relative importance of ritual in comparison with love, so enthusiastically confirmed by the main character in the name of the kingdom he proclaimed, signalled the subversion of all that Jerusalem-based religious authority stood for, as Mark portrays it.

22. In treating of location Rhoads and Mitchie, in *Mark as Story*, 68–70, recognise the significance of Galilee's accessibility to gentile territory, but they do not seem to have fully grasped the overall significance of Galilee for the development of the plot in Mark.

3. Jesus and his Movement in Galilee: the Main Character's Origin and the Outcome of the Plot

Jesus' proclamation concerning the advent of the reign of God was Mark's way of initiating the story, and even though the expression does not occur frequently thereafter, it must be presumed that it is the master symbol that controls the whole narrative.[23] It is introduced by the formula 'the time is fulfilled', presupposing that it has had a pre-history of being awaited which is now over. Later we are informed by Jesus, with his superior knowledge of God's will, that some of those present would not see death 'before the kingdom of God comes in power' (9:1). Thus, story-time, that of the kingdom, extends beyond plot-time, the narrative about Jesus, both backwards and forwards.[24] Therefore, the present of the plot is all-important for an understanding of the author's particular portrayal of the symbol's meaning as this is manifested in the life of Jesus. The symbol is by no means self-explanatory, and repentance and faith are called for from the very beginning (1:15). The gospel of the kingdom proclaimed to all becomes the mystery of the kingdom, the understanding of which is given to some (4:10), chief among whom are the Twelve, that is those 'whom he would himself', who are chosen to be with him (3:13). For others, designated 'those outside', everything happens in riddles ἐν παραβολαῖς, but even insiders find it difficult to grasp the meaning of the parable/riddle that has been given to them (4:13; 7:17), since this calls for attentive, generous and courageous hearing of the word (4:14–30). Thus a paradox of good news that is mystery hangs over the whole narrative and invests it with a genuine dramatic tension.[25] The struggle for understanding is

23. See W. Kelber, *The Kingdom in Mark: A New Place and a New Time*.

24. See N. Petersen, *Literary Criticism for New Testament Critics*, 49–80, on story time and plotted time in Mark.

25. The various approaches to the messianic secret in Mark are well documented in C. Tuckett, ed., *The Messianic Secret*, London: SPCK, 1985. Those who have considered it to be a Marcan construction receive strong confirmation by the recognition in our present approach of the way in which various aspects of the mystery, as expressed in the Marcan text, fit in with other authorial and narratorial hints to the reader that dominate the whole work. For the view that parable, especially in relation to mystery, is a suitable designation for the Marcan opus, cf. J. Donahue, 'Jesus as Parable of God in Mark's Gospel', *Interpretation* 32(1978) 369–86; also M. Boucher, *The Mysterious Parable. A Literary Study*, CBQMS 6, Washington D.C.: The Catholic Biblical Association of America, 1977.

given a mythic dimension by the author/narrator, as incomprehending or obtuse disciples fail to grasp the obvious (cf. e.g. 6:52; 8:14–21), or are under the spell of Satan, whose kingdom is under attack, and must surely fall (3:24f.), but who can still snatch the seed that has been sown from the unwary hearer (4:15), or who uses a disciple in order to impede the main character from going the way that is destined for him (8:33).[26] The ideal reader, who has shared the mystery that is good news in a way that even the chosen ones within the narrative do not, is thus drawn into the deepest mythic level of the narrative and into the struggle to understand.

If Galilee is the place of disclosure and manifestation, Jerusalem is the theatre where the paradox of the Kingdom reaches its climax. On the way there Jesus is asked by two of his chosen, Galilean disciples for special places in the glory to come, only to be told that a share in his baptism and cup is theirs but a seat in his glory is only granted by him to whom the kingdom belongs, namely God. The other members of the Twelve are indignant, only to be told that 'lording it over others' and 'exercising authority' was not the way in this particular kingdom. Instead, the Son of Man giving his life for others becomes the new model of kingship that is to emerge from the career of Jesus. Through the three predictions of the suffering and resurrection that lie ahead, acting as signposts for 'the way' of Jesus, the author has prepared for the ironic enthronement of Jesus as king in the trial and crucifixion scenes.[27] In these scenes, where the plot reaches its climax, the use of irony is pervasive.[28] The mockery of the opponents

26. On the pervasive presence of the demonic in Mark, cf. J.M. Robinson, *The Problem of History in Mark*, London: SCM, 1957, especially 51–4, in relation to the ongoing struggle with the disciples. For a treatment of the disciples in Mark against the background of apocalyptic and mythic patterns cf. my article, 'The Disciples in Mark and the *maskîlîm* in Daniel. A Comparison', *JSNT* 16(1982) 7–23.

27. Norman Perrin's treatment of these three predictions from a redactional point of view, showing a threefold development of a conscious pattern, in *What is Redaction Criticism?*, Philadelphia: Fortress, 1969, thus corresponds with and receives its full significance from a reader-oriented approach in which repetition as a conscious pattern should be seen as a definite wink to the reader.

28. Irony, it is increasingly coming to be recognised, is a highly important literary technique employed by all the evangelists, especially in dealing with the death of Jesus. Wayne Booth's treatment of irony has been highly influential, particularly the understanding that irony on the part of the author involves an invitation to the reader

proclaims the truth about Jesus in a way that is concealed from them, but for which the ideal reader has been well prepared, even if the final vindication of Jesus' claim that the Son of Man will be seen seated 'on the right hand of power and coming on the clouds of heaven' (14:62), must await the fullness of story time (cf. 9:1; 13:26). For the present the only seeing that is possible, even for the ideal reader, is that of the centurion at the cross (15:39), or that which has been promised to the disciples in Galilee (16:7).

Since the vindication of the claim about the kingdom belongs to the incompleted action of the story, the present takes on even greater significance. Here in particular Galilee as the place of final disclosure for the time opened up by the plot becomes particularly significant, especially in view of the final injunction to the disciples: 'Go tell the disciples and Peter that he goes before you to Galilee; there you will see him as he told you' (16:7). This is perhaps the most vital clue for the reader, with its promise of fulfilment of the prediction made to the disciples at 14:28.[29] The promise of seeing Jesus in Galilee is highly significant because of the manner in which sight and blindness are woven into the narrative in terms of understanding events and sayings. As ideal readers, striving to pick up the signals of the author/narrator, we will ignore this important nod in our direction at our peril. The question is, how are we to realise the full potential of the clue in our reading of the narrative? To put the matter differently, what particular contours of the kingdom of God have emerged in the presentation of the ministry of Jesus as a ministry of disclosure in Galilee of him, who for our author/narrator embodies the kingdom and its presence?

to enter a higher level of awareness regarding the plot and its outcome, see *A Rhetoric of Irony*, Chicago: University of Chicago Press, 1974. With regard to Marcan irony in general see Fowler, *Loaves and Fishes*, 96–9. 155f.; in regard to irony in the passion narrative see J.R. Donahue, *Are You the Christ? The Trial Narrative in the Gospel of Mark*, Missoula: Scholars Press, 1973, and D. Juel, *Messiah and Temple*, Missoula: Scholars Press, 1977, 47–9.

29. As well as Struthers Malbon in 'Galilee and Jerusalem', Petersen in *Literary Criticism*, 77, has emphasised this point: 'The narrator has unequivocally directed the reader to the impending story-time incident in Galilee. By doing this principally through the use of an unfulfilled prediction, he also brings to bear on this anticipated moment the whole weight of his major plot device of prediction and fulfilment'.

In the light of our earlier exploration into the social world of Galilee as portrayed in the narrative, as well as the nature of Jewish religious affiliation that is assumed for the province, the following lines of enquiry suggest themselves: i) Galilee, though thoroughly Jewish in character, was relatively unencumbered by the presence of restrictive religious affiliation, thus allowing for easy access to and from the gentile world in a way that was precluded in a Jerusalem setting; ii) with its essentially rural character, consisting of villages rather than cities for the most part, Galilee offered the possibility of portraying an itinerant ministry of healing and teaching that was detached from any central holy place, in contrast to Jerusalem, which in Mark's view was identified with the temple and those religious authorities immediately associated with it; iii) Galileans were the first followers of Jesus, who, despite their sharing religious and social assumptions both with the crowd and the opponents, were still chosen to be agents of the kingdom as preached by Jesus. Each of these motifs can be traced separately within the narrative, though obviously they are closely interrelated.

i) *Galilee and the Breaking Down of Barriers.* The Marcan Jesus is portrayed as having scant regard for boundaries, especially those established by scribal authority or Pharisaic piety. This dimension of his understanding of the kingdom is already implied in his unconditional call to repentance on announcing its advent (1:14), and is graphically demonstrated in the call of a tax-collector to share the intimacy of his small band of permanent followers, among whom were the former fish-traders, with whose class the tax-collector would be likely to have had unfriendly dealings. Table-fellowship was to be shared with others of his ilk as well as with sinners (2:13–17). Subsequently, the narrator lists both Jewish and gentile regions among the places from which people came to follow Jesus. Thus, not merely were inner-Jewish barriers being broken down, but also those obtaining between Jew and non-Jew.

As the narrative progresses the main character is made to exploit fully Galilee's central location in the midst of thriving gentile regions. First he crosses to the land of the Gerasenes, where the natives' inability to deal with a particularly bad case of demonic possession is underlined by a detailed description of his condition. 'No one was able to bind him', we are told rather pointedly, in view of the fact that the same image—binding—was used earlier to indicate Jesus' superiority over Satan (5:3f.; 3:27). The successful outcome of this brief excursion into gentile territory is assured when the demons in the guise of swine hurtle headlong into the deep, the place where they belong, and of which Jesus, just previously in the narrative, had shown himself to be master (4:35–41). Thus, the gentile land is also purified and the cured man prepares the way for further movement of the main character in gentile territory, as he goes through the Dekapolis proclaiming all that Jesus had done for him (5:20).

It has been noted by Elizabeth Struthers Malbon that Mark has consistently used the word θάλασσα, sea, rather than λίμνη, lake, to describe the northern expanse of water that forms the centre of the stage for Jesus' mission in Galilee. She sees this choice as deliberate, giving our author a much richer symbolic and mythic pattern to exploit in the narrative.[30] Sea and dry land are opposed to each other in biblical imagery, but in Mark Jesus proves himself to be lord of the sea, and his various crossings are important in establishing the reconciliation that his ministry as a whole achieved. His first journey to gentile territory had, we have seen, this effect, and thereafter the sea is no longer a threatening barrier, but a bridge between two hitherto opposing ways of life. Other journeys follow, sometimes to gentile territory (6:32f.,35,42–55; 7:24,31; 8:9f.,13f.,22–7), dominating the so-called bread-section. In one summary that is not noted for its topographical accuracy the narrator succeeds in including all the surrounding gentile territory—Tyre, Sidon, Dekapolis, ending at the sea of Galilee (7:31).[31] Through the whole section, the movement to break down Jew/gentile barriers begun at 5:1 is

30. 'The Jesus of Mark and the Sea of Galilee', especially 375f.

31. See F. Lang 'Über Sidon mitten ins Gebiet der Dekapolis. Geographie und Theologie in Markus 7,31', *ZDPV* 94(1978) 145–59, who concludes that Mark's primary concern in this summary was theological, in that Jesus is presented as the originator of the mission to the gentiles, even though the journey is in principle not impossible; M. Hengel takes the same view in *Studies in the Gospel of Mark*, 46 and 148 n. 51.

carried forward, as a story of Jesus' mastery of the deep (6:45–51) is interspersed with the account of the cure of a Syrophoenician woman's child (7:24–8) and several references to meals (6:32–42; 7:27f.; 8:1–10), the symbol previously used to remove the barrier between just and sinner within Judaism (2:16f.). On two occasions the use of spittle to perform a cure shows a further disdain for the purity laws (7:33; 8:22).[32] And throughout this whole section Jesus is surrounded by enthusiastic crowds on both sides of the sea (6:33, 54–6; 7:24, 36f.; 8:1), whose needs are cared for, even when the chosen disciples would have it otherwise (6:34–6).

It is no surprise therefore, to find that it is in the heart of this section that the author has located the one serious critique of scribal traditions that the work as a whole contains, provoked, as we have seen, by the arrival of scribes from Jerusalem. Indeed the use of the phrase 'all the Jews' to characterise those whose views are to be criticised, wittingly or not, betrays the gentile point of view of the narrator. Not that he wishes to portray a gentile Galilee, but one that is open to non-Jews and in which intermingling with gentiles does not create any false problems, even for somebody as important as a synagogue leader. Trouble in this regard stems from one quarter only, namely the scribes (and Pharisees by association in the author's mind) and their centre is Jerusalem, not Galilee.

The main character's criticism centres on a distinction between the commandment (word) of God and the tradition of men, which focuses attention on the externals of religious worship rather than the essentials. In passing, it is noteworthy that the example which is given of how scribal traditions nullify the intention of God's word is taken from the area of the temple, a gift for which releases an individual

32. See J. Neyrey, 'The Idea of Purity in Mark's Gospel', *Semeia* 35 (1986) 91–127, especially 108 in regard to spittle, using a model of purity proposed by Mary Douglas. While Neyrey's analysis is useful in highlighting the way in which the Marcan Jesus contravenes the Jewish purity laws in terms of their boundary-setting function, it would seem to be potentially misleading to speak of Jesus setting up new boundaries for his group that rigidly separated insiders from outsiders (123). In this regard his article is an example of an over-rigid application of a model to the point that the nuances of Mark's treatment of the crowd or other individuals in relation to the disciples are missed.

from other obligations such as caring for one's parents. After this frontal attack on scribal attitudes, the narrator has Jesus summon the disciples and the crowd for further instruction of a proverbial nature, thereby subtly distancing the crowd from the scribes and aligning it instead with his followers. Subsequently in the house, as Jesus explains his proverb (παραβολή/*mashal*) to the disciples, the narrator intrudes himself once again to declare that Jesus by his explanation had made all foods clean (7:19). Thus the scribal and Pharisaic points of view which created a social and a religious boundary between Jew and non-Jew are explicitly rejected.

It is not that the people of Jerusalem should feel excluded from the new movement either. They are listed among those whom the narrator reports had come to Jesus from every quarter (3:8), and they are eager supporters of the Baptist, unlike their religious leaders who did not believe in him (1:5; 11:30–32). Jesus' teaching received an enthusiastic reception from them also (11:18; 12:35,37). Yet despite the narrator's best efforts to vindicate the Jerusalem populace, we cannot help noting that they were not the beneficiaries of any of Jesus' mighty deeds, only hearers of his teaching, rather like the experience in Nazareth, where he was not able to perform any of his works of power because of their lack of faith (6:5). As the pressure on Jesus from the leaders begins to mount, the crowd who heard him gladly in the temple disappears from view, only to resurface at the trial before Pilate, persuaded by the high priests to ask for the release of Barabbas, rather than Jesus (15:8–11). Nowhere in the Galilean context does the crowd disappear or prove disloyal, and the final journey of Jesus has him passing through Galilee, not wishing that anyone should know he was there (9:30f.), implying that, as usual, a crowd would quickly assemble, should his presence be known. Thus a real contrast is set up between the freedom of the Galilean crowd, with its unbounded enthusiasm for Jesus to the end, and the people of Jerusalem, who though interested, are eventually brought under the control of their religious leaders, despite the reported fear of the crowd on the part of the authorities, should they move against Jesus, when first he arrived in the city (11:32; 12:12).

As he pronounces on the trading in the temple courtyard, the Marcan Jesus cites Is 56:7 in full: 'My house will be called a house of prayer *for all people*'.[33] As depicted, however, there is never any likelihood of such an equal gentile presence there. All is rigidly controlled by scribal and priestly interests which, as we have seen, were in constant opposition to Jesus in the Jerusalem setting.[34] While one naturally expects that the priests alone will control the temple as their preserve, this is not Mark's point of view. The scribes, who as early as 3:22 had been established by the narrator as Jesus' main opponents, are always included with the priests at the crucial points in the Jerusalem narrative, even when Jesus visits the temple (11:27). Apart from Pilate, who is portrayed as being at least sympathetic to Jesus (15:19f.), the one gentile who has an encounter with him in a Jerusalem setting is the centurion at the foot of the cross, who recognises him as son of God in the moment of death, while the chief priests and scribes stand by, calling on the Christ, the king of Israel to come down from the cross, 'that we may see and believe' (15:32,39). As mentioned previously, the use of irony reaches its climax in the final scenes of the trial and crucifixion and, as privileged readers, we are well equipped to appreciate the correctness of the centurion's identification (cf. 1:1,11; 9:7) and the ironic treatment of the mockery of the Jewish leaders (14:61). Thus the author passes final judgment on these Jerusalem notables, depicting them as tragic figures, caught up in their own blindness in not recognising the truth of their identification of Jesus. There is a touch of black humour also, as, unwittingly,

33. Fowler in *Loaves and Fishes*, 217 n.34, rightly remarks with Kelber, *Kingdom in Mark*, 101f., that cleansing of the temple is not a correct rubric for this episode, since Jesus' action, in obstructing the temple vessels being carried, effectively brought about a cessation of temple cult. Certainly such a radical stance fits well with e.g. the friendly scribe's remark which won Jesus' commendation.

34. As Cook in *Mark's Treatment of the Jewish Leaders*, 78, points out, Mark consistently has priests, scribes and elders as one set of conspirators against Jesus and the Pharisees and Herodians as another, and he never breaks this pattern when dealing with the threat to Jesus' life. At a purely literary level the combinations are a perfectly understandable pattern in that the Pharisees and Herodians are essentially anchored in Galilee and their appearance in Jerusalem is not directly conspiratorial, whereas the priests, scribes and elders are anchored in Jerusalem. This pattern helps to highlight the centrality of the scribes in Mark's view, since their attack on Jesus can occur in both locations.

by having Jesus condemned, they are aiding him in achieving the divine will in his regard.[35]

It is quite clear that the scribally controlled point of view can see no good in Jesus, having attributed his powers to the source of evil. Clearly then they have no will to either see or believe, despite their final protestation. The author's judgment is that the seeing, which throughout the narrative was regarded as essential if one were to capture the reality of the kingdom present in Jesus, could never take place in a religious environment dominated by their point of view. The gentile centurion can see and make the proper identification in an open profession of faith, thereby giving confirmation to the 'Galilean' point of view, which sought to include gentiles too within the range of the kingdom.

ii) *Galilee and an Itinerant Ministry.* If a Galilean setting allowed for the extension of the kingdom's range beyond that of narrow scribal limits, the region also offered the possibility, indeed the necessity, of portraying a different type of ministry to that which is depicted in Jerusalem. For practical purposes Jesus' ministry in the holy city is confined to the temple, in the Marcan view. True, he is portrayed as moving back and forth from Bethany, but this merely serves to underline the fact that he spent his days in the temple, since on each occasion a visit there is the reason for re-entering the city (11:11,15,27). It is there that he meets the various representatives of Jewish religion, including the scribe who is declared to be not far from the kingdom because of his recognition of the primacy of love over cultic observance. It is there also that he is repeatedly said to teach (11:18; 12:35; 14:49), and there that he observes the widow casting in her two mites, 'her whole life' (12:41). The only exception to this location is the address to his disciples about the fate of the temple, but even this address is located by the narrator on the Mount of Olives, 'opposite the temple' (13:1–3). As a final comment on his Jerusalem sojourn, Jesus himself declares: 'I

35. Thus R. Tannehill, 'The Gospel of Mark as Narrative Christology', *Semeia* 16(1979) 57–95.

was with you daily in the temple teaching, and you did not arrest me' (14:49).[36]

What is notable about this presentation, especially when viewed from a Galilean perspective, is the concentration on teaching alone, which of necessity is confined to one place, and excludes the performance of mighty deeds. Thus, while the author may not have fully prepared us for the repeated charge of destroying the temple (14:57; 15:29), we cannot but suspect that the point of the Jerusalem narrative as a whole was to portray the main character as having taken over the temple and used it for his own purposes. At the same time, in the name of the gospel of the kingdom which he proclaimed, he enthusiastically endorses the relativising of temple cult, and actually prophesies the temple's destruction (12:32–4; 13:2). The concentration on a teaching ministry only would appear to be highly significant, even ironic, since the scribes are portrayed as the official teachers of Judaism. Now, Jesus enters the place which defined their role, namely the temple, and respectfully undermines its centrality to Jewish faith. The passage from Isaiah that he cites when formally prohibiting actions necessary for the maintenance of cultic activity describes the temple as a house of prayer only, thus preparing the way for the friendly scribe's declaration. But even then Jesus prays elsewhere also—in Galilee in a desert place or on a mountain (1:35; 6:46). During the ascent (ἀναβαίνειν/*aliah*) the sacrificial language of the sin-offering (λύτρον) was used to interpret his own death as Son of Man, which was to be accomplished at Jerusalem (10:35f.,46); yet in Galilee, as Son of Man, he had claimed authority on earth to forgive sin, without any reference to temple-sacrifice, and all the people performed the cultic gesture of glorifying (δοξάζειν) God at the declaration (2:10f.).

If, then, the author, with his developed sense of irony, wishes to inform us through the charge that Jesus has in fact destroyed the temple and is about to build another one, that new one is certainly 'not made with hands', but signifies an altogether different view of religion to that associated with

36. It is one of the strengths of Juel's study, *Messiah and Temple*, that he has convincingly shown how the themes of Messiah and temple are interwoven at the level of Mark's literary production.

the old temple dominated by the scribes. This is dramatically highlighted by the author who takes us rapidly from Calvary to the temple mount at the moment of Jesus' death to report that the veil of the temple was rent in two, from top to bottom (15:38). The Jerusalem scribes are well portrayed, therefore, in recognising this attack on temple-religion as they defined it and attempting to discredit him in Galilee. We must go down with them, and see how the Galilean setting has aided the author in bringing about this transformation of the central symbol-system of Judaism as his narrative has developed.

The initial meeting with the main character in Galilee found him on the move—from Nazareth, to the Jordan, to Galilee—in order to proclaim his message. This mobility is maintained throughout the Galilean ministry, something that is highlighted by the frequent occurrence of verbs of movement, often qualified by the adverb εὐθὺς, immediately, giving a slightly breathless pace to the narrative. Consequently, there is a particular significance in the description of his invitation to individuals to join him as a call to follow (ἀκολούθειν; cf. 2:15; 3:7; 9:32; 15:41). It is very much in character then that the final mention of Galilee (16:7) also contains a verb of movement: he goes before you (προάγειν) to Galilee. We could scarcely have expected otherwise from this elusive presence.

As a result of this mobility the narrator does not assign to him any one location, even if Capernaum, rather than Nazareth, is singled out for special mention: 1:21; 2:1; 9:33. However, he refuses to return there, when told that all are searching for him, declaring instead that his purpose was to visit the neighbouring villages (1:38). At Nazareth he also visited the villages round about (6:6). Likewise, when other geographical locations are mentioned the narrator does not confine the movement to a single place, but implies instead that Jesus visited the whole territory in question. Thus he is reported to have visited the territory (χώρα) of the Gerasenes, or the land (γῆ) of Gennesareth (5:1; 6:53), or the region (ὅρια) of Tyre (7:24), or the villages (κώμαι) of Caesarea Philippi (8:27).

Corresponding to this geographical spread with its suggestion of total coverage of the region, the narrator takes us in the company of the main character to a variety of special locations. Some of these suggest the rural terrain of Galilee—sea and sea-shore, mountain, desert place and fields, whereas others reflect various forms of social grouping—synagogue, house, village, boat. As the narrative progresses, various patterns begin to emerge in relation to the different locales. The desert is the place of quiet refreshment and prayer (1:35; 6:31); the mountain too is a place of quiet (6:46), but also of election and disclosure (3:13; 9:2). It is along the sea-shore that the crowd usually assembles (2:13; 3:7; 4:1; 5:21; 6:34, 45,55), but it can appear elsewhere also: around the house (1:33; 2:2,15; 5:24) or in a desert place (6:31). The house and boat on the other hand serve for more intimate meetings with the disciples. It is in these places that table-fellowship is established (2:15; 6:10; 14:3,14) and mysterious utterances are explained through special instruction (4:10; 7:17; 9:13). The synagogue, we suggested earlier, was replaced by the house as the place of meeting, and while it occurs in the summary of 1:39 as a place that Jesus visited on his tour of Galilee, the indications are that for the author it is a hostile place both for Jesus (3:6) and his followers (13:9).

'What is this wisdom that is given to this one so that mighty deeds are done through his hands?' (6:2), is the fundamental question which the Galilean ministry of Jesus raises for those who have experienced him, according to the author. Together with the corresponding question of 1:27, 'What is this? A new teaching?', also left unanswered, it is intended as a question which the ideal reader will have little difficulty in answering. The combination of wisdom and mighty deed or teaching and exorcism that is implied, shows that from the point of view of the author, deed and word are simply two facets of the same reality, something that makes the absence of any mighty deeds in the Jerusalem setting all the more pointed. Galilee affords the author a suitable range of possibilites to manifest a full repertoire of Jesus' wisdom at work—cures and exorcisms, nature miracles and desert feedings, as well as parables, proverbs and mastery of scriptural argument. Though it occurs only once, the term 'wisdom' has an inclusive connotation to cover all these varied forms of ministry of word and work, even if it is the deeds that seem best to illustrate the impact of the main character which the author wishes to convey.[37]

For Jesus wisdom was a gift received, it is suggested (δοθεῖσα, 6:2), just as elsewhere the source of his power is attributed to the Holy Spirit which he had received at the baptism (1:10; 3:28–30). His authority is clearly contrasted with that of the scribes, which is based on the tradition of the fathers, and is therefore 'from men' (7:8,13). His authority on the other hand is 'from heaven', and, understood as wisdom, is universal in its scope, unlike theirs which is particular and therefore ethnocentric. Jerusalem, in the author's view, could not contain such universality, and hence Galilee is exploited to the full as the proper setting for portraying this new mode of divine presence which is no longer to be localised, and hence knows no boundaries. Any house can now be 'the house of prayer for all nations', since the old temple, with its structured order so rigidly controlled, could not function as God had intended.

iii) *Galileans and a New Understanding of the Kingdom.* The servant maid of the high-priest recognised Peter as a Galilean and so identified him as follower of Jesus (14:70). By refusing to elaborate further, the author allows us to decide for ourselves as to the significance of this identification, having already given many clues throughout the narrative. While people from Jerusalem come to Jesus in Mark, the permanent band of Jesus' followers, 'those whom he himself wished' (3:13), are Galilean, and it is in Galilee that they are expected to see him again and thus achieve the purpose of

37. In his highly stimulating study, *Jesus the Teacher. A Socio-Rhetorical Interpretation of Mark*, Philadelphia: Fortress Press, 1984, Vernon Robbins has shown that this composite portrait is an adaptation of aspects of teacher/disciple relationships in both Judaism and Graeco-Roman tradition. According to him the important consideration was not whether a person performed healings or exorcisms, but the social identity in which he performed them, and for Robbins that identity was as teacher (114–17, e.g.). While agreeing that Mark certainly wishes to situate the healings etc. in a larger context, thus avoiding any misunderstanding of their author, there is no denying the preponderance of deeds in the Galilean section, which the designation 'teacher' does not quite capture. It is noteworthy that though 'teacher' is a frequent designation for Jesus on the part of both disciples and others (12 times in all), it does not appear in the list of reactions to his ministry at 8:28. We shall have occasion to discuss the issue with Robbins in greater detail in part two of this study.

their call, namely,'to be with him, and to be sent' (3:14). The fact that this restoration is not part of the plot time does not mean that it is any less important for the author, since it is the underlying assumption of his whole story. Unlike the other gospel writers the author leaves the reader to complete that final injunction to Peter and the disciples. Yet this does not mean any rejection or even implied criticism of the group on his part, but is the result of his dramatic technique, which communicates its message through suggestive scenes rather than attempting to make everything explicit. We agree with Robert Tannehill, that too much narrative time has been invested in the disciples, and the hero's credibility is too much at stake for them to be regarded as failures by the author.[38]

One highly significant aspect of the disciples' role already appeared in considering the activity of Jesus in Galilee, namely, their radical detachment from family and possessions, similar to that of the main character. This is highlighted in the original call to the two pairs of brothers, as well as to Levi (1:16–20; 2:13f.), all of whom were engaged in secular activity when they were summoned to follow. Subsequently, the Twelve as a group are given very specific instructions not to take anything with them on their mission, but to rely on the hospitality of those whom they would visit (6:7–12). Yet this is only one side of the pattern that the author seeks to establish through the narrative. There is also the sharing of function with the main character, which means sharing in his authority (3:14f.; 6:7). Within the time of the plot they can be said to achieve this only to a limited degree (6:30; 9:29), yet the use of such important terms from the author's point of view as κηρύσσειν (to preach), ἀποστέλλειν (to send) and δαιμόνια ἐκβάλλειν (to cast out demons), all of which are used to describe Jesus' activity, is a clear indication of how the author wishes us to understand their

38. 'The Disciples in Mark: the Function of a Narrative Role', *JR* 57(1977) 134–57. Cf. also E. Best, 'The Role of the Disciples in Mark', *NTS* 23(1976) 377–401; H-J Klauck, 'Der erzälerische Rolle der Jünger im Markusevangeliums', *NT* 24(1982) 1–27. The view that Mark is critical of the disciples is particularly associated with T. Weeden, 'The Heresy that necessitated Mark's Gospel', *ZNW* 59(1968) 64–77, followed by among others W. Kelber, most recently in *The Oral and Written Gospel*, 97f.

role. It is in plot time rather than story time, however, that they will fulfil their function properly (10:29f.; 13:9–13).[39]

The fact that they have been specially called is stressed repeatedly (3:13; 4:10), or assumed (8:14–21), yet this does not give them any pre-eminence, but lays a further obligation on them to grasp the meaning of the mystery entrusted to them and imitate the master's pattern of self-giving service. This emerges most clearly in the threefold prediction of the passion, directed explicitly to the small permanent group of followers. On each occasion, either the group as a whole or representative figures from it show that they have understood nothing of the divine necessity by which the main character is impelled to go to Jerusalem, there to suffer and later be vindicated. Each time a general instruction, not just to them but to all who would be followers, stresses the need for a total reversal of human values if one wishes to be a genuine disciple (cf. 8:31–8; 9:30–37; 10:32–45).[40] The account of the formation of the disciples into a symbolic group, the Twelve (3:13–19), is wedged between a narratorial summary of enthusiastic crowd-following (3:7–12) and rejection by Jesus' own (οἱ παρ' αὐτοῦ), who at least for the narrator would appear to be equivalent to 'his mother and his brothers' (3:20,31). A real transition in the development of the plot would seem to have been arrived at with this account, especially in the wake of the conspiracy to destroy him (3:6).[41] Yet if the author wishes to suggest any particular significance to the Twelve, especially in a Galilean setting where the symbolism of Israel's forefathers might be expected to have particular resonances, it is a covert one, since as the narrative progresses the Twelve and the disciples are virtually interchangeable (9:31,35; 11:11,14; 14:14,17), and it is the aspect of their being with Jesus that is particularly highlighted, and hence their homelessness and mobility (10:28).

Nevertheless, the relation of this group of permanent followers to the larger audience is carefully, if subtly deve-

39. Cf. my study, *The Twelve: Disciples and Apostles. An Introduction to the Theology of the first Three Gospels*, London: Sheed and Ward, 1968, 138–48.

40. Robbins, *Jesus as Teacher*, 155–66.

41. Freyne, *The Twelve*, 63–72; more recently, K. Stock, *Boten aus dem Mit-Ihm-Sein. Das Verhältnis zwischen Jesus und den Zwölf nach Markus*, AnBib 70, Rome: Pontifical Biblical Institute Press, 1975.

loped by the narrator. On the one hand the Marcan Jesus cannot avoid crowds, it would seem, and yet the narrator repeatedly stresses the dangers of over-exposure and his desire for privacy (1:44f.; 3:10; 4:1–2,32f.; 6:31; 7:24,36). The commands to silence after certain cures and the attempt to achieve privacy in the performance of others (5:37; 7:33; 8:23) help to underline for the reader the author's point of view, namely that enthusiasm alone cannot penetrate the mystery that is unfolding in the events being narrated. In order to highlight this dimension of the proclamation more fully we are repeatedly being taken inside the house (4:10; 7:17; 9:33) or away in a boat (4:35–40; 6:40–45; 8:14–21) or on the way (9:33; 10:17,32), as privileged insiders with the disciples. Thus, apart from the crowd, we witness special manifestations of power, have parabolic utterances unravelled or the role of suffering explained.

Yet strangely, the disciples' performance seems to be in inverse proportion to the special attention which they receive. They are twice accused of hardness of heart, a condition ascribed to those who sought to destroy him (6:51; 8:14; cf. 3:5), and their leader, Peter, is called Satan for objecting to the path that the Son of Man has predicted for himself (8:33). Compared with such failures, the over-enthusiasm of the crowd seems negligible indeed. We are not surprised then to hear that the crowd too can be called on occasion (7:14; 8:34), or that Jesus insists on caring for it because it is like sheep without a shepherd, even when the disciples would have him dismiss it (6:34,36).[42] Yet despite this blurring of the lines between the disciples and the crowd the narrator persists in portraying the constancy of the main character to the small group. In his final meal with them, they, and not as earlier, the crowd, are designated the sheep who will shortly be deprived of the shepherd (cf. 6:34), but with the promise of subsequent restoration in Galilee, presumably to complete in

42. For a perceptive and careful analysis of the crowd, especially in relation to the disciples in Mark, cf. E. Struthers Malbon, 'Disciples/Crowds/Whoever: Marcan Characters and Readers', *NT* 28(1986) 104–30, especially her conclusion: 'the disciples and the crowd—especially when taken together—do evoke a composite image of the followers, the fallible followers, of Jesus... the Marcan narrative message is plain: discipleship is both open-ended and demanding; followership is neither exclusive nor easy' (123f.).

the story-time the tasks that have been designated for them already within the plot.

This fluctuating picture of the disciples' performance—now separate from and responsible for the crowd, now one with them in their incomprehension, and yet again far less understanding in their reaction than the crowd—dominates the Galilean section of the story. It thus helps to underline their relative obscurity in the Jerusalem section. We are already prepared for this change by the narrator's report that on the way up to Jerusalem 'Jesus was going ahead of them, and they (the disciples) were amazed and those who followed were afraid' (10:32). Amazement and fear occur elsewhere in the narrative as reactions that are less than full and perfect trust in Jesus, and by sharing with us the intimate emotions of Jesus' followers at this moment of transition the narrator has alerted us to what lies ahead.[43] Mention of the Twelve with its foundational symbolism for the group, related to Israel's past, seems altogether inappropriate at this moment. We hear of the ten being indignant with the two (James and John) who had sought precedence over them (10:35,41), and later still there is the group of the four (13:3), and then the three (14:33), adding to our sense of unease that all is not well with the group. This is confirmed for us when Judas turns traitor and Peter denies Jesus three times, as had been predicted (14:20,30). It comes as no surprise then to hear that they all abandoned Jesus and fled, since this too had been predicted (14:27,50). Their absence at the foot of the cross is in sharp contrast to other Galileans, those women who had followed Jesus in Galilee, ministering to him, and who had made the pilgrimage ascent to Jerusalem with him (15:40f.). With the possible exception of Peter's mother-in-law (1:31), we have not encountered these women in the Galilean phase of the story, and so their presence now only helps to underline for the author the scandal of the absence of the chosen disciples, whose very function it was 'to be with Jesus'.[44] By the use of

43. Amazement (ἐκθαμβεῖσθαι): 1:27, everyone; 9:15, the crowd; 10:24, the disciples; 14:32, Jesus himself; 16:5, the women at the tomb; fear (φοβεῖσθαι): 5:15, 33, the crowd; 4:41; 6:50; 9:6, the disciples; 16:8, the women.

44. E. Struthers Malbon, 'Fallible Followers: Women and Men in the Gospel of Mark', *Semeia* 27 (1984) 29–48.

the technical language of discipleship the narrator wishes to describe their role in quite formal terms, thereby ensuring that we do not miss the negative contrast as far as the chosen disciples are concerned. And yet these women, too, are Galileans, and their role within the narrative is to ensure that their fellow-Galilean disciples will be restored with Jesus in Galilee.

In the light of this portrayal of the Galileans as disciples we are justified in detecting a note of irony in the maid-servant's remark: 'Truly you are one of them, for you are also a Galilean' (14:70). The disciples share a common place of origin with the main character, and as such they have no place in Jerusalem. Their failure there was as necessary to the plot as it was predictable in the light of the narrative. Their performance as portrayed enables the author to illustrate the deep paradox that is at the heart of his plot, namely, that in failure lies success, in death there is life. And so it is in Galilee, not Jerusalem, that there is 'resurrection'. Failed disciples who are capable of being restored in Galilee, that is, in terms of the plot, those who are open to the Galilean perspective of the main character, are vital to the continued viability of the story, to which the narrative about Jesus the Galilean bears witness. It is in this way that they fulfil the function that was given to them within the narrative, namely, to represent the mystery of Jesus the Galilean as a continuous, if ambivalent, sign of the presence which he proclaimed once in Galilee.

CHAPTER THREE

Galilee as Portrayed by Matthew and Luke

MARK'S gospel was chosen as the starting point for an investigation of the portrayal of Galilee in the gospels because for centuries it was overshadowed by the longer accounts of Matthew and Luke. Inevitably, then, the perspectives of one or both are brought to bear on the reading of what most commentators accept to be the oldest gospel. In the first century it was quite the reverse, however, as Mark had a considerable, some would say a controlling, influence on the way the later evangelists presented their story of Jesus. Recently, Robert Fowler has reframed the question of synoptic interdependence in a fresh and challenging way, by asking whether, because the later gospels appear to copy from Mark so extensively, they are, therefore, necessarily saying the same thing, playing the same language game?[1] Certainly, in dealing with a location such as Galilee we could easily fall into the trap of thinking that, beause it is so flatly described, it functions in a similar manner in all the gospels. Our reading of Mark suggests that such an assumption would be erroneous, since that precise location had a genuine shaping effect on the Marcan narrative and the way in which the plot developed.

In this chapter we shall once again concentrate on the internal dynamics of the narrative as constructed by Matthew and Luke rather than examine the possible external factors that caused each writer to recast the story of Jesus in their different ways. This should, hopefully, better attune us to

1. 'Reading Matthew, Reading Mark: Observing the First Steps toward Meaning-as-Reference in the Synoptic Gospels', SBL Seminar Papers, ed. K.Richards, Atlanta: Scholars Press, 1986, 1–16.

answering the question posed by Fowler, thereby uncovering the multivalence of the symbol Galilee for the early Christians. In consciously adopting this literary approach we cannot, of course, ignore what source and redaction criticisms of the gospels have taught us, particularly the fact that both Matthew and Luke had access to collections of sayings of Jesus which Mark either did not know or chose not to use. At the same time each has developed the Marcan story backwards and forwards in terms of an account of the infancy of the main character and his restoration with his disciples after the resurrection. This additional material together with the extended story-line have considerably enhanced the possibilities in regard to location, plot and characters, and we must now attempt to delineate these for each writer in turn, avoiding insofar as is possible any 'intertwining' with the Marcan treatment.

1. Matthew

i) *The Galilean Social World.* It has long been recognised that in rewriting the Marcan narratives Matthew has adopted a style that is less vivid, more hieratic and distanced than that of Mark.[2] This observation also applies to the Matthean summaries which are both general and repetitive in tone: 'healing every kind of sickness and every disease among the people' (4:23; 9:35; 10:1). This sense of detachment that Matthew's narrative style conveys is further underlined by his compilatory technique which collects similar material into large blocks, e.g. the five discourses or the collection of mighty deeds, chs 8–9. Thus the rapid flow of the narrative is interrupted as the reader is invited to rest with the disciples and listen to a lengthy discourse from the main character. Furthermore, Matthew's preoccupation with the 'Jewish Question', something that dominates the whole narrative, makes the work less reflective of regional differences, as the whole Jewish people becomes involved in the plot. In this regard the use of the designation 'Israel', even when Galilean audiences are being addressed (8:5; 9:35; 10:5,23; 15:24),

2. Cf. e.g. X.L. Dufour, in 'Les Évangiles Synoptiques', *Introduction à la Bible. II. Nouveau Testament*, ed. A. Robert and A. Feuillet, Tournai: Desclée, 1959, 170–72.

shows that the author's interests are essentially theological rather than geographical[3]

Nevertheless, interesting insights do emerge which help to enlarge considerably our view of the Galilean social world. Already in the infancy narrative a clear distinction emerges between the political realities of Galilee and Jerusalem. Herod and all Jerusalem were greatly disturbed on hearing from the Magi about the birth of the king of the Jews (2:3), and the family of Jesus were warned in a dream not to settle in Judea, on returning to 'the land of Israel', because Archelaus ruled there in the place of his father Herod; instead they are to settle in Galilee (2:22). The fact that we are assured by the narrator that this movement which brings them to Galilee is divinely directed (by dreams, cf. 1:20), alerts the reader to the importance of Galilee for shaping the story from the very outset. Herod and his family give the narrative a political colouring, despite the fact that it is the Sadducees, not the Herodians, who join forces with the Pharisees in plotting against Jesus in Galilee (12:14; 16:12). According to Matthew it is only in Jerusalem that the Herodians are linked with the Pharisees against Jesus (22:15), and then significantly, on a political issue about paying taxes to Caesar.[4]

The sermon on the mount is Matthew's first and longest collection of instructions for disciples, which from the point of view of the narrator takes on a special significance from being delivered on a mountain, which is firmly located for us in Galilee (4:23).[5] It is frequently assumed that Matthew's

3. For the significance of the term Israel in Matthew cf. W. Trilling, *Das Wahre Israel*, *SANT* 10, 3rd edn Munich: Kösel, 1964, 130–37.

4. J. Dean Kingsbury, 'The Developing Conflict between Jesus and the Jewish Leaders in Matthew', *CBQ* 49(1987) 57–73, has shown how that characterisation of Herod in this episode is similar to that of the Jewish leaders in Matthew, and as such he is the precursor of their attitudes within the narrative. However, this does not exclude political overtones to the episode also, especially since Herod, like Pilate later (27:11, 17, 22, 29, 37), is concerned with the political implications of the Christ, the king of the Jews (2:2,4,13,16). Cf. Kingsbury's earlier study of the titles of Jesus in *Matthew: Structure, Christology, Kingdom*, Philadelphia: Fortress, 1975, 96–9, especially 97.

5. Cf. the redaction critical study of T. Donaldson, *Jesus on the Mountain. A Study of Matthean Theology*, Sheffield: JSOT Press, 1985, especially 111-21, where he shows the theological importance of the mountain setting based on the eschatological Zion tradition. From a purely literary point of view the connection between this mountain scene at the beginning of the Galilean section and one at the end 15:29–31, which is beside the sea of Galilee, will not be lost on the attentive reader, since the narrator, it would seem, has this in view, as is shown by the phraseology of his summary.

opening utterance, 'blessed are the poor in spirit', is a deliberate spiritualising of a more radical statement, preserved by Luke, 'blessed are the poor'. This assumption then dictates the subsequent reading of the sermon, which traditionally has not been thought of as having overtly political concerns. However, recent interpretation from a more political perspective has challenged such a 'spiritual' reading of the sermon and alerted us to the very concrete social realities that lie behind many of its injunctions.[6] In this reading 'poor in spirit', far from being a spiritualisation of a more radical statement about poverty, now becomes an affirmation of blessedness for those who are not just poor, but who have taken that condition to their very heart, by not allowing themselves to be deceived by the attraction of wealth, instead trusting their lives totally to the heavenly Father (5:25–34). When read in this larger context of the sermon itself, the blessing falls into line with other pronouncements of the main character on the dangers of wealth, and on the ideal of perfection—selling all and giving it to the poor—that is proposed in the story of the rich young man (19:16–30). Possessions are dangerous since they create a desire in the human person to entrust oneself to them rather than to God (6:19,24; 19:22). Jesus' own detachment from everything becomes the model for all would-be disciples: the Son of man has nowhere to lay his head (8:20; cf. 10:19–21; 19:16–30). Thus, in Matthew's view, the poor who are really poor, that is in their very spirit, are a challenge to those who live their lives on assumptions such as those expressed in the injunction of 6:19f., namely storing up wealth in terms of money or fine clothing (cf. 11:8). Such an injunction assumes an affluent social world, where these temptations are real. Elsewhere, Matthew will instruct his disciples that anyone who provides them with even the most insignificant material thing —a cup of cold water—or offers them hospitality because they are disciples of Jesus, will also receive their reward (10:40–42).

6. Cf. in particular S. Van Tilborg, *The Sermon on the Mount as an Ideological Intervention. A Reconstruction of Meaning*, Assen: Van Gorcum, 1986; R. Horsley, 'Ethics and Exegesis: Love your enemies' and the Doctrine of Non-Violence', *JAAR* 54(1985) 3–31. The fact that both of these studies are concerned in different ways with the extra-textual referents does not prevent them from alerting us to the social dimension of the text and the assumptions of the author/narrator.

Thus the poor in spirit and the wandering disciple who follows the life-style of Jesus are pointers to a social world where the opposite values must be presumed to be operative. As disciples of Jesus both serve as models for the alternative rewards that the kingdom he preaches has to offer.

Other beatitudes turn out to be no less informative of the assumed social world of the author/narrator. The evils of political domination (5:4), social injustice (5:5f.), sexual licentiousness (5:8) and violence (5:9) are all presumed to be present in Matthew's social world, and throughout the work we are given a clearer picture of the forms these actually take. We have already met Herod, whose slaughter of the innocent children left many mourning in Bethlehem and its environs (2:16–18), but the brutal killing of John the Baptist (14:1–10) is a warning to Galileans that even closer to home similar oppression can take place against those whose religious stance is perceived as a political threat (10:16–20).[7] The presence of this political power in the immediate setting is graphically described by the one who can compel others to carry their burdens along the road (5:41; cf. 27:32). The absentee landlord's son who lost his life so that wicked husbandmen might inherit his land without any respect for the property rights of others (21:38) is one example of somebody who is the victim of injustice in Matthew's story. Within the overall development of the plot he becomes the image of 'the meek' king who enters his city to take possession of it (21:5); he is also a symptom of the social problems that Matthew assumes for his readers in the society he is depicting. Violence, both physical and sexual, are also part of that society and litigation an everyday occurrence, based on the teacher's instructions to avoid retaliation, lust, even in the heart or recourse to a judge (5:24–36,40; 5:38–42; 5:27–28,31f.).[8]

Thus, Matthew, through his reporting of the detailed instruc-

7. This is particularly true because of the close connection the narrator in Matthew makes between John's movement and that of Jesus: the disciples of John tell Jesus about the Baptist's fate (14:12), presumably because they had previously been sent to Jesus by John and heard the encomium of their master (11:2–15). Cf. J. Meier, 'John the Baptist in Matthew's Gospel, *JBL* 99(1980) 383–405.

8. For a discussion of the social background of these sayings cf. Horley, 'Ethics and Exegesis', 21ff., and chapter 5 below. R. Tannehill's discussion from a rhetorical perspective is also highly significant: *The Sword of his Mouth*, Semeia Studies, Missoula: Scholars Press, 1975, especially 60–88.

tions of the main character for everyday life, has succeeded in suggesting a social world caught up in various forms of human exploitation, despite his own narratorial distance. What is particularly informative for our discussion is the fact that the picture is gleaned from the ideals that are being proposed for his followers by the main character, whose conduct is therefore seen as an alternative to that of the society at large, even earning them opprobrium in their own families: 10:21f., 35f.

Yet, despite this picture that in many respects is more specific than that of Mark, the imagery remains thoroughly rural, or small-town. The selection of parables is extended considerably and we meet the jealous farmer who sows weeds in his neighbour's grain crop, fishermen sorting out their catch, an agricultural worker unexpectedly finding a treasure-trove and the travelling pearl-merchant hoping for a good bargain (13:24–30,44–48). Day-labourers in the village square are waiting to be hired for a minimum wage (20:1–15), and servants in debt, who themselves become ruthless money-lenders, fill out the picture further (18:21–35). In the village squares we encounter the festive celebrations or tragic dirges of small-town rituals (11:17), and thievery and begging are accepted facts of life (6:19; 5:42). Human relations are described in images from the countryside—wolves and sheep—and the disciples are expected to know the characteristics of the serpent and the dove (10:16). The sun and the rain are important factors in the lives of people (5:45) and figs and thistles are natural images for the good and evil life (7:15–19). The image of entering by the narrow gate (7:13) picks up the symbol of the city seated on a mountain at the beginning of the sermon (5:14), but presupposes a rural, if not indeed a pilgrimage motif, as cities were usually located on hills for reasons of safety and control of the surrounding countryside.

Apart from this picture of a mainly rural setting for the story, the author/narrator is familiar with the geographical setting of Galilee. Thus the fact that the report about Jesus reached all the region of Syria is an addition to the geographic information supplied by Mark (4:25). Besides, the proximity of Samaria is noted (10:5–6), as well as Tyre and Sidon and the Dekapolis. The journey of Jesus, reported by Mark at

7:21, is simplified by Matthew (15:21). Three Galilean locations are called cities (πόλεις) even though the author is familiar with the distinction between city and village in a general way (9:35). There is an implied contrast between these Galilean cities and Tyre and Sidon in terms of the relative amount of attention they have received in the ministry of Jesus, suggesting that while Matthew certainly has no desire to exclude gentile contacts, he wants us to consider that it is 'the lost sheep of the house of Israel' that are the main concern throughout the Galilean ministry (10:6; 15:24). Furthermore there is an implied criticism of gentile ethical standards, at least in terms of those being proposed by Jesus (5:47). Who these gentiles are is not specified further, but on the basis of the overall ethical code of the sermon on the mount they would appear to be of the Cynic variety, with their disregard for their physical appearance and detachment from material goods. The disciples of Jesus are also not to be concerned about their clothing (6:28), but they should comb their hair and wash themselves (6:16f.). It will be important to see whether this change of focus to Galilee as part of Israel will have repercussions at other stages of our enquiry also.

ii) *Religious Attitudes in Galilee.* Matthew's story is about the coming of Jesus the messiah to Israel and Israel's mounting rejection of him, which reaches its narrative climax in the Jerusalem section. Yet this rejection is already apparent in the Galilean section, and a judgment similar to that foretold for Jerusalem (23:34f., 37f.) is also predicted for the Galilean cities (11:20–24). Inevitably then there is a levelling of the religious attitudes displayed within the story, as the author/narrator takes a temporal stance in relation to his narrative that is between the resurrection and the Parousia (24:15; 27:8; 28:15)[9]. In addition, the tone of the narrative is highly polemical against the Jewish religious authorities, and this generates a rhetoric of *vituperatio*, a favourite ploy of which is to generalise in order to discredit.[10] For these reasons one

9. Cf. J. Dean Kingsbury, *Matthew as Story*, Philadelphia: Fortress, 1986, 34.

10. Cf. my article, 'Vilifying the Other and Defining the Self: Matthew's and John's Anti-Judaism in Focus', in '*To See Ourselves as Others See Us*'. *Jews,Christians, Others in Antiquity*, ed. E. Frerichs and J. Neusner, Chico: Scholars Press, Studies in the Humanities 1985, 117–44.

does not expect a discriminating treatment of Galilean Jewish affiliations. Yet, as we observed in regard to the social world, a considerable amount can in fact be gleaned from a careful reading of the text and the signals that the author gives us.

Matthew does recognise some regional differences in his narrative. Indeed, the transition from Galilee to Judea is more carefully noted than it is in Mark:'And it happened when Jesus had finished these words he moved from Galilee and came to the region of Judea beyond the Jordan (19:1; cf. Mk 10:1). At other important points in the previous narrative we are reminded of our Galilean location: 4:23; 15:29; 17:22; the former two are matching narratorial summaries preparing for two mountain scenes in which the crowd is taught and has its sick and infirm healed, and the latter provides the setting for the second prediction of the passion, presumably to the disciples, who, the narrator tells us, were greatly saddened by the announcement. However, it must also be said that the regional locations for the narrative do not seem to coincide with the other indications of the overall structure of the work, at least as this is proposed by Kingsbury.[11] Perhaps it is a mistake to impose rigidly one particular understanding of the structure on the narrative, to the exclusion of other possibilities, since even Kingsbury is prepared to admit that the author/narrator has given several different indicators of important internal movements. Foremost among these are those marking the end of each of the five major discourses, and 19:1, the transition from Galilee to Judea, is one such.[12] In that perspective four of the five discourses are all deliberately given a Galilean setting, and the fifth, as a farewell discourse, had of necessity to be located in Jerusalem. We are

11. Cf. e.g. his *Matthew. Structure, Christology, Kingdom*, 1–36, where he convincingly argues that the repetition of the formula, 'from that time on Jesus began to...' (4:17 and 16:21) marks the major divisions of the gospel according to the evangelist's salvation-historical perspectives. It is presumably for this reason that even in his most recent study of Matthew from a reader-perspective, *Matthew as Story*, geographical location features minimally in his analysis (27f.).

12. For a different view of the structure of Matthew, based on the five discourses, cf. J. Meier, *The Vision of Matthew: Christ, Church and Morality in the First Gospel*, New York: Paulist, 1979.

encouraged then by this initial probe to search further for the religious significance of Galilee for Matthew.

The most striking feature comes at the very outset—the need to justify Nazareth, Galilee and Capernaum as suitable places for the origin and activity of Jesus the Messiah by an appeal to Scripture. The fact that all four geographic locations in ch.2 are authenticated by a Scriptural citation containing the name of the place arrived at in the itinerary of the new-born child, was noted by Krister Stendahl. In addition, Kingsbury has pointed out that the move from Nazareth to Capernaum at the beginning of the ministry is validated in exactly the same way as the move from Bethlehem to Nazareth on the part of the child and his parents (2:22f.; 4:12–14), thus supporting his claim that the author/narrator wants us to see the whole section 1:1 – 4:16 as a presentation of Jesus the Messiah.[13] As is well known, Matthew's gospel is dotted with citations of scriptural passages, all introduced by a standard formula, showing that the whole career of Jesus is in accordance with God's purpose. For the reader they function as reliable commentary, guiding an understanding of the events taking place and ensuring that all is in accordance with God's word.[14]

Thus, Galilee and Capernaum, his own city (9:1), are not just a safe haven for the main character, the reader is reliably informed; they are actually the divinely willed theatres for the career of Jesus. Capernaum is given a double description—beside the sea and in the territory of Zebulun and Naphtali—and so its location corresponds to the first two geographical notations in the Isaian text that is quoted in full. It thus becomes the centre of the messianic visitation which the text promises for Galilee of the gentiles. However, the reader has already been informed that as far as the author/narrator is concerned Galilee is not gentile but part of the land of Israel (2:20–22), and this is confirmed by the divine authority of the

13. K. Stendahl, 'Quis et Unde? An Analysis of Matthew 1–2', reprinted in *The Interpretation of Matthew*, ed. G. Stanton, London: SPCK, 1983, 56–66, especially 57f.; Kingsbury, *Matthew: Structure, Christology, Kingdom*, 15f.

14. Freyne, *The Twelve*, 174f.; Kingsbury, *Matthew as Story*, 34.

angelic-dream messenger.[15] That does not mean that the reference to the gentiles has no significance for the subsequent development of the story, however. Even though Matthew is less concerned with the gentile links of Galilee at the level of the social world, as we have seen, he does not exclude gentiles from contact with Jesus there in the narratorial summaries of 4:23–5 and 15:21, and the final point of view of the author on the place of the gentiles in the community of Jesus is expressed in Galilee also.[16] Galilee, therefore, has been blessed with a messianic visitation in the career of Jesus, seen as a light for those in darkness.

The outcome of that visitation only gradually emerges as the Galilean ministry unfolds. In Mark the opponents surfaced almost immediately and their downfall is rapid indeed. In Matthew, however, it is only after the author has given a lengthy sample of Jesus' teaching, in which the most explicit contrast is made between the righteousness based on his words and that offered by the scribes and Pharisees, that the authority of Jesus is lauded by the crowds, in words identical to those that were expressed in Mark on the very first day of the ministry (7:28; cf. Mk 1:22). Matthew has diffused the dramatic impact considerably but the outcome appears ominous already. John the Baptist, a highly reliable character from the reader's point of view, having been confirmed by the narrator with a scriptural citation, had already intimated the

15. The Nazareans, a Jewish-Christian group, whose gospel shows affinities with that of Matthew, cited by Jerome in his commentary on Isaiah, dropped all explicit reference to Galilee from this text, using instead the translation of Symmachus who renders *galîl haggoyîm* by ὅριον τῶν ἐθνῶν. Thus they can make a twofold application of the text: Jesus removed the heavy yoke of Jewish tradition from the land of Zebulun and Naphtali, and afterwards Paul brought the gospel of Christ to the borders of the gentiles. In this instance their understanding differs from that of Matthew. Cf. A.F.J. Klijn, 'Jerome's quotations from a Nazarean Interpretation of Isaiah', *RScR* 60(1972) 241–55.

16. We cannot agree with O. Lamar Cope, *Matthew A Scribe Trained for the Kingdom of Heaven* CBQMS 5, Washington: The Catholic Biblical Association of America, 1976, 84, that the citation of Is 8:23 simply informs us of Matthew's knowledge of ancient geography without any influence on surrounding material, and therefore does not qualify as a mid-point text in his terms. The text points backwards to the coming to Galilee in the infancy, and forwards to the summary of 4:23–5, which Matthew has carefully constructed to suggest the dawning of eschatological light for Jew and gentile on a mountain in Galilee, something that is confirmed as the author's point of view by the final commission 'to make disciples of all the nations' (ἔθνη), also on a mountain in Galilee. Cf. Donaldson, *Jesus on the Mountain*, 114.

outcome with his scathing attack on the Pharisees and Sadducees (3:7–12). As Jesus proceeds to show his authority not just in words but in deeds also (chs. 8–9), the scribes and Pharisees are present, thinking evil thoughts in their hearts (9:3,34), or questioning his disciples (9:10f.,14), but avoiding any confrontation with the main character, despite the evil thoughts of both groups in his regard.[17] Matthew then has no qualms in locating both scribes and Pharisees in Galilee, and the fact that the Sadducees are also mentioned twice by the narrator outside the Jerusalem setting (3:7; 16:12), even if they do not feature in any actual episode, would seem to indicate that identifying the opponents of Jesus in terms of geographic location plays no part in his scheme.

What he does portray however, is a deterioration in the opponents' relations with Jesus as the Galilean ministry develops and his permanent group of followers begin to have a clearer identity within the narrative. As recipients of the revelation that Jesus is prepared to share with them, the disciples are designated little ones and contrasted with the wise and understanding, a thinly veiled description of Jesus' opponents as the false teachers of Israel. These show their true colours when the crowds who had witnessed a healing miracle begin to wonder if Jesus might not be the son of David (12:24). There is no need for Matthew to introduce Jerusalem scribes with the charge against Jesus of being in league with Beelzebul; the Galilean Pharisees had had such private thoughts already (9:34), the reader will remember, and now they utter them openly. In responding to them, Jesus uses images employed earlier also, a brood of vipers (John) and good and bad fruit (Jesus) to discredit them, both in their words and their actions, thereby describing them as evil, the 'root trait', as Kingsbury calls it, by which their character is defined.[18]

Later, while still in Galilee, scribes and Pharisees come from Jerusalem to put the question about handwashing violations to Jesus, and in condemning their legalism they are designated 'blind guides' (15:14), a description that is twice repeated in the Jerusalem setting (23:16,24). It is not clear

17. Kingsbury, 'The Developing Conflict', 68f.
18. 'The Developing Conflict', 58–60.

whether this designation is intended for Jerusalem scribes only. Certainly the note of opposition and hostility to Jesus is to be found in Galilee quite independently of their arrival. The impression which had previously been given in terms of the contrast between Jesus' teaching and that of the scribes now comes clearly into the open. Blindness is a charge that makes them inappropriate leaders, and it is repeatedly levelled at the opponents as a way of discrediting them. The attentive reader will not have missed the point that it was in restoring sight and speech to a blind mute that the charge of being in league with Beelzebul was first made against Jesus. It is surely ironic, then, that those who make the charge are now deemed blind, and their blindness as leaders/teachers is specified in the repeated question.: 'have you never read in the Scriptures?' (9:13; 12:7; 19:4; 21:16,42; 22:29–33). For the ideal reader whose understanding of the events surrounding Jesus' career is being carefully charted by scriptural quotations, the point of this question will not be missed.

It seems then that Matthew does not wish to distinguish sharply between Jerusalem scribal attitudes and those of Galilee, nor to differentiate between scribal and Pharisaic concerns. In this regard his combinations of opponents—scribes, Pharisees, scribes and Pharisees, Pharisees and Sadducees—appear to be quite mixed, with little specific significance attached to individual instances.[19] As well as the scribes and Pharisees from Jerusalem, we also meet those who collect the temple-tax at Capernaum (17:24), suggesting that there is a struggle going on for Galilean loyalties between the traditional Jewish positions generally and Jesus and his group of disciples, who are pointedly designated as 'scribes discipled in the kingdom', and therefore capable of bringing forth from their treasure things both new and old (13:51f.). The difference between the two points of view emerges in the scribe who wishes to follow Jesus but is warned that the Son of Man has nowhere to lay his head (8:19f.). The contrast with Mark's sympathetic scribe is striking, as the implications are that for Matthew there is little possibility of movement from

19 For a detailed discussion cf. D. Garland, *The Intention of Matthew 23*, Leiden: Brill, 1979, 43–6, 218–21.

the one position to the other, and following Jesus is not something that one can take on oneself but comes as a call from him.[20]

It is the Galilean crowds that are being sought by both groups of teachers. Initially, a great crowd is gathered in Galilee for the first sermon of the teacher, and the same crowds are to be found at the end of the Galilean ministry, having their sick healed by Jesus (15:21). The Matthean crowds are not as colourful as those of Mark, whose constant use of the singular, ὁ ὄχλος, gives the group a more distinctive definition. But in Matthew also they are enthusiastic about Jesus, contrasting his teaching to that of their scribes (7:28). They hail him as a prophet, declaring on one occasion that never was anything like this seen in Israel (9:8; 12:23; 15:31; 21:8–11,46; 22:23), and they are combined with the disciples as audience for Jesus' most scathing attack on the scribes and Pharisees (23:1), just as they have been witnesses to the disputes between Jesus and their leaders throughout the gospel: 9:18; 12:22–32; 15:1–20; 21:10–17, 23–7; 22:23–33. As far as the main character is concerned they are 'like sheep without a shepherd' (9:35), thus castigating their blind leaders. Jesus and his specially chosen disciples have a mission to these crowds who, as the abandoned sheep, are in danger of becoming 'the lost sheep' (10:6; 15:14). Yet, even as he heals their ills, thereby fulfilling in their regard one of the servant prophecies of Isaiah (42:1–4; cf. Mt 12:18–21), the suggestion is clear that his mission will eventually encompass the gentiles who 'will hope in his name'. Thus, as already intimated, even as Galileans are being ministered to as part of the lost sheep of the house of Israel, a broader definition of Israel is emerging, based on the scriptural promises, and Galilee, not Jerusalem, provides the eschatological mountain where this can take place. The prophetic judgment of the main character on the Galilean towns, including Capernaum, his own city, matches the judgment on Jerusalem later (23:37–9). Consequently the reader is not surprised to find the Matthean crowd under the control of the opponents at the

20. Cf. G. Bornkamm, 'The Stilling of the Storm in Matthew', in G. Bornkamm, G. Barth, and H.J. Held, *Tradition and Interpetation in Matthew*, London: SCM, 1963, 52–7.

end (27:20), as all—crowd and leaders alike—constitute this evil and adulterous generation, who formally, as the λαὸς, or people, call down the blood curse on themselves, in what amounts to a derogation of the Sinai covenant (27:25; cf. Ex 24:8).

iii) *Jesus and his Movement in Matthew's Galilee.* Since Matthew presents the story as a polemic between Jesus and the Jewish teachers, even in Galilee, the portrait of Jesus that emerges is highly polemical also. As we have seen, no direct confrontation takes place between him and his opponents until the author has established for the reader beyond any doubt the validity of Jesus' claims, both in terms of his teaching and his mighty deeds. The ideal reader received vital clues about his identity from the very outset through the genealogy, the birth and the flight into Egypt. Jesus is son of David, his very name has salvific significance and, as the one who fulfils the Emmanuel prophecy from Isaiah, he is in fact 'God with us', according to the interpretation of the Hebrew word which the narrator gives for our benefit (1:23). The Egyptian sojourn establishes further that he is God's son, something that is confirmed for us by the voice from heaven at the Baptism (2:15; 3:17). Finally, the temptation shows how, unlike old Israel that was unfaithful in the desert, he is God's obedient son, rejecting the offer of all the kingdoms of the world and their splendour, a vision of which is granted to him 'on a very high mountain' (4:8f). We observed also in passing that news of his birth had caused great disturbance in Jerusalem, and that in seeking to be rid of him secular and religious authorities—Herod, the chief priests and the scribes—had joined forces in trying to eliminate him.

With all this information at our disposal, we have little difficulty in acknowledging the truth of the claims that Jesus makes for himself or that the narrator makes on his behalf, as well as a clear premonition of the outcome (5:17–20; 7:28; 8:17; 9:6). But characters within the narrative also have little difficulty in grasping the identity of Jesus, least of all his disciples who, in sharp contrast to Mark's presentation, understand all that they are witness to (cf. e.g. 8:25; 13:16f.,

51f.; 16:5–12).[21] Even the crowd's reactions, we saw, were positive, climaxing in the question, 'could this be David's son?' (12:24), a question which they themselves answer positively as Jesus enters David's city (21:9,15). The bad faith of the blind leaders is all the more culpable in the light of such evidence, and the main character does not spare them in the use of apocalyptic language of exclusion to describe their final fate.[22]

But it is the influence of the Galilean setting in the way Matthew presents the career of Jesus that is our real concern. In the final mountain scene in Galilee, Jesus, now claiming for himself the universal authority he had refused to accept from Satan in the first mountain scene, sends his chosen (eleven) disciples to make disciples of all the nations, 'teaching them to observe all that I commanded you' and baptising them (28:16–20). Thus a direct link is established with other teaching occasions in the gospel, chiefly, one suspects, the great discourses, all but one of which is located in Galilee. Yet when the question is put to Jesus about his messianic status by the Baptist, on hearing of the works (τὰ ἔργα) of Christ, he replies by giving a veritable list of his deeds up to that point in the narrative, adding by way of conclusion: 'the poor have the gospel preached to them' (11:2–5). A final remark, 'blessed is the one that shall not be scandalised in me', at once makes it clear that not all will be convinced by what they have heard and seen, and invites the reader to understand both the deeds and the words of Jesus in a fuller context.

After replying to John, and by implication to all who care to ask the obvious question, Jesus goes on to discuss his own fate as Son of Man and that of the Baptist at the hands of this generation; they are both rejected, but for opposite reasons, thus showing the lack of seriousness of those involved. Nevertheless, we are assured, 'wisdom is vindicated by her works (ἔργα, 11:19). The woes on the Galilean towns that have experienced his works of power (δυνάμεις) clarifies the reference to the rejection of the Son of Man, and links up with the Baptist's question about the works of the Christ, and the

21. Cf. Freyne, *The Twelve*, 198–205; U. Luz, 'The Disciples in the Gospel according to Matthew', reprinted in *The Interpretation of Matthew*, 98–128.

22. Cf. Freyne, 'Vilifying the Other and Defining the Self', especially appendix 1.

reference to the deeds of wisdom. Finally, as wisdom incarnate, Jesus claims a privileged knowledge of God that only a son can have, and is grateful that this is shared with the little ones while being hidden from the wise and understanding. In an implied contrast with the opponents' teaching, later to be made explicit (23:4), he invites all to come and learn of him.

By thus skilfully weaving a web of allusions to various scriptural figures—Christ, Son of Man, wisdom—and identifying them with Jesus in his ministry of deed *and* word in the Galilean setting, Matthew can now formally introduce the opponents. Through an open confrontation with the main character further aspects of his person and mission emerge more clearly. At the centre of the treatment is the long citation from Isaiah explaining the servant of Yahweh's care for the broken reed and the smouldering flax, and his role in bringing justice and judgment (κρίσις) to the gentiles. This double role that the scriptural reference indicates, constitutes it as a mid-point text, in terms of the analysis of O. Lamar Cope, providing a number of connecting links with the passages that precede and follow it.[23] On the one hand, Jesus, as someone greater than the temple, puts the demands of love above those of the Sabbath (12:6f.), thereby not crushing the bruised reed, in contrast to the Pharisees, who need to learn from Hosea that love is more important than cultic observance. On the other hand, endowed with the spirit of God, Jesus is greater than Solomon, and so those who came to hear Solomon's wisdom will rise in judgment (κρίσις) against this generation, typified by the Pharisees, who attribute Jesus' powers to Beelzebul (12:24,42).

Once again, Matthew has subtly linked a number of scriptural allusions to interpret further the significance of Jesus' Galilean career. The contrast with Solomon, the father of wisdom in Israel, links up with the declaration about Jesus being wisdom incarnate of the previous chapter. And since it was Solomon who had built the original temple, Jesus can

23. For his analysis of ch. 12 cf. *Matthew. A Scribe Trained for the Kingdom of Heaven*, 32–52. Though his discussion is conducted very much in the context of redaction criticism, his linear form of analysis, attempting to trace the logic of the evangelist/author's intention at the level of the completed text, has many resemblances with the reader-oriented approaches.

now claim superiority over it also, declaring in his wisdom that the needs of people are more important than cult or Sabbath. The ideal reader will recall that at his birth Jesus, as Emmanuel, was described as God-with-us, and Jerusalem, its scribes and chief priests, were disturbed by the news. As Matthew has interwoven his own commentary into the narrative of Jesus' ministry in Galilee, the reason for their unease is becoming clearer. By declaring his superiority over the original son of David, Solomon, and his achievements as the wise one who built the temple, this son of David is in fact subverting the system that was based on Jerusalem, and thereby undermining the position of those whose lives were dependent on it. The only possible reaction is to attempt to discredit him by denying the source of his power in God, attributing it instead to the prince of demons. In doing so they are cutting themselves off from God irrevocably, however.

It comes as no surprise to find that in the final confrontation in Galilee between Jesus and his opponents, Jerusalem is represented in the persons of its scribes and Pharisees (15:1). In reply to the charge that his disciples transgress the tradition of the elders, Jesus accuses them of transgressing the word of God by their own traditions, using the same example as Mark to show how temple piety can lead to violation of one of the central love commands of the decalogue. The Pharisees, we are informed, were scandalised on hearing this, only to be further castigated by Jesus as blind guides, plants not planted by the heavenly Father, and so destined for destruction (15:12f.). This final judgment by the main character on his opponents within the Galilean narrative links up with the earlier statements of the author, and it is presumed that the reader will be sufficiently in tune to make the connections. In responding to John's question, Jesus had said that those who would not be scandalised in him would be blessed, and now we hear that the Pharisees were scandalised; as the son who knows the hidden things of God, Jesus can judge the plants that his heavenly Father has not planted; in the controversy over Beelzebul they were described as being both blind and evil and now they are declared blind guides, so that those who follow them must know their own fate also.

By developing his narrative in this way during the Galilean

phase, Matthew was able to mount an attack on the Jerusalem centre of Jewish faith and the authoritative guardians of its temple and tradition there. Thus the plot comes to its inevitable conclusion in the Jerusalem setting, as Jesus is rejected, not just by the leaders but by all the people. We have seen that this casts a shadow over the Galilean ministry also, since that region too pertains to the house of Israel, whose destruction and desolation is now foretold in the most explicit terms possible (23:37–9). Likewise, however, Jerusalem must receive the full benefits of Jesus' ministry, and so, unlike in Mark, we find Jesus performing cures in the temple (21:14f.), much to the annoyance of the chief priests and scribes, as well as teaching there on a daily basis (26:55). The one new element that emerges in Jerusalem is the role of the high priests, who until now were only encountered as advisers of Herod on the birth of the child (2:3). However, once the narrative reaches Jerusalem, they, together with the elders, become central to the plot, but without any diminution of the role of the opponents from the Galilean phase.[24] It appears as though the narrator wants to bring them into contact with each of the other three groups of opponents in turn as soon as Jesus reaches their territory, the temple: at 21:15 the high priests and scribes are disturbed at the enthusiam for Jesus' healings in the temple; at 21:23 the chief priests and the elders of the people query Jesus about his authority, and at 21:45 the chief priests and Pharisees recognise that the parables of the two sons and the wicked tenants have been spoken against them.

Thus at the crucial point of the plot all the strands of Jewish opposition are brought together with the chief priests at the centre, involved to the last in trying to discredit the good news about Jesus, so that the word that his body had been stolen had gone abroad among the Jews to the day in which

24. The most frequent combination is 'chief priests and elders', occuring 9 times in all and always in conjunction with the death of Jesus which they both plot and see through to its completion: 16:21; 21:23; 26:3,47; 27:1,3,12,20; the chief priests appear on their own 3 times as those primarily in charge of the arrest and execution: 26:14; 27:6; 28:11; together with the scribes alone 3 times: 2:4; 20:18; 21:15, and with the scribes and elders twice: 16:21; 27:41; they join the Pharisees twice: 21:45; 27:62. Finally, at 26:59 we hear of the chief priests and the whole sanhedrin seeking false witness against Jesus.

the author had written his story (28:11–15). In this way the author takes his stance over against all the various segments of Jewish faith who, despite their differences, are united as 'the Jews' simply in their rejection of Jesus.

There is an alternative ending, however, that of the commissioning of the eleven in Galilee. Because Matthew is so heavily involved with the Jewish question the emergence of his own group of followers in Galilee does not obtrude itself into the narrative in quite the same way as it did in Mark. One reason for this has been dealt with in passing already, namely the fact that the truth about Jesus is open to all and clearly documented as the narrative progressed; there could be no mistaking his identity, either for followers or opponents. The disciples appear as it were from nowhere. This is certainly true of the twelve disciples, since Matthew omits any separate call to this group, summoning them rather for the task of mission to Israel at an appropriate point in the narrative after Jesus' purpose has been clearly described in terms of a ministry of word and deed. The crowds are like sheep without a shepherd, soon to be designated 'the lost sheep of the house of Israel' (9:35; 10:6), and the twelve disciples/apostles are sent to perform the self-same tasks as Jesus—proclaiming the nearness of the kingdom of God and healing every disease and every infirmity among the people (10:1,7). As Galileans (cf. 26:69,73) they participate in the mission of Jesus to Israel, sharing in his rejection also (10:16–33), even to being thought to be in league with Beelzebul. Later in the Jerusalem section, designated as prophets, wise men and scribes, those whom Jesus sends will be rejected and persecuted by Jewish authorities (23:34–6), so that the fate of Jesus and his disciples becomes part of a larger pattern of rejection in Israel's history. Presumably, it is this rejection that wins for them the role of judging the twelve tribes of Israel in the apocalyptic reversal that is awaited with the glorious return of the Son of man (19:28; 25:31).

The final commissioning indicates that the twelve disciples have another role also within the story. As disciples they themselves have been discipled (13:51; 27:57), and as the Twelve they evoke for the reader the original Israel as a twelve-tribe people (Mt 19:28). They are not directly designated as Israel however, since Matthew has reserved that name for those to whom they are sent, who unfortunately, in their rejection of Jesus and his emissaries, forfeit the right to be Israel. Instead it is around them and their leader Peter that the ἐκκλησία of Jesus is gathered, in the midst of which Jesus himself will be present to the close of the age (16:18; 18:17,20). This name too has scriptural warrant as the *qahal Yahweh*, thereby claiming that the community so designated is the alternative Israel.

The story of the original followers of Jesus is not an idealised one by any means in Matthew. They are beset by 'little faith' (ὀλιγοπιστία), which is a crippling fear in the moment of crisis rather than a lack of understanding (8:26; 14:31; 16:8; 17:20), and is contrasted with mustard-seed faith, that is faith worthy of the kingdom (cf. 13:31). In this regard Peter, the rock, is all too typical, being guilty of little faith (14:31), of a restricted understanding of the love command (18:21) and of denying his Galilean associations with Jesus, despite his accent (26:69–75). Yet he is also the recipient of the revelation promised to the little ones (11:25–7; 16:17), and it is in this role of the little ones that the disciples of Jesus have a special function within the community of disciples. Under the related images of babes, children, little ones, the ideal of authentic discipleship continues to be put before the reader at crucial points of the narrative (10:40–42; 11:25–7; 18:1–14) and so we are equipped to judge the achievements and failures of the symbolic group and individuals at the centre of the disciples. Essential to these images is the idea of total trust in the heavenly Father's care for his creation, and accordingly, the lack of preoccupation with material goods. In the farewell discourse the wandering missionaries in their homelessness, lack of material possessions (especially clothing) and open confession leading to imprisonment, are the ones who best portray the ideals for all disciples enunciated earlier (6:19–34; 10:16–33), ideals which were such a radical challenge to the social world assumed by the author.

By way of summary we may briefly contrast the picture of Galilee that emerges with that of Mark previously delineated. Matthew also has a highly positive evaluation of Galilee, as is clear from his desire to validate its claims to having had a messianic visitation in the career of Jesus. These claims are further reinforced by the final reunion and commissioning scene in Galilee. As the presentation of Jesus and his ministry unfolds, Galilee recedes from view, and the reader's attention is directed instead to the lost sheep of the house of Israel, about to reject Jesus, the messiah of Israel, son of God and Son of man—God's wisdom among them who reveals things hidden from the foundation of the world, and God's servant who carries their burdens. Yet, even though no distinctive Galilean point of view emerges, in contrast with Mark, we are never allowed to forget the Galilean perspective, as judgment is passed on Galilean cities and Galilee is finally left behind only after the community discourse had been addressed to the ἐκκλησία of Jesus in Capernaum (19:1).

Because of the determining role that Jesus' struggle with all the forms of Judaism has had on the shaping of the Matthean narrative, the local colouring of the Marcan treatment is lacking. Opponents are found equally in Galilee and Jerusalem, and judgment falls on all insofar as they reject their shepherd. Yet the imagery of the house in the description of the mission to Israel (10:6; 15:24) naturally evokes Jerusalem and its temple, David's city, whose first temple was built by Solomon, his son. Even more overtly than in Mark, Jesus' Galilean ministry is presented as an attack on that institution, since in Jesus' words and works something greater than both the temple and Solomon the wise is present, as Matthew describes them.

As Jesus is rejected, his community of disciples with the twelve disciples at its centre, emerges as the *qahal Yahweh*, an alternative to unfaithful Israel. Those disciples who are discipled in the kingdom, that is, those who have taken on themselves the easy yoke of Jesus' radical teaching, are called scribes, in a deliberately provocative contrast with the most influential teachers of Israel. As the Twelve, the Galilean followers share Jesus' rejection by Israel and are promised a share with him as judges of Israel in the future. As disciples who model their lives on his in the present, in terms both of lack of concern for material things and of complete trust in divine providence, they demonstrate an ideal of discipleship for all. Their life-style makes them specially dear to the heavenly Father, and, insofar as it is replicated, it allows Christ to be present in his community as Emmanuel, God-with-us, to the close of the age.

The importance of Galilee to this picture is not that Matthew exploits its gentile associations during the ministry as in Mark, but rather that as part of Israel, a ministry that was conducted there once can now be justified as a messianic visitation to Israel, which is also to encompass all the nations, as the Isaianic prophecies had foretold.

2. Luke

In discussing Luke's treatment of Galilee we are faced with the enigmatic situation that, although all commentators agree that Galilee is highly important in his presentation, there is no absolute agreement as to the extent of his Galilean section.[25] As early as 4:44, even before the call of the first disciples, we are informed by the narrator of an active ministry in Judea, and this has suggested to some commentators that the Galilean phase is already over, since Luke was interested in it only as the place of beginning (23:2; Ac 10:37).[26] Were that the case there would appear to be little point in examining the Lukan narrative for a distinctive understanding of Galilee, since the author would scarcely have been interested in developing a contrast between Galilee on the one hand and Jerusalem/Judea on the other. In that event we could not reasonably expect any developed treatment of the Galilean social and religious worlds as having any significance in the narrative.

Must we, however, take 4:44 to mean that in Luke's view Jesus has abandoned Galilee finally? The response to this question depends on the meaning given to Judea in 4:44—the southern region as opposed to the north, or the whole of the

25. H. Conzelmann, *The Theology of St. Luke*, E.T. London:Faber, 1960, 41, is a notable exception to this statement about the importance of Galilee for Luke. Cf. Freyne, *Galilee*, 364–7 for a detailed criticism; also J. Fitzmyer, *The Gospel according to Luke I—IX*, Anchor Bible, New York: Doubleday, 1985, 164–71.

26. H. Schürmann, *Das Lukasevangelium* I, HTKNT 3:1, Freiburg, 1969, 260; M. Völkel, 'Der Anfang Jesu in Galiläa. Bemerkungen zum Gebrauch und zur Funktion Galiläas in den Lukanischen Schriften', *ZNW* 64 (1973) 222–32.

Jewish territory.[27] In deciding between these two alternatives it is often pointed out that the former seems to be Luke's general usage, thereby distinguishing the southern part of the country from Galilee: 1:39; 2:4; 3:1; 5:17; 17:11; cf. Ac 9:31. However, Luke can also use Judea in the larger sense to encompass all the regions of the country: 1:5; 7:17; 23:5. In this latter instance the phrase 'throughout the whole of Judea beginning from Galilee' seems to suggest Luke's own point of view as a generalised summary.[28] It seems that Luke can slip from the narrower to the broader usage rather easily, but the attentive reader will have little difficulty in recognising from the general context or from other hints which meaning is intended. The fact that a number of Galilean place-names and other associations occur after 4:44 (cf. 5:1; 7:1; 8:2,22,26; 9:7–9), clearly implies that the author/narrator wants us to think of Galilee as the actual location of the story up to the major break of 9:51.[29] We are justified then in probing further for a clearer picture of how Luke envisages Galilee, especially since the expression 'beginning in Galilee' shows a genuine concern with the past and with Galilee as the originating point of the ministry.

i) *The Galilean Social World.* The political setting which Luke highlights for the ministry of Jesus is the clearest indication for the reader that he wishes us to take the regional aspect of the story into account. The birth of John, we are informed, took place in the days of Herod, king of Judea (1:5). Judea here would seem to encompass the whole region,

27. That 'Ἰουδαία is the *lectio difficilior* at 4:44, and is therefore to be preferred is now generally accepted. Cf. B. Metzger, *A Textual Commentary on the Greek New Testament*, London-New York: United Bible Societies, 1977, 137f.

28. Cf. Freyne, *Galilee*, 381 n.6. Pliny writes: 'Supra Idumaeam et Samariam Judaea longe lateque funditur. Pars ejus Syriae juncta, Galilaea vocatur' (*Natural History*, V, 70.).

29. F. O Fearghail, in 'A Study of the Role of Lk 1:1–4:44 in the Composition of Luke's Two-Volume Work', Doctoral Dissertation (to be published in Analecta Biblica) presented to P.I.B. Rome, 1987, argues that the Galilean section begins at 5:1, since there is a thematic and literary unity in the first four chapters which gives them the role of an anticipatory introduction to the whole work. Thus, the reference to Judea in 4:44 does not stand in chronological sequence to the immediate context, but includes the whole territory covered by Jesus' ministry. Despite the convincing arguments that O'Fearghail gives for his thesis, it still remains true that Nazareth and Capernaum, two Galilean locations, are chosen as suitable sites for this introduction, just as Jerusalem had previously functioned in that capacity (2:46f.).

north and south, since in the subsequent narrative the appearance of the angel to Mary takes place in a city of Galilee called Nazareth (1:26), but she goes to the hill country of Judea, (1:39), only to return home later (1:56). In this way the narrator conveys a sense of close bonds between the regions, reinforced subsequently when we hear that Mary and Joseph have again to leave Galilee and go to Judea in order to fulfil the census requirements (2:4). For Luke then, Galilee is not just a safe outpost, as in the case of Matthew, but rather an integral part of the territory of Herod, with close religious and human bonds with Judea in the narrow sense.

Thirty years later this situation has changed somewhat, we are informed, as the rulers of the different regions of the country, including Galilee, are listed (3:1,23), among them two characters—Herod Antipas and Pilate—who will have an important bearing on the story of Jesus. Some Pharisees intimate that Herod is a threat to Jesus (13:31–3), but the fact that Joanna, the wife of his steward, Chuza, is part of Jesus' permanent retinue (8:2), suggests that the threat may not be all that real. We meet no Herodians in Galilee plotting against Jesus, and when eventually Herod does get to meet Jesus he is presented as a shallow figure, more interested in having his ego suitably flattered than in removing any potential threat (23:6–12). Pilate is quite a different figure, since in the very same context in which Jesus receives the warning about Herod we hear of those 'Galileans whose blood Pilate had mingled with their sacrifices' (13:1), a rather ominous note in view of the fact that a little later we are told that Jesus journeyed through villages and towns making his way to Jerusalem (13:22). The reader is thus suitably warned about the likely outcome of the story that is firmly anchored to the political realities from the outset. Jerusalem can be a dangerous place for Galileans, especially when they are on a religious mission.

As already mentioned, Luke seems to move easily from Judea in the broad sense to the more narrow, regional understanding. This does not mean that the author/narrator is unconcerned about location, however. Most noteworthy is the fact that Jesus does not travel in extra-Galilean territories such as Tyre and Sidon, the Dekapolis or the region of Caesarea Philippi, something that is quite remarkable in view of the declared interest of the main character in both Jews and gentiles from the outset (2:32). True, people from the sea-coast of Tyre and Sidon are present to hear the sermon on the plain, together with those from Jerusalem and Judea (6:17), thus avoiding any sense of xenophobia. Yet, when Jesus does visit the country of the Gerasenes we are reminded by the narrator that it is 'opposite Galilee' (8:26). The journeys of the main character are internal to Galilee, therefore, and we are constantly reminded that he is on the move, thereby preparing us for the journey section proper (4:30; 4:43f.; 6:1; 7:11; 8:1–3).

If surrounding gentile territories do not feature prominently in Luke, he is unique among the Synoptists in adverting to the Samaritan influence on the story. Their relations with the Galileans are not very cordial because of religious differences, since the Galileans are among those who worship in Jerusalem (9:53). Thus the narrator subtly prepares us for the shock of the main character's use of a Samaritan as the hero of one of his stories, which is pointedly, if provocatively, located on the Jerusalem/Jericho road and clearly implies criticism of temple personnel and their concerns (10:25–37). A location somewhere between Galilee and Samaria is chosen for extolling the Samaritan leper; alone of the ten who were cured he returned to give thanks (17:16). Thus Samaria is portrayed in different colours in its relation to the main character, rejecting him as a Jerusalem-based pilgrim, yet accepting his healing ministry. What is most interesting is the way in which the author has woven into the story an awareness of the general relations between the two regions, something which increases the reader's sense of the importance of the depicted social world for the plot.[30]

On turning to the economic and social realities, we note

30. The fact that Samaria features as a place where the early Christian missioners are received in Acts (8:4–25) does not falsify the assumptions of the gospel narrative, since those who are accepted are hellenistic Jews who have been rejected in Jerusalem, and Samaria was a thoroughly hellenised city. Cf. J. Jervell, *Luke and the People of God. A New Look at Luke-Acts*, Minneapolis: Augsburg, 1972, 115–17.

how Luke speaks about cities rather frequently, even though he is aware of villages also.[31] Yet this usage is deceptive since the social world that is depicted is rural rather than urban, and the overall picture that emerges is no different from that of other gospels—a rural Galilee whose economy is based on agriculture and related labour. Admittedly, if we take into consideration the special Lukan parables from the journey section, there does seem to be a preference for city characters (14:21; 18:2,3; 19:17,19,31), but even then these are matched by rural settings also (13:6f.; 15:25f.). The phrase κατὰ πόλεις κὰι κώμας (8:1; 13:22) seems to be Luke's favourite one to suggest a total coverage, but at 8:1 we hear of crowds travelling to Jesus κα τὰ πόλιν to hear parables with a rural flavour in a rural setting. All the places mentioned as cities—Nazareth, Capernaum, Naim, Bethsaida—do not, even in Luke's narrative, possess the institutions one normally associates with a hellenistic city, and it is doubtful if he really wishes to convey the impression that they do.[32] Instead, the dominant pattern of social relationship that is featured is that of a village society in which people have close ties of kinship with each other, sharing goods (11:5–11) as well as familial joys and sorrows (7:11–14; 15:6,9). Even the fish industry is conducted on a co-operative basis (5:1–11) and not on hired labour as in Mark. Besides, there is a reserve and a hostility towards outsiders because of limited horizons (4:42; 9:52–6). The leaders are described as elders (7:1–10) though mention of a ruler (ἄρχων, 14:1) is suggestive of city structures; we also meet the synagogue leader who appears to have a representative role in the village because of shared religious belief (8:41; 13:14).

The economy is essentially rural also, and the chief commodoties are fruit, grain, oil and cattle (13:6–9; 12:16–21; 15:23,29; 16:1–9). Yet the primary resource of the land is not

31. Nazareth, Capernaum, Naim and Bethsaida are all called cities. Though Jesus goes κατὰ πόλεις καὶ κώμας the Twelve and the Seventy (Two) are sent to cities (9:5; 10:1,8,11,12). In dealing with the region of Samaria he speaks of villages only both in the gospel and in Acts.

32. The fact that in Acts Luke concentrates the mission exclusively to cities, except in Samaria (8:25), may have influenced the terminology of the gospel also, thus continuing the parallelism between the two works.

shared equally. At one end of the scale there are the large landowners who have hired servants (μίσθιοι, 15:17) or a steward (οἰκονόμος, 12:42; 16:2), and at the other end we meet day-labourers (10:2), slaves (12:35–8; 14:17–22; 15:26; 17:7–10) and the destitute who do not participate at all—the beggars, the blind, the maimed and the lame (14:23, 16:3). In between are the small landowners or share-croppers, living in one-roomed houses with their families (8:4–8; cf. 11:5–8; 16:4ff.). Nevertheless, it is an economy that is based, partly, at least, on money (12:6,59; 15:8), and debt seems to have been a fact of daily life (7:41f.; 12:58f.; 16:34). In such a limited goods economy in which debts were incurred to meet the pressing needs of land-owner or other tax-collector there was always the danger of exploitation or brigandage: 3:14; 6:29; 10:29–37; 11:21f. The ἀγορά is a place of meeting rather than of trade and commerce (11:43; 20:46), and when this does take place it is the occupation of the well-to-do, Herodian class (17:28; 19:11–27). As depicted then, this is a society of great inequalities where wealth can be acquired by good fortune (12:16) or hard work (19:12–16) on the one hand, or alternatively, by robbery and exploitation. There is a stark contrast between the affluence of the rich and the penury of the poor (16:19–31), and the implied criticism of the rich man is not that he is wealthy but rather that he refuses to share goods with the needy—a constant injunction throughout the gospel (3:12; 6:29f.; 11:8ff.; 15:16).

This theme of sharing goods with the needy—in Lukan terms 'giving alms'—helps to highlight a dominant aspect of Luke's economic picture as the reader encounters this in various characters. The gentile military commander has built a synagogue for his Jewish subjects (7:5); wealthy Pharisees give meals and Jesus is invited (7:36; 11:37; 14:1); the rich tax-collector, Zacchaeus, is delighted to have Jesus dine with him (19:6). This repeated pattern, expressed in different scenes throughout the narrative, underscores for the reader the fact that our author wishes to describe a limited goods economy which can only be maintained through the generosity and sharing of the wealthy with the less well-off. Unfortunately, the reverse is all too frequent as greed manifests itself in the desire to share only with one's social equals, whereby a return of some kind can be anticipated (11:39; 14:12; 16:27). In these scenes one catches a glimpse of the patron/client relationship which was so dominant a social pattern in Roman society, the assumptions of which Jesus and his movement cut across, as we shall see.

Luke's treatment of the Galilean social world gives the most detailed account of the economic realities of any of the gospel writers. The parables that are unique to this gospel help considerably in filling out this picture with their characters enmeshed in economic and social affairs. Clearly, this aspect of the narrative world is much more important for Luke's version of the story than is the case for the other evangelists. It is a world of great contrasts in which the well-off in their condition of affluence and the poor in their deprived state are deliberately juxtaposed. At several points the author makes it clear that his sympathies lie with the underprivileged. 'Those who are dressed in fine clothes and live in luxury are in the houses of kings' (7:25), is the utterance of the main character as he lauds John the Baptist, whom Luke introduces as preaching a message of social justice and non-exploitation of the weak. The rich man who is so unfavourably contrasted with the poor Lazarus is also described as being lavishly attired (16:19), whereas Jesus' instruction to his disciples is that they are to travel with only one tunic and without money or food (9:3; 10:2). The reader has been well prepared for this definite option of the author, in that God, whose plan for history is being brought to completion in the narrative about Jesus, is also the one who 'fills the hungry with good things and sends the rich away empty' (1:53). It is wholly consistent with this point of view that the main character, Jesus, depicts his own mission as one of good news for the poor, in terms drawn from the socio-economic realities of the year of Jubilee (Lk 4:18; Is 61:1–2; 58:6). We must now examine the religious world in which this social and economic picture is so firmly embedded.[33]

ii) *Religious Attitudes in Galilee.* The concentration on social realities by the main character does not diminish the

33. On the links between the Nazareth pericope and the Jubilee cf. J.A. Sanders 'From Is 61 to Lk 4' in *Christianity, Judaism and Other Greco-Roman Cults. Studies for Morton Smith at 60,* 3 vols., ed. J. Neusner, Leiden: Brill, 1975, vol. 1, 75–107.

essentially religious colouring of the story from the outset. The infancy narratives set the tone in this regard with representative figures awaiting the consolation of Israel, and the Jerusalem temple is the focal point of their piety. The fact that the parents of Jesus, as Galileans, together with their kinsmen and neighbours, also make the pilgrimage journey regularly (κατ' ἔτος) to Jerusalem suggests that Galileans, less than Judeans, shared the same pious hopes (2:41,44).[34] It is, then, not surprising to find that the main character's life is firmly directed towards Jerusalem from the very beginning, and when he reaches the city the temple is the focal point of his ministry. In this regard the fact that the Samaritans do not accept him as one 'whose face was set to go to Jerusalem' (9:53) shows how much Luke wishes to present Jesus as a pilgrim like so many of his fellow-Galileans (cf. 13:1).

Even though the pilgrimage and the temple dominate the narrative in a highly positive manner unlike Mark's negative evaluation of Jerusalem, the internal Galilean religious scene comes into focus also in a highly distinctive fashion.[35] The public ministry of Jesus is presented in an anticipatory way by the two contrasting receptions in Nazareth and Capernaum (4:14–42). Here we are taken inside a synagogue by the narrator for a detailed description of the service. The suspense is palpable and our eyes as well as those of the people in the Nazareth synagogue are on Jesus as he adopts the seated position for teaching after reading from the book of Isaiah (4:20; cf. 2:46, but contrast 6:19). We are informed that attendance at the synagogue on the Sabbath was customary

34. On the question of the observance of the law in Luke cf. C. L. Blomberg, 'The Law in Luke-Acts' *JSNT* 22 (1984) 53–80. who explains the picture of law-abiding Jews in the opening chapters as part of a developing pattern in which Luke seeks to portray a gradual movement from law-abiding to freedom from law as the narrative progresses in terms of the establishment of the new covenant in the ministry of Jesus and the early church. For a different view of the same phenomenon in terms of a common cultural concern of respect for ancestral customs cf. G. Downing, 'Freedom from the Law in Luke-Acts', *JSNT* 26(1986) 49–52.

35. On Luke's positive appropriation of Jerusalem as the city of salvation cf. I. de la Potterie, 'Les deux noms de Jérusalem dans l'évangile de Luc' *RSR* 69 (1981) 59–70; M. Bachmann, *Jerusalem und der Tempel*, BWANT Stuttgart: 1980, 132–70, who argues rather one-sidedly for the identity of temple and city. For a contrasting point of view cf. F.D. Weinert, 'Luke, the Temple, and Jesus' Saying about Jerusalem's Abandoned House (Luke 13:34–5)' *CBQ* 44 (1982) 68–76, for whom, οἶκος does not mean the temple, but the Judean religious leadership.

for Jesus (4:16), something that the subsequent narrative bears out, both through individual episodes (5:17–26; 6:6–11; 7:1–10; 13:10–17) and narratorial comment (4:43f.). He performs cures on behalf of the gentile centurion who had built a synagogue for the Capernaum Jews (7:1–4), as well as the synagogue ruler Jairus (8:41). Yet, despite such frequent contacts, the location in the end is no more favourable for Jesus than in any of the other accounts. He must leave the Nazareth synagogue under threat, and at Capernaum he transfers to the house where we find the Pharisees and lawyers seated around him listening to his teaching (5:17). It is on the plain that the author/narrator locates his teaching of the crowd in the most important single address within the narrative, and the significance of the house as a private place of instruction, a feature of Mark's narrative as we have seen, is abandoned (cf. Lk 8:14–21 in contrast to Mk 3:22–4:32).

Apart from the greater emphasis on a synagogue ministry the author also devotes more narrative space to Jesus' dealing with the Pharisees in a Galilean setting. The reader who is attuned to opposition coming from scribal jealousy on the basis of Mark's narrative will be surprised to find that this is not such a marked feature in Luke's account. There is no implied contrast with scribal teaching on the occasion of his first visit to the Capernaum synagogue (4:32,36 in contrast to Mk 1:22,27), and since Luke does not report the hand-washing episode with the scribal presence from Jerusalem, the overall effect of their opposition in Galilee is somewhat muted. They do appear together with the Pharisees in the disputes about the Sabbath (14:3), the forgiveness of sins on the occasion of the cure of the paralytic and the table-fellowship with tax-collectors and sinners (5:21,30; cf. 15:2), but even in that context the narrator has intimated that Pharisees and teachers of the law had come from every village of Galilee and Judea and from Jerusalem, and were seated listening to Jesus (5:17).

This information is highly significant on two counts. Not merely are we informed about an active presence of Pharisees and scribes throughout Galilee, with the emphatic ἐκ πάσης κώμης τῆς Γαλιλαίας but in addition we are to assume that they are interested in discoursing with Jesus. While the final outcome in terms of their attitude to Jesus may not be very different, the Lukan narrator is preparing us for further encounters, with the Pharisees alone, as it transpires. It is only in the Jerusalem section that the scribal opposition comes into its own, and repeatedly we find them as opponents of Jesus together with the chief priests and elders, leading ultimately to his death (9:22; 19:47; 20:1,19,39,46; 22:2,66; 23:10). But in Galilee their importance is downplayed, not merely by the fact that they are variously named—νομοδιδάσκαλοι (5:17), γραμματεῖς (5:21,30; 6:7; 11:53) and νομικοί (7:30), thereby diffusing somewhat their impact on the narrative as an organised group based essentially in Jerusalem (cf. 2:46)—but also by the particular highlighting of the role of the Pharisees in the Galilean context.

In dealing with the social world, Luke, we saw, was interested in using typical characters as a way of illustrating a particular situation, and he employs a similar strategy in dealing with the religious scene also. Instead of the Pharisees we meet a certain Pharisee named Simon (7:36,40), a certain Pharisee concerned with hand-washing (11:37) and a Pharisee described as a ruler (ἄρχων, 14:1). In this way a much clearer profile of the Pharisaic movement emerges, and for Luke this movement is firmly rooted in Galilee, since apart from one brief appearance (19:39), they play no part at all in the Jerusalem setting. The impression of Galilean Pharisees is further accentuated by the warning given to Jesus by some Pharisees that Antipas was out to destroy him (13:33). However we interpret the incident—a subtle ploy to be rid of Jesus or a genuine concern for his safety—it assumes that Pharisees are active in his territory, right up to the highest court circles, it would seem.

While Luke's Pharisees have definite religious concerns—hand-washing, sabbath observance and purity laws (6:2,7; 7:39; 11:39; 14:13)—a closer examination of the scenes in which Jesus encounters individual Pharisees shows how completely they are integrated into the social world that is depicted. In the first incident in the house of Simon, the host is shocked that Jesus allows a notorious woman sinner to touch him, and questions his status as a prophet (7:39). A rather different understanding of prophecy had already surfaced in the spontaneous reaction of the crowd that a great prophet had arisen among them and God had visited his people, after the raising of the widow's son at Naim (7:16). When measured against that view of prophecy the limitations of the Pharisee's understanding are blatantly exposed. For him prophecy had to do with protecting himself from undesirables as defined by a particular set of religious assumptions, whereas the author/narrator sees it as a divine visitation that benefits the underprivileged—widows, sinners, outsiders of various kinds. By contrast with the sinful woman, whose lavish deed of oriental hospitality is vividly depicted, the Pharisee is without love, and this shows itself in his parsimonious behaviour of not providing properly for his guest on arrival. The parable which is addressed to the Pharisee, highlighting the magnanimous debtor's generosity, has in the context a decidely pointed edge by underlining Simon's tight-fistedness. Separatist religious assumptions and social exclusivity are subtly intertwined in this story which suggests that the Pharisaic religious point of view is closely related to rank and social control.

The second instance of Jesus' visit to a Pharisaic house (11:37–54) shows the same conjunction of religious attitudes about purity and socio-economic realities. Here the charge is quite explicit—the Pharisees are guilty of rapaciousness (ἁρπαγῆς) and evil, even though they are concerned about purity; if on the other hand they would give alms from their possessions (τὰ ἐνόντα), all would be pure. Thus the categories of pure and impure are re-defined in terms of socio-economic concerns in which sharing one's possessions makes those categories devoid of any real meaning. The separatism generated by those very purity laws is removed in a more equitable system in which justice and the love of God are the fundamental values.

Finally the Pharisaic ruler who is concerned about healing on the Sabbath has his narrow world-view challenged, but again in socio-economic categories of sharing his hospitality outside the narrow confines of his own family and social class (14:12–14). Instead of inviting his own kind to a meal, those who are in no position to return the invitation are to be invited—the poor, the lame, the crippled and the blind. Once again the same picture of the Pharisees emerges: their closed religious system creates social élitism based on their refusal to share their goods with the less well off.

This criticism reaches its climax with the description of the Pharisees as lovers of money (16:14). The charge occurs in a context in which money is called mammon of unrighteousness (ἀδικίας), and it is emphatically declared that you cannot serve God and mammon. Riches then take on the category of a religious power, and in serving money the Pharisees are accused of idolatory. The story of the rich man and Lazarus, whose fortunes are reversed in the world to come, forms a fitting climax to this chapter, since it graphically illustrates the real perversion of not sharing one's riches with the needy—the selfish rich (here surely the Pharisees are intended) will be incapable of hearing even Moses and the prophets, it is declared by no less a figure than Abraham himself.[36]

Mention has already been made of the episode in which some Pharisees warned Jesus about the danger from Antipas (13:31). In view of the sustained criticism of Pharisaic religious attitudes by Jesus throughout the work it is difficult to imagine how Galilean Pharisees could be portrayed as friendly towards him.[37] Perhaps the author does not wish to castigate all Pharisees by singling out individual members of the sect on the one hand, and on the other stressing the fact that some (τινες) were friendly to Jesus. This would be consistent with the portrayal of friendly Pharisees and Christian Pharisees in Acts (5:34; 15:2; 21:21).[38] On the other hand the inclusive tone of the charges in 11:39–44 ('You Pharisees'), as well as the stereotyping of Pharisaic attitudes

36. There are several indications that link the Pharisees with this story of the rich man and Lazarus. Luke consistently presents them as believing in the resurrection of the dead (cf. Acts 23:6–9), yet that belief is declared to be of no avail to the rich within the story. In addition the Baptist had earlier warned that claiming to be children of Abraham would be useless without a genuine sense of social justice (3:7–14), and we hear that the Pharisees and scribes rejected John and his baptism (7:29); in the story Abraham cares for the poor man and has no comfort for the rich.

37. Cf. A. Demaux, 'L'hypocisie des Pharisiens et le dessein de Dieu: Analyse de Lc XIII, 31–33', in *L'Évangile de Luc. Problèmes Litteraires et Théologiques*, ed.F. Neirynck, Louvain, 1983, 244–85.

38. J. Ziesler, 'Luke and the Pharisees', *NTS* 25(1979) 146–57, especially 146–8.

(18:10–14), suggest that the Pharisees in general represent an unacceptable version of Jewish faith for Luke, unless genuine conversion can be shown to have occurred in terms of a changed outlook on their social obligations.

As depicted by Luke, Galilean Judaism is both intimately linked to Jerusalem and its temple, and controlled by Pharisaic élitism, more concerned with socio-economic factors than with religious issues of a genuine kind. In this regard 5:17 represents an extremely important summary from the narrator's point of view, with its explicit mention of Pharisees and law-teachers from every village of Galilee. The specific encounters with individual Pharisees give them a much more prominent role as controllers of the existing social world than in any of the other gospels. This is all the more significant in that scribes play a less important part in Luke's Galilean section, and the author/narrator seems to differentiate clearly between the two groups, even when they can be coupled together at certain points (cf. 11:45). However one regards the Pharisees, the attitude of the people as a whole is positively portrayed, despite the negative impression of the synagogue experiences, especially that in Nazareth. By the repeated designation of Jesus' audience as 'the people' (ὁ λαός), the author/narrator has adopted a very positive point of view towards the crowds around Jesus.[39] Unlike their leaders they are quite capable of forming a part of the messianic people that will be gathered from all peoples—ἐξ ἐθνῶν λαός (Ac 15:14)—thereby forming a genuine continuity with the Jewish people of Old Testament hopes (Lk 1:10,17,26,68,77; 2:10,31f.; 3:15,18,21). While it is clear from Acts that the author sees the messianic people being comprised of both Jews and gentiles (cf. Ac 18:10), the absence of any gentile emphasis in the Galilean section, with the single exception of the mention of the sea-coasts of Tyre and Sidon (Lk 6:19), is all the more remarkable. Luke can concentrate on a Jewish Galilee since in Acts there is plenty of

39. 6:17; 7:1; 8:47; 9:13; 16:29; 18:43; 19:26,45,48; 20:1,6,9; 21:23,38. Cf. P. Minear, 'Jesus' Audiences according to Luke', *NT* 16(1974) 81–109; J. Dupont, *Teologia della Chiesa negli Atti degli Apostoli*, Bologna: Edizioni Dehoniane, 1984, 51–6.

narrative space to show the true dimensions of 'the people for his name' in all its ethnic and cultural diversity.[40]

iii) *Jesus and his Movement in Luke's Galilee.* According to Luke, Jesus' activity in Galilee is seen in contrasting colours by the Jewish assembly and by the leader of his permanent retinue, Peter. The former, highlighting his teaching activity, considers it to be subversion of the people (23:3,14), whereas the latter, focusing on his healing and exorcism ministry, describes it as doing good (Ac 10:37). As actually described, however, it is impossible to separate these two aspects of his career—teaching and healing—since the word of grace that proceeds from his mouth (4:22) covers a range of activity from instruction to proclamation to commanding of evil spirits whom he encounters throughout his journeys. These different facets of the one ministry are highlighted in the progammatic scene in the Nazareth synagogue when Jesus applies to himself the Isaian passage (a combination of Is 61:1–2 and 58:6, in fact), only to repeat the main elements—healing and proclamation of good news to the poor—in his reply to John the Baptist's query concerning his true identity (7:22). Again and again, in various summaries and individual stories the key terms of these responses are repeated in order to remind the reader that the programme that has been announced is indeed being accomplished.[41]

How then can Jesus' 'doing good' be seen as subversive? Certainly his success gives rise to a growing and widely diffused reputation, as we are informed repeatedly by the narrator: 4:37; 5:15,17; 6:17f.; 7:17. The spontaneous reactions after individual episodes are also indicative of a similar pattern: 4:36; 5:26; 7:16, 9:43. The activity of Jesus clearly raises fundamental questions about his identity for the intratextual participants. However, the reader has been well prepared for these events through the infancy stories in which various reliable characters have presented the birth of the

40. This reading of Luke's attitude towards the Jewish people differs radically from that of J. Sanders in several articles and most recently in *The Jews in Luke-Acts*, London, SCM, 1986, who sees Luke as anti-Jewish and presenting a picture of the Jews as finally rejected by God. Cf. n.50 below.

41. Cf. R. Tannehill, *The Narrative Unity of Luke-Acts. A Literary Interpretation,* Vol 1, Philadelphia: Fortress, 1986, 79f. and 82–5.

child as a divine visitation which Israel eagerly awaited (1:68,78), and now in his career his deeds are recognised by the crowd in precisely these terms (7:16).

For Luke the term prophet seems a particularly appropriate designation for Jesus in his Galilean ministry. Yet, as already noted, the title prophet is susceptible of different interpretations, and the sense in which the author/narrator intends it needs to be carefully traced. Twice Jesus uses 'prophet' as a self-designation, but in both instances the note of rejection and death is firmly associated with the term. However, the rejection of prophets takes place in Jerusalem, not Galilee (13:34; cf. 4:23; 11:47–51). Others too think of him in this role, more specifically as Elijah or as one of the prophets of old who has risen from the dead (9:7,19), and the raising of the widow's son at Naim is narrated by Luke in a manner that directly imitates one of Elijah's miracles (1 Kgs 17:17–24; cf. Lk 4:25–6)[42] In this regard Lk ch. 9, coming as the climax of Jesus' Galilean ministry, is seen as particularly significant, since it is here that the true identity of Jesus as prophet is amply confirmed for the attentive reader.

In addition to Herod's and some other people's view that 'one of the prophets of old has arisen', the mountain scene is also highly significant. In Luke this scene has been consciously depicted in the light of Mt Horeb. In the Deuteronomic account God's voice is heard from a cloud, preparing for the journey ahead for God's people, and announcing the fate of his prophet Moses that is intimately bound up with the successful outcome of that journey.[43] Similarly, Jesus' journey and its outcome are hinted at with the reference to his ἔξοδος, even as his true identity is established once more, as an aid to the reader in the trials that lie ahead. In this way the author has set up a tension between a popular perception of Jesus as a prophet and a more adequate understanding of that

42. See L.T. Brodie, 'Towards Unraveling Luke's use of the Old Testament: Lk 7:11–17 as an *Imitatio* of 1 Kgs 17:17–24', *NTS* 32(1986) 247–67.

43. This has been argued in particular by D. Moessner, 'Luke 9:1–50: Luke's Preview of the Journey of the Prophet Like Moses of Deuteronomy', *JBL* 102(1983) 574–605, particularly 582–7 on the mediatorial role of Moses' death on behalf of Israel. Cf. Ac 4:22f.

designation as applied to his ministry and its eventual outcome.[44]

What then are the dimensions of Jesus' career, as narrated by Luke, that make the designation 'prophet' particularly apt as a description of the Galilean ministry and what hints are we given about his future fate? That his words and works form an inseparable unity in Luke's view is quite clear from the closing testimony to Jesus of the two disciples on the road to Emmaus: 'he was a prophet mighty in deed and word before God and all the people (Lk 24:19). This inner unity is equally apparent in the main character's estimation of his career according to the quotations from Isaiah that he applies to himself (4:18; 7:22)—proclamation of good news and opening of the eyes of the blind. The Spirit that comes on Jesus at the Baptism (3:22), an event that is subsequently described as an anointing (4:18; Ac 10:38), plays a very vital role in the conduct of this ministry. The Spirit is both the source of Jesus' power to perform cures (4:14; cf. the reference to δύναμις in 4:36; 5:17; 6:19; 8:46; 9:1) and the inspiration for his whole ministry (10:21; 11:3). Peter describes Jesus' ministry as 'doing good, and healing all who were enslaved by the devil' (Ac 10:38) and this turns out to be an accurate description of the various cures performed by Jesus, as Luke narrates them. They are not just displays of superior power, though the Holy Spirit (Luke's contant usage) is directly opposed to unclean spirits and their leader (11:20). Luke emphasises the sense of caring for those being healed, their families and friends on the part of Jesus, and sickness is understood as enslavement by the devil, from which people should be released (4:38; 13:10–17).[45]

Far from explaining how the career of Jesus can be seen as subversive, this portrayal only heightens the paradox. Where-

44. For a general discussion of Luke's redactional activity in this chapter cf. Fitzmyer, *The Gospel according to Luke*, vol. I, 757–821. R.F. O'Toole, 'Luke's Message in Luke 9:1–50', *CBQ* 49(1987) 74–89, sees the intention of Luke's composition in this chapter as going beyond the Moses typology by highlighting the heavenly Father's identification of Jesus as his Son who first must suffer in order to enter his glory, in preparation for the fulfilment of Peter's confession earlier in the chapter.

45. Tannehill, *Narrative Unity*, 89–96. Peter's description of Jesus' ministry as εὐεργετῶν in Acts recalls the hellenistic-Roman figure of the benefactor.

in lies the real offence? The words of Jesus in the Galilean context have as their centre-piece the sermon on the plain (6:19 – 7:1). Here the message of good news for the poor is given very concrete expression in the beatitudes and woes which articulate God's care for the outcast, in terms of eschatological reversal for the hungry, the poor, the mourners and those who weep in the present. Several of the subsequent stories such as the raising of the widow's son, the feeding of the crowds in the desert, the parables of the banquet and the rich man and Lazarus, illustrate that judgment taking place in the career of Jesus already. Other instructions in the sermon concerning loving one's enemies and sharing with those from whom one has no hope of receiving in return (6:35) are also directly implemented in the subsequent narrative. Thus the gentile centurion, a traditional enemy, has loved (ἀγαπάν) the Jewish people and built a synagogue for them (7:5), in sharp contrast to the Pharisaic leaders who were either parsimonious (7:44) or who invited only those from whom they could expect hospitality in return (14:12). Both had appealed to religious values based on the purity laws to cloak their social élitism and lack of generosity. Yet the woman who 'loved much' is declared blessed rather than the Pharisee Simon, and the poor, the blind, the maimed and the lame are assured of a place at the final banquet, even if they are excluded in the present (14:13,21; 16:25).[46]

Thus the instruction of Jesus repeatedly finds its fulfilment in the Galilean narrative of Luke. Those who mourn are comforted (7:11–17; cf. 6:21); the hungry are fed (9:10–17; cf. 6:21a; 4:25); sinners and other outcasts are included in his retinue (7:47–9; 8:1–3; cf. 7:34); those who are enslaved are set free (4:38; 5:23; cf. 4:18); lepers are cleansed (5:12–16; 17:11–19; cf. 4:27). In short, there is an intimate link between the words and works of this prophet whose career is both religiously radical and socially subversive.[47] The norms and

46. In an as yet unpublished MS, *Luke and the Pharisees,* which he very kindly allowed me to read, Professor H. Moxnes (Oslo) has highlighted the manner in which social élitism and rigidity in religious observance are intimately connected in Luke's account of the Pharisees and their value system.

47. See L.T. Johnson, *The Literary Function of Possessions in Luke Acts*, SBL Dissertation Series 39, Missoula: Scholars Press, 1977, especially 96–103, on the pattern of speech fulfilled in action as a characteristic of Luke's treatment of the Galilean section.

values of those who control the limited goods society which the author has graphically depicted through typical characters and situations, are under attack, and the religious system that gave legitimacy to them is being dismantled. Here lies the reason for the charge of subversion which came to its final expression in Jerusalem.

What of the reception in Galilee? The Nazareth pericope is generally recognised as being particularly important for Luke's overall point of view, and the rejection there is quite explicit, without the intervention of any of the alternative leaders. The programme outlined on the basis of the Isaian text is too radical, it would seem. Nevertheless, the attentive reader will not fail to recognise the deliberate contrast with Capernaum, where Jesus' appearance in the synagogue is favourably received (4:32,36), and those who are captive are actually released (4:38), thus inaugurating the programme announced at Nazareth.[48]

As yet we have not met any religious leaders in Galilee, only two contrasting receptions in the synagogue. Even when scribal and Pharisaic opposition is encountered, it is somewhat muted, so that the overall relationship is not absolutely clear. On the one hand the scribes and Pharisees from all Galilee are seated around Jesus who is in a seated, that is, a teaching position (5:17), thus recalling his appearance in the temple as a twelve-year-old in the midst of the teachers (2:46). In the end, however, the narrator has a highly negative evaluation of the Galilean scribes and Pharisees: they rejected the plan (βουλή) of God by refusing to undergo John's baptism, unlike the people (λαός, 7;29–30). This judgment had been well prepared for by the presence of scribes and Pharisees in various situations in which Jesus had broken the Sabbath or purity laws (6:2,7; 5:30), or, more significantly still, had declared sins forgiven (5:21; cf. 7:47–49). The author/narrator who is constantly privy to the people's internal feelings and emotions in a most striking way, tells us that they were filled with ἄνοια, a term that suggests not just lack of understanding but a frenzied condition of extreme

48. By describing the condition of Peter's mother-in-law as συνεχομένη πυρετῷ μεγάλῳ (4:38) Luke stresses the notion of sickness as a form of captivity, presumably by Satan (cf. 13:16).

anger and frustration (6:11).

It is in the individual scenes with the Pharisees that the clash of perspective between Jesus and the Jewish religious leaders comes into focus most clearly. Though couched in religious terms, the criticism is directed more against their social élitism than their false teaching or hypocritical behaviour. Hence, the subversion that Jesus is accused of in Jerusalem can only be an undermining of the social control that these groups exercised within Luke's narrative world, especially in Galilee. In this portrayal Galilee is 'part of the whole country of the Jews' (Ac 10:37), and the division between the religious leaders and the people as a whole which is such a marked feature of the Jerusalem phase of Luke's narrative, both in the gospel and in Acts, is a factor in Galilee also. The 'friendly Pharisees' who suggest that Jesus escape from Herod are told that the prophet cannot abandon his designated course, even if that means inevitable death in Jerusalem (13:31–3). Accordingly, there can be no compromise between the two points of view—that of the Pharisees and that of the prophet, Jesus—once the latter's message is translated into a programme of action in Galilee that challenges the value-system of the wealthy Pharisees.

For Luke also, Jerusalem is the climactic setting for the final confrontation, yet his perspective on the holy city is quite distinctive in comparison with the other evangelists, especially Mark. From the very beginning, close links between the city and the countryside are assumed, and the temple is the setting from which the narrative originates (1:5–25). The birth of the main character is later proclaimed there as the fulfilment of both Jerusalem's and Israel's hopes, even if there is also a recognition that his coming would occasion the rise and fall of many in Israel (2:25–28,34). Furthermore, in these opening chapters we find the main character 'at home' (ἐν τοῖς τοῦ πατρός μου) in the temple, and by divine necessity (δεῖ). Thus, a much more positive attitude towards the holy city is established from the start, despite the recognition later that it is the place where prophets meet their doom. It is altogether in keeping with the overall tone of Luke's work that this first volume should end where it began, with the disciples of Jesus praising God joyfully in the temple (24:50–52).[49]

In view of this positive presentation of Jerusalem and its temple at the centre of Israel's hopes and the joyous realisation of those hopes in the messianic career of Jesus, it is quite significant to find that Jerusalemites are present during the Galilean phase of Jesus' career already: 5:17; 6:17. On the first occasion Jesus is surrounded by Pharisees and teachers of the law from every village of Galilee, as well as from Judea and Jerusalem. As previously mentioned, the scene is reminiscent of Jesus' visit to the temple as a twelve-year-old, but the reaction now is quite unfavourable, even if, as yet, it is only in their hearts that the Jewish teachers think evil of Jesus. By contrast, on the second occasion, a great multitude of the people (λαός) from Jerusalem and Judea are present as part of the crowd that is gathered around Jesus and his newly appointed apostles, as, in a standing position, he addresses them on the plain, about the values that are to operate in his community. This deliberate contrast between the Jerusalem people and their religious leaders' attitudes to Jesus, already in Galilee, prepares for later events, and it is no surprise to find that many of the inhabitants of Jerusalem are numbered among this (new) people on the first Pentecost day (Ac 1:8). It is in Jerusalem also that Jesus will accomplish his great ἔξοδος, later described as his ἀναλήμψις, or ascension (9:31,51). Thus, the Galilean ministry is enclosed between two visits to Jerusalem, the one under Satan's direction, during which his will is rejected (4:9), and the other to accomplish God's will there. Thus, for Luke, the Galilean ministry, far from being in opposition to that at Jerusalem, is part of the one mission which is seen as God's visitation of his people, centred on Jerusalem and the temple, which, tragically, will only be partly successful.[50]

49. I. de la Potterie, 'Les deux Noms de Jérusalem dans l'Évangile de Luc', especially 60f. on the association between the hopes of Israel and Jerusalem.

50. This reading of Luke-Acts on the role of Israel within the work does not concur either with that of R. Tannehill, 'Israel in Luke-Acts: A Tragic Story', *JBL* 104(1985) 69–85; or with J.T. Sanders, *The Jews in Luke-Acts*, see n. 40 above. The former sees Luke as sympathetic towards the Jews, despite their tragic rejection, whereas the latter regards the author as essentially anti-semitic. For a more positive understanding of the role of Israel within the work, cf. F. O'Fearghail, 'Israel in Luke-Acts', *PIBA* 11(1988) 23–43, who sees the question of Israel's conversion as being left open by the author, following a pattern of the continuing role of Israel in God's universal plan of salvation and the divisions that this creates within Israel, with the consequent warnings to the unrepentant element.

In view of this treatment of Jerusalem within the narrative, it is highly significant that Luke has deliberately transformed Mark's 'way theme' into a pilgrimage journey: 9:51,53; 13:33; 17:11; 18:31; 19:28, thus underlining the continuities with Israel's religious life and the hopes associated with it, which Jesus' ministry represents. Nevertheless, as the journey progresses, the negative role of the city begins to surface for the reader. This may already be symbolically expressed in the story of the man 'going down' from Jerusalem to Jericho—the direct inversion of Jesus' journey (10:30; 18:35–19:11; 19:28). Jerusalem can symbolise danger, as the incidents of the fall of the tower of Siloam and the slaughter of Galileans at the hands of Pilate suggest. Both episodes are used to stress the need for repentance, (13:1–5), an ominous suggestion about Jerusalem's fate in view of the failure of its spiritual leaders to take John's call to repentance seriously (7:29f.; 19:41–4; 23:27–31).[51]

In this regard the lament for Jerusalem, 13:31–5, is particularly important, since it links Jesus' ultimate fate with the holy city, and appears to offer a totally negative view of its role in salvation history: a prophet cannot die outside Jerusalem. However, the concluding remark—'but (the adversive δε) I say to you, "You shall not see me until the time comes when you will say: blessed is the one who comes in the name of the Lord"'—strongly suggests that, even while laying the charge of killing the prophets at Jerusalem's door, Luke does not wish to present the main character as rejecting Jerusalem irrevocably.[52] Indeed this earlier hint is confirmed on the arrival of the main character at the city (19:37). The same cry of blessing on Jerusalem as he had spoken, is uttered now by the whole crowd (πλῆθος) of his disciples, combined with the words of the whole crowd (πλῆθος) of the heavenly host at the birth of Jesus (19:39b; 2:13f.). There is one slight, but significant adaptation—peace is proclaimed now for heaven, not for earth as the angels had done at the birth of the saviour

51. R. Maddox, in *The Purpose of Luke-Acts*, Edinburgh: T. and T. Clark 1985, 47f., does not seem to have fully appreciated the positive aspects of Luke's treatment of Jerusalem, however.

52. Cf. F.D. Weinert, 'Luke, the Temple and Jesus' Saying about Jerusalem's Abandoned House', *CBQ* 44(1982) 68–76, especially 73f., arguing that the οἶκος in question is the Jewish religious leadership rather than the temple.

child, thereby suggesting that Jerusalem cannot now expect immediate peace. Still, Jesus' visit to the temple is one of great authority. The narrator informs us that he taught the people there and proclaimed the good news, just as in Galilee (19:47; 20:1,9), but significantly, there is no mention of healings. In Luke's version of the prophecy of destruction, Jerusalem will be surrounded by an army and trodden under foot by the gentiles until the times of the gentiles are fulfilled (21:21,24), but there is no comment on the profanation of the temple, and the question of Jerusalem's ultimate restoration is left open (cf. 21:28).

By various hints and comments, then, Luke is able to convey to the reader a sense of concern for Jerusalem and the hope that its symbolic role for Israel might be realised. Yet, and this is the tragic irony of the situation, it is also guilty of killing the prophets, and others sent to it. In terms of Luke's full story these are Jesus, Stephen and the other Hellenists, and James the Son of Zebedee. It is the scribes in particular who are identified with this murderous attitude, and long before his arrival in the city Jesus had condemned them for withholding the key of knowledge, neither entering themselves nor allowing others to enter (11:52). Though the actual destination to which this key leads is not specified, the presumption from the context must be that it is Wisdom's house (cf. the mention of σοφία in v. 49). It was in the temple that Jesus first encountered the Jewish teachers, and this prepares us for finding them, and not the priests, in charge of that house when eventually Jesus arrives in Jerusalem. For Luke the temple was primarily a place of prayer (1:10; 2:27; 19:45; 24:53), but also of instruction. By having him teach a large and enthusiastic crowd there, Luke suggests that Jesus has usurped the scribes' position as the ones who possess the key of knowledge that leads to Wisdom's house. In view of the fact that the Pharisees were joined with the scribes in a violent reaction to Jesus' earlier condemnation (11:53f.), it is all the more surprising to find that they are virtually missing in the Jerusalem setting, apart from 19:39, where, we are told, some Pharisees asked him to silence his disciples' enthusiastic chant at the triumphal entry to the city. By contrast, the scribes are constantly present in the Jerusalem setting, together with the traditional opponents, the elders and the priests. Their opposition is particularly pronounced during the sojourn in the temple (20;1,19,39,46), but they are also actively engaged in the arrest and trial (22:2,66; 23:10).

In these final chapters the relation of the scribes (and other leaders) to the people (λαός) is somewhat ambivalent. The admiration and enthusiasm of the people for Jesus is repeatedly mentioned by the narrator, as well as the fear of the religious authorities to move against him because of the people (19:48; 20:1,8,19,26,45; 21:38; 22:2; but cf. 20:39). Briefly, during the trial and crucifixion scenes, the chief opponents are much less differentiated, and the people also are actively involved (22:47–66; 23:13). In the end, however, the crowds are respectfully contrite, 'beating their breasts' (23:48). Thus, in a manner consistent with the pattern established in Galilee, the reaction to Jesus is divided between a favourable crowd, sometimes designated 'the people', and hostile religious leaders, notably the scribes, whose position as official instructors of the people he has usurped. The Pharisees, too, must be included among the opponents of Jesus, not for their role in Jerusalem, but because of their rejection in Galilee of the values of the prophet, Jesus, which challenged their world and the control that they were able to exercise there.

It is significant that there is no return to Galilee for a reunion with the chosen disciple/apostles as in both Mark and Matthew. Instead, one of the angelic figures whom they encountered at the empty tomb admonished the Galilean women to remember what they had been told in Galilee by Jesus, and they duly reported this to the eleven (24:6–8). In this way Luke is able to maintain his positive understanding of Jerusalem as the centre of the drama of salvation according to the Scriptural promises, and at the same time integrate fully the Galilean experience of the disciples into his narrative.

It is from the perspective of Acts that we can best evaluate the significance of that experience as he presents it within his total narrative. As is well known, Luke, alone of the evangelists, designates the Twelve as apostles from the moment of their special election (6:13). The significance of this designation emerges from the fact that, apart from two references which appear to be a more generalised use of the term as applied to Paul (Ac 14:4,14), ἀπόστολος is reserved for the Twelve alone. Whatever the reason for this special use in the context of Luke's ecclesial experience,[53] its intra-textual significance emerges from the conditions that were laid down for the appointment to the Twelve of a successor to Judas, namely, 'someone from among those men who were gathered with us in all the time that the Lord Jesus had gone in and out among us, beginning from the baptism of John until the day on which he was taken up from us, a witness of the resurrection' (Ac 1:23). On these terms Paul could not have been included among the apostles, even though he is clearly the hero of the second half of Acts. Peter, the leader of the Twelve, is reported as proclaiming all that the Lord had done, 'beginning from Galilee', in the house of Cornelius, and he is conscious that he and his fellow-apostles were chosen beforehand, so that they could be witnesses of the resurrection (Ac 10:37–41). Equally, Paul is made to acknowledge the fact that it was 'to those who had made the ascent with him from Galilee to Jerusalem', that the risen Lord had appeared (Ac 13:31). Thus, the Galilean ministry is clearly designated by Luke as essential for the proper comprehension of the story of Jesus, and, as he tells that story, the experience of the first Galilean disciples/followers was foundational.

Not that Luke idealises them or their experience. Indeed his account of the disciples during the Galilean period is noteworthy for two distinctive features. Firstly, Luke alone tells us that women were part of his permanent retinue in Galilee (8:1–3), and corresponding to this role, they are the ones who act as the first, vital link in the proclamation of the good news about the resurrection after their encounter with the angelic messengers (24:8f.). In addition Luke also narrates the sending of other missionaries with almost identical instructions to those given the Twelve (10:1–11), thereby indicating clearly that, however important this group was in

53. Cf. Freyne, *The Twelve*, 207–58 for a detailed discussion, and a position that differs from that of G. Klein, *Die Zwölf Apostel. Ursprung und Gehalt einer Idee*, Göttingen: Vandenhoeck and Ruprecht, 1961, who attributes Luke's development of the idea to second-century, anti-gnostic tendencies.

symbolic terms, others could and did share in the mission of Jesus. Indeed the very fact that as the narrative of Acts proceeds, they depart from the scene, to be replaced by Paul, suggests that it is Luke's sense of history that has caused him to highlight the significance of 'the men of Galilee' (Ac 1:11), and their memory in the initial period of the movement whose development he has chosen to narrate.

During the Galilean period less narrative time is spent on the group than in Mark. We are reminded of their presence with Jesus on one of the intra-Galilean tours, but others, including women, are part of that retinue (8:1–3). The so-called 'great omission', namely, the fact that Luke does not include in his narrative material corresponding to Mk 6:45–8:26, means that we are never given a sense of the Twelve apostles' incomprehension as to the identity of their master or of his frustration with them, which was such a feature of Mark's account. Their only failure in this regard has to do with the passion (9:44f.), and then it is the disciples generally who are said not to have grasped the meaning of the saying. This is highly significant, since Luke, much more clearly than the other writers, specifies that the Twelve were chosen from a larger crowd of disciples (6:13), and at the triumphal entry to Jerusalem we hear of a large crowd of disciples praising God for all that they had seen (19:37). Thus, the Twelve apostles are part of a larger Galilean following in Luke's story, and their presence and identity is submerged in that more general picture in the narrative.

Nevertheless, they do receive special instruction for the task ahead—in Jerusalem and at table. In that setting, just like the Pharisees, their unworthy attitudes in regard to rank are criticised (22:14–38, especially vv. 24–8). They are, however, designated 'those who have remained with me in my trials' (v. 28), and are therefore given a special role in his kingdom, that of judging the twelve tribes of Israel. As Luke's story develops, this role is a present, rather than a future, task for them, in that they are called to present the good news of salvation in Jesus at the very centre of Judaism, by calling Israel to repent and accept the claims of Jesus (Ac 2–6).

In this task they are not unsuccessful with the people (Ac 2:37–42; 3:11ff.; 5:12–16), despite the hostility of the 'rulers and elders and scribes', whose role of religious leadership of Israel they are effectively usurping (Ac 4:5–11; 5:27–32).[54] After the persecution of the Hellenists they stay on in Jerusalem, but send their representatives to Samaria to ensure that the new converts there receive the spirit, which Luke regards as the possession of Israel (Ac 8:14–24). Their leader, Peter, has the task of officially opening the gentile mission—the Pentecost of the gentiles according to Luke (Ac 10)—but only after Paul, the apostle of the gentiles, had been previously legitimated by the whole group (Ac 9:26ff.). Thereafter, they disappear from the picture, apart from a brief appearance at the Council of Jerusalem in order to validate the admission of gentiles to this people (Ac 15), to be replaced by Paul as the one who will complete the mission 'to be my witnesses in Jerusalem and in all Judea and Samaria and to the end of the earth', which had been entrusted to them by their departing Lord (Ac 1:8).

The importance of the Galilean experience in Luke's view, becomes clear, therefore, from the narrative role of the twelve apostles within the missionary plan of Acts. That plan is one that encompasses Jew and gentile in the one people, as determined in particular by the prophecies of Isaiah concerning the servant of Yahweh. The restored of Israel and the nations are to be included within the one vision (Is 49:6,12; Lk 2:30–32; 13:27–30; Ac 1:8; 13:47). It is this vision that shapes the narrative account of the Galilean Jesus' mission and that of his Galilean followers. Luke, it would seem, has his own distinctive view of the significance of the phrase 'Galilee of the Gentiles', even though he never actually cites that text, and paradoxically, his account of the Galilean ministry restricts Jesus' movement to Galilee, as part of all Judea, despite the depiction of his precursor, Mark. The narrative space he has allowed himself in writing a two-volume work means that, more clearly than any of the other evangelists, he was able to highlight the bridging role of the twelve Galileans in assembling the one people from the nations, that was central to their leader's prophetic vision from the outset.

54. See J. Jervell, *Luke and the People of God*, 75–113.

CHAPTER FOUR

Galilee and Galileans in the Fourth Gospel

OF all the gospels, that of John would win widespread recognition as being a genuine literary creation, with its distinctive language and style, its subtle word-plays and its use of irony. Even if recent studies from source and redaction critical points of view have seriously challenged the assumption that it is the work of one hand, 'woven without seam from top to bottom', most would admit that there is a distinctive Johannine point of view which receives a genuine literary expression in this work.

This recognition of the literary features of the Fourth Gospel does not at first sight hold out any great prospects for the approach adopted in this study of discovering the narrative treatment of Galilee in the gospels. John, it would seem, is too ethereal to be concerned about the geographic setting of the main character's life and ministry. Yet the prologue-hymn that begins by extolling the pre-existent Word returns sharply to earth with the proclamation that, 'he came to his own and his own did not receive him' (1:11). Behind such a statement, one suspects, lies a human story that will involve details of space and time.

And so it proves to be. Despite the Fourth Gospel's widely recognised theological concerns there is a surprising amount of detail as the work develops, especially of a geographical nature.[1] Places like Cana in Galilee, Aenom near Salim with its plentiful supply of water, Sichar and its well, the pool of Bethesda (Betzata) having five porticoes, the Lithostratos or Gabbata, are all known to us because John chose to include them in his narrative. The story of Jesus, as he tells it, is

1. Cf. the study of C.K. Barrett, 'St. John: Social Historian', *PIBA* 10 (1986) 26–39.

interwoven with such locations, often now invested with symbolic significance within the narrative. The most profound statement of Johannine, indeed Christian theology, 'the Word became flesh and pitched his tent (ἐσκήνωσεν) in our midst', demands that we take the author seriously in the human dimensions of the story, even when he uses those very human aspects to elevate us to the lofty spheres of his own faith and thought. Coming as it does, at the outset of John's work, it can be read not just as a theological, but as a literary statement also, in which we are being summoned to take seriously the whole human colouring of the narrative if we, like the author and the group for whom he speaks, are to see the glory of the only-begotten of the Father, full of grace and truth.

When all that is granted we must be careful not to demand of this author, above all others, more than he is prepared to tell us. Since the Jesus of the Fourth Gospel is more interested in establishing his own true identity than in giving detailed instructions for the way of discipleship, there is an absence of concrete social description, which was so clearly present in the sayings attributed to Jesus, especially in Luke and Matthew. Missing also is the sense of Herodian presence in Galilee, and therefore, the political context of Jesus' career. Even the religious situation has been drastically simplified, to the point that often we hear simply of the Jews when the author wishes to describe the opponents of Jesus. We must then, to borrow a phrase from J. G. Dunn, 'let John be John', and not read his version of the story of Jesus the Galilean through synoptic-tinted glasses.

1. Galilee and the Journeys of Jesus in the Fourth Gospel

Attention to the geographical data of the Fourth Gospel immediately highlights the amount of movement by the main character within the narrative, something that is surprising at first sight, since the unity of style and theme gives a static impression to the whole. Galilee is usually the point of arrival or departure of these journeys, and a discussion of the way in which these movements of the main character relate to other

2. 'Let John be John—A Gospel for its Time', in *Das Evangelium und die Evangelien*, WUNT 28, ed. P. Stuhlmacher, Tübingen: J.C.B. Mohr, 1983, 309–40.

developments within the plot will help in determining the way in which Galilee and Galileans are characterised within the narrative. Not that there is general agreement about the pattern of these journeys, yet the attempt to impose a more logical order by transposing chapters six and seven should be resisted, since there is no MS evidence for any such rearrangement. We must, as C. H. Dodd reminds us, attempt to make sense of the text as it has come to us, including ch. 21.[3]

Most of Jesus' journeys are centred on going to Jerusalem for the great Jewish feasts (cf. 2:13; 5:1; 7:1–10; 12:12), and it is there that most of the dialogue occurs. There are, in all, four clusters of such movements, with Galilee playing a decisive role in three of these. In the final movement it is missing at first, since the progression is from the place where John was baptising (10:40), through Bethany (11:17f.) to Ephraim in the wilderness (11:54), back again to Bethany (12:11) and finally to Jerusalem (12:12). However, the apparent break in the earlier pattern only highlights the return to Galilee that ch. 21 presupposes, thereby implying a criticism of Jerusalem which a more careful examination of the whole structure reveals.[4]

Ostensively, the journeys to Jerusalem have to do with the Jewish feasts, but on each occasion there is an open and prolonged confrontation between Jesus and his opponents, usually designated the Jews, but sometimes also as the Pharisees, who in John are characterised as the official watchdogs of an orthodox Jewish point of view.[5] One can also detect an increasing hostility with each visit, as Jesus' challenge to the claims of Jerusalem becomes more explicit, climaxing in the final movement to his death. It is this hostility that forms the backdrop to the various retreats to Galilee.

On the first occasion Jesus goes to Jerusalem for the feast

3. See *The Interpretation of the Fourth Gospel*, Cambridge: University Press, 1953, 289f.

4. B. Olsson, in *Structure and Meaning in the Fourth Gospel: A Text-Linguistic Analysis of John 2:1–11 and 4:1–42*, Lund: C.W.K. Gleerup, 1974, 27–35, highlights well the internal movements within the text.

5. Jn 1:24; 3:1; 7:32,45,48; 9:16,40; 11:47,57; 18:3. Cf. K. Wengst, *Bedrängte Gemeinde und verherrlichter Christus*, Neukirchen-Vluyn: Neukirchener Verlag, 1983, 40–44, for a summary of the evidence and its relation to the Johannine community's situation within Judaism at the time of writing.

of Passover, and proceeds to cast out of the temple those who bought and sold there, claiming that this was his Father's house (2:15f.). The Jews challenge him for a sign to validate such claims, something that is perfectly understandable in the circumstances. Yet the reply of Jesus strongly suggests that the author wants us to understand the question as a direct threat to Jesus, since his response is unprepared for within the narrative: 'Destroy this temple and in three days I will raise it up again'. That the protagonists are clearly at cross-purposes emerges from the mention of the building of the temple taking forty-seven years and the question of how it could be rebuilt in three days. In order to underline the points that the author wishes to make, the narrator informs us directly that Jesus was speaking of the temple of his body. This allusion was intelligible to his disciples, we are informed, admittedly in a post-resurrection perspective, which is the same as that of the author, clearly. Thus they were able to believe in his word and in the Scriptures, corresponding to their positive response at Cana previously.

Despite this clear indication of the divisions that lie ahead the first Jerusalem visit for the feast of Passover was not a complete failure, since the narrator tells us that 'many believed in him, seeing the signs which he did' (2:23). Yet curiously none of these signs are reported for us, in direct contrast to the detailed account of the Cana story. Furthermore, Jesus' reaction was not to trust himself to them. Thus a tension is established between Jesus and the Jews as the inhabitants of Jerusalem, with the temple the focal point of their differences. The arrival of a man of the Pharisees by night (νυκτὸς, 3:2) only confirms our initial impressions of opposition, and there is a clear contrast implied between the faith of his disciples on the one hand (2:23) and that of the Jerusalemites on the other, which Jesus did not trust. Eventually Jesus went to the Judean country and conducted a baptismal ministry similar to that of John the Baptist, with great success, it would seem, since the disciples of John express some dissatisfaction: 'all are going to him' (3:26). Yet an air of uncertainty hangs over this success also, since a dispute had arisen between the disciples of John and a Jew over purification (3:25), and hence by implication between

Jesus and the Jews also, particularly in view of the fact that Jesus had earlier used the jars which were filled with water for purificatory purposes, in accordance with Jewish custom, for his wine-making miracle at Cana (2:6f.).

In view of these various hints of emerging opposition it comes as no great surprise to hear that Jesus left Judea and went *again* to Galilee (4:3). Still the narrator gives us the reason for the withdrawal explicitly: 'As soon as Jesus knew that the Pharisees had heard that Jesus was making more disciples that John, and baptising ... he left Judea'. A further parenthesis stresses that in fact Jesus himself did not perform baptisms, but only his disciples.

In view of the fact that over-packing of a narratorial summary can function as a signal for the reader that highly important information is being conveyed, we shall do well to give this summary our special attention.[6] The clarification that Jesus did not himself baptise may well have a polemical intention in relation to the Johannine and Baptist communities, but it has an intra-textual meaning also. The fact that Jesus is said to come *again* to Galilee points backwards to his first journey there. This occurs at 1:43, when, we are informed, he wished to go to Galilee to find other disciples in addition to those who had already joined him from John's circle. The contrast between John and Jesus indicated by this transfer of disciples as well as by the utterances of the Baptist himself (1:26,33), shows that Jesus is not to be compared with John, and it is a measure of the superficiality of the Pharisees' approach that they judge Jesus in terms of his relative success by comparison with the Baptist. The narrator wants to disassociate the reader from any such comparisons, since Jesus can in no sense be properly seen as a rival of John's.

On his first visit to Galilee Jesus encountered Nathanael whom he designates 'an Israelite in whom there is no guile', clearly indicating that here indeed is a genuine disciple.[7] Galilee and the making of disciples are then associated in the reader's mind. But the linking of the Pharisees' knowledge of

6. See R. Fowler, *Loaves and Fishes*, 160f.
7. S. Pancaro, "The Church and Israel in St John's Gospel", *NTS* 21 (1975) 386–405.

his success with the departure is also ominous. They had first appeared within the narrative in an investigative role, querying John the Baptist as to his identity (1:19–28), and the fact that one of their number, Nicodemus, as an honest enquirer, was constrained to approach Jesus by night, is a further pointer to their potentially hostile role. As the narrative progresses their suspicious nature will turn to open hostility, and Jerusalem is clearly seen as their centre of operation, from whence they exercise their religious control.

Though Galilee was explicitly mentioned as the goal of Jesus' journey, he was diverted to Samaria, of necessity (ἔδει), we are told. The subsequent narrative has its own internal set of movements, both spatial and temporal, leading eventually to many Samaritans believing in him as the saviour (σωτήρ) of the world. This universalist confession has special significance in the light of the declaration of the main character that the hour was fast approaching when the true worshippers would worship the Father neither on Mount Gerazim nor in Jerusalem, but in spirit and in truth (4:21–3). This statement is highly charged in view of the earlier episode of Jesus' implicit appropriation of the Jerusalem cult centre. Now in the name of the salvation which is 'of the Jews', and soon to be declared the saviour of the world, he disqualifies both Jerusalem and Gerazim as the proper places and modes of worship of his Father. Galilee differs from both places in not having a formal place of worship, and it is there that Israelites, that is, in terms of the author, those who are prepared to join the messianic community of Jesus, are to be found. As well as being a place of refuge from hostile forces, it also has positive overtones in terms of Jesus' mission and purpose, therefore. Thus the journey down takes on the character of a pilgrimage (cf. ἔδει of 4:4), a reversal of the synoptic presentation of the journey to Jerusalem.

After this successful Samaritan sojourn, the journey to Galilee, announced at 4:3, is now completed (4:43–5). The information that the Galileans received him (ἐδέξαντο αὐτὸν) seems to be highly significant for understanding the overall point of view of the author, even if it is based on signs which he had done in Jerusalem and which the Galileans had also experienced on the occasion of the festival (4:45). Those very signs had led many to believe in his name while in Jerusalem (2:23), but he did not entrust himself to them in that setting. The absence of any such hesitation in a Galilean setting is all the more noteworthy therefore. This would seem to be confirmed by the application to the situation of the proverb about the prophet not receiving honour in his own (ἴδιος) country, which in the context can only refer to his rejection in Judea, not Nazareth (or Galilee) as in the Synoptics.[8] The fact that the subsequent miracle in favour of the ruler is called by the narrator a second σημεῖον done at Cana, thus explicitly linking it to the previous one which had such positive effects in terms of the faith of the disciples (2:11; 4:54), would seem to confirm this understanding. Still there is no unqualified acceptance of Galileans as such, since a general condemnation of faith based on signs and wonders (σημεῖα καὶ τέρατα) is uttered before the miracle is actually performed.[9]

The next journey of Jesus to Jerusalem is for an unspecified feast (5:1), when a miracle performed there gives rise to a theological dispute of the most serious kind. Jesus is not merely accused of violating the Sabbath, but of blasphemy by making himself equal to God. Far from withdrawing, he proceeds to reiterate the claim, justifying it by an appeal to both his works which have their origin in God and the Mosaic scriptures which bear witness to him. While there is no explicit mention of a retreat to Galilee, it comes as no surprise to find Jesus across the sea of Galilee, which is Tiberias, even

8. For recent discussions of this saying in the Johannine context which arrive at rather different conclusions as to its import, compare J.M. Bassler, 'The Galileans: A Neglected Factor in Johannine Community Research', *CBQ* 43(1981) 243–57, especially 248f. with J.W. Pryor, 'John 4:44 and the *Patris* of Jesus', *CBQ* 49(1987) 254–63. The former opts for Judea as the πάτρις of Jesus, as being more in accord with the logic of the work as a whole, whereas the latter argues for Galilee insofar as it shares in the Jewish rejection of Jesus. Bassler's line of argument is more convincing, especially in view of the fact that she does not insist on a rigid Galilee/Jerusalem opposition in terms of belief and rejection, something that would appear to be precluded by the story of ch. 9 in a Judean setting as well as the rejection by Jesus in the synagogue at Capernaum in a Galilean context. Pryor fails to distinguish between superficial acceptance and downright rejection.

9. The plausible suggestion has been made by R. Fortna that the expression καὶ τέρατα in this phrase is epexegetical, that is explanatory of a particular, non-Johannine understanding of signs: signs that are the equivalent of miracles, 'Source and Redaction in the Fourth Gospel's Portrayal of Jesus' Signs', *JBL* 89(1970) 153, n.8.

as the feast of Passover approaches (6:1–4). It is at this point that some have proposed a rearrangement of the existing text because, it is alleged, this would make better geographical sense and also because 7:14–24 alludes to the miracle of healing on the Sabbath performed in ch. 5 and carries forward the discussion there about Moses as a witness to the claims about Jesus. However, such rearrangement of the text is not necessary nor indeed warranted. In terms of the emerging pattern of the contrast between the reception in Galilee and Jerusalem, the present order is in fact demanded and corresponds to the author's intention as we have been able to decipher this within the first movement. Once again there is no unquestioning affirmation of Galileans as such, since in ch. 6 the typical Jewish response of a totally superficial appreciation of Jesus and his claims, climaxing in the rejection in the Capernaum synagogue, is found in a Galilean context also.

The third journey of Jesus from Galilee to Jerusalem is for the feast of Tabernacles (chs. 7–8). It is introduced by a discussion between Jesus and his brothers as to whether or not he should go to Jerusalem for the feast. They exhort him to go and show his deeds openly to the world, but he counters that his time is not yet ready and that therefore he cannot go up. Their time was always ready, however, and hence there was nothing to prohibit their going to Jerusalem. This opening dialogue already sets up a clear tension between the time (καιρός) of the main character on the one hand and that of his brothers on the other. The narrator informs us that they did not believe in him, and hence their point of view is to be rejected. Jesus cannot go to Jerusalem on their terms (7:1–9).

With this introduction it is surprising, to say the least, to find that Jesus is actually present in the temple at the feast. On both the middle and last great day he appears in the temple precincts (τὸ ἱερόν), and his presence and utterances give rise to a lively debate, both directly with his opponents and backstage in the higher councils of the Jews. Once again two differing points of view emerge that can be labelled Galilean and Judean, even though the geographical locations are subservient to the perspectives that are espoused on either side. The law-abiding Pharisees and chief priests are ironically shown to be in violation of the very law they claim to cherish in seeking to put Jesus to death without a trial. When one of their own colleagues, Nicodemus, reminds them of this they accuse him of being a Galilean for appearing to be sympathetic to Jesus.[10]

The underlying assumption throughout this whole discussion is that the Galileans do not know the law and are not, therefore, law-abiding. When Jesus first appears on the scene they are surprised at his knowledge, since he has not been taught (7:15). Those who believe in him—by implication Galileans (cf. 4:45)—are described as 'this people who know not the law and are accursed' in contrast to the members of the Sanhedrin and the Pharisees. As Jesus continues to challenge their understanding by his increasingly outspoken declarations about his own identity (couched in terms of the actual symbolism of the feast) he is described as being a Samaritan and being possessed (8:48). Thus a deliberate chain of pejorative epithets is established—unlettered in the law, Galilean, Samaritan and possessed—the first three of which, ironically, have the total approval of the author/narrator, something the reader can scarcely have failed to grasp, particularly with the sympathetic treatment of the Samaritans by the main character in ch. 4.[11]

As already mentioned, Galilee does not feature explicitly in the final cycle of movements by the main character, which originates instead across the Jordan (10:40–42). On approaching the city he is enthusiastically greeted by those who had 'gone up for the feast'. It would appear that we are to assume the presence of Galileans among them, since a little later we hear of Greeks who hoped to meet Jesus at the festival making their approach to him through Philip who was from Bethsaida in Galilee (12:21). Once the city has been

10. Bassler, in 'The Galileans', correctly, in my view, stresses that the primary symbolism functions not at the level of locale but at that of people, even though Galileans are always to be found in Galilee. Outside the actual territory those who believe in Jesus are designated in some other way. Thus the question to Nicodemus, Μὴ καὶ σὺ ἐκ τῆς Γαλιλαίας εἶ should be understood adjectivally: 'are you also a Galilean' (253, n.36).

11. See W. Meeks, 'Galilee and Judea in the Fourth Gospel', *JBL* 85(1966) 159–69, especially 163–6.

entered the geographic tension is dropped in favour of other oppositions, yet Jesus is remembered as being from Nazareth in the inscription on the cross (19:19). Nevertheless, the completed story which includes ch. 21 has the main character returning to Galilee for a final meeting with the disciples and their commissioning for the tasks that lie ahead. In this farewell scene Nathanael from Cana in Galilee is explicitly mentioned as being present, true to the designation he received in the opening encounter, as an Israelite in whom there is no guile. (21:2; 1:45).

2. Galilee within a Jewish Religious Perspective

This first reading of John has concentrated on the movements of Jesus, and the various reactions to him that are associated with the journeys to and from Jerusalem within the narrative. The main action, apart from ch. 6, is located in Jerusalem, yet the few glimpses of Galilean response that the author has chosen to give us have on the whole been positive, but without any idealisation. Judea and Jerusalem on the other hand are associated with opposition to and rejection of Jesus, so that he cannot trust himself even to those who make a positive response in that setting (2:24; 7:25–30). This initial probing prompts the further question as to the assumptions which the author makes about Galilee and its religious affiliations. To be sure the picture is sketchy in the extreme in view of the minimal amount of narrative space that is given to Galilee, yet for that very reason the glimpses we are given are all the more significant for our purpose.

As already mentioned the opponents are often designated simply as 'the Jews', yet other distinctions do occur. In particular, the Pharisees, we saw, were authoritative figures who took the initiative for maintaining a law-centred observance. It is only in the trial scenes that the chief priests and elders surface (7:32,45; 11:47,55), and we never hear of the Sadducees or any other Jewish party. John's Pharisees then take on the role of the scribes in the other gospels. They send emissaries to investigate the identity of John (1:19,24) and they are obviously concerned about the success of new religious movements (4:1); they send servants to arrest Jesus (7:32ff.); they cross-examine the parents of the man born blind and it is they who will be responsible for expulsion from the synagogue (9:13ff.); they are deeply involved in the decision to have Jesus removed, actually summoning a meeting of the council (11:46f.). In this role they are not indigenous to Galilee, but to Jerusalem, and hence the author/narrator is able to locate an alternative point of view within the province, while maintaining its essentially Jewish character.

Because of the Jewish contours of the story the author shows little interest in the gentile associations of Galilee. The ruler (τις βασιλισκὸς) whom Jesus befriends (4:46,49) is more likely Herodian than gentile, though in a synoptic story that seems to be related from a traditio-historical point of view (Mt 8:8–13; Lk 7:1–10) he is clearly a gentile, but this aspect is not at all developed. Instead his faith, based on Jesus' word, is exemplary of true Johannine faith (4:53). When Jesus tells the hostile Jews that they will seek him and not be able to find him they wonder whether he will go to the Diaspora and teach the Greeks, in a context where his Galilean origins are being particularly highlighted (7:35). Finally, there are those Greeks from Bethsaida in Galilee who approach Philip with a view to meeting Jesus. None of these gentile associations are developed, however, and they are not at all essential to the narrative and its main thrust.

In view of the fact that Judea is described as the πάτρις of Jesus some have suggested that either he or his followers were from the south and were not Galileans.[12] Yet this seems to be an unwarranted assumption even in terms of the narrative. True, we first encounter Jesus outside Galilee in Bethany beyond the Jordan where the Baptist was active. Later, John is located at Aenom near Salim, which is said to be in Judea (3:22f.), and in Perea across the Jordan (10:40). It seems to be assumed that John too had a mobile ministry, but confined to the Jordan region. However, the fact that Jesus' first followers come from among the disciples of John, does not mean that they were not Galilean in the author's view. It is

12. E. Schillebeeckx, in e.g. *The Christ. The Experience of Jesus as Lord*, 312–21, following Cullmann, Martyn and others, locates the beginnings of Johannine theology among believers from non-official Jewish circles, emanating close to Stephen and the Hellenists in Jerusalem. This would explain the presence of so many Judean/Jerusalem traditions in the gospel and the relative scarcity of Galilean ones.

explicitly stated that Peter and Andrew were from Bethsaida in Galilee, as was Philip (1:44; 12:21); Jesus too was from Nazareth, it is recognised (1:45), and Galilean origins are repeatedly assumed for him and for his family (2:1,12; 6:42; 7:44,52). The narrative portrayal, then, is not of Judean origins, but rather of Galileans in search of religious meaning outside Galilee. Indeed 1:41–5 presents them in search of a messianic figure as disclosed in the scriptures.

Apart from these indications of a religious search among Galileans, the Cana story with the six pitchers of water—for the purificatory rites of washing before meals, presumably—presupposes a degree of halachic observance that does not easily tally with the description of this mob who do not know the law and are accursed (7:49), which in the context seems to be aimed at the Galilean crowd present for the festival. The observance of the pilgrimage regulation is thereby assumed, and this is explicitly asserted of the brothers of Jesus as well as of Galileans generally (4:45; 7:1–9; cf. 12:55).

The presence of these aspects of more orthodox Jewish practice in the author's Galilee raises the question of the Ἰουδαῖοι in the synagogue at Capernaum (6:41,52). The attempt to give this term the purely geographical meaning of 'Judean' is unsustainable, as are efforts to restrict it to the Jewish authorities only.[13] Undoubtedly the term has negative connotations within the narrative for the most part, and can easily fade into the more general 'the world' or become more specific as the Pharisees, but almost always denoting opposition to Jesus. Yet one can encounter Ἰουδαῖοι in Galilee also, once the term is stripped of the ethnic or geographic associations which it undoubtedly carries in pagan literature of the period, and is given the religious valuation which John wishes it to have, namely, those children of Abraham who are totally closed to the idea of a messianic visitation in Jesus. For the author, these Jews are identifiable by their strict adherence to inherited practices which they trace back to Moses,

13. M. Lowe, in 'Who were the Ἰουδαῖοι?' *NT* 18(1976) 101–30 defends the former position and U.C. von Wahlde, in 'The Johannine 'Jews': A Critical Survey', *NTS* 28(1982) 33–60 espouses the latter point of view. For a much more nuanced treatment which forms the basis for the reading proposed here cf. J. Ashton, 'The Identity and Function of the ἸΟΥΔΑΙΟΙ in the Fourth Gospel', *NT* 27(1985) 40–75.

but which in our author's view misinterpret the real meaning of what Moses wrote. To be a Galilean does not preclude one from being a 'Ἰουδαῖος in John's perspective, even when the presupposition is that one is open to a divine manifestation that goes beyond any knowledge of torah, as in the typical case of Nathanael of Cana, seated under the fig tree, but yet prepared to accept Jesus' word and so be declared a true Israelite. The 'Ἰουδαῖοι, on the other hand, are found in the synagogue, and as such are identified with the Pharisaic point of view, which cannot tolerate within its ambit those who recognise Jesus, whether they be Galilean or Judean.

3. The Reception of Jesus in Galilee

Comment has already been made on the fact that the actual Galilean ministry of Jesus receives a minimal coverage in contrast to the Judean ministry with its hostile or suspect reactions. This can only be attributed to the ironic stance of the author which is such a feature of the work as a whole, especially in view of the favourable reception which the Galileans gave to Jesus.[14] The Two Cana miracles form the high points of the Galilean ministry, and are highlighted as taking place in Galilee (2:1,11; 4:46,54). Yet neither receives any commentary in terms of a typical Johannine monologue, which is such a feature of the Jerusalem episodes, often helped along by the misunderstanding of one of the audience or the need to respond to hostile reactions. The one exception is ch. 6, in which the feeding miracle is followed by the bread of life discourse and climaxes in the rejection in the synagogue of Jesus' claims, leading to a division even among his own disciples. This outcome was in part prepared for by the over-enthusiastic reaction of the crowd after the feeding miracle, when they sought to take Jesus by force and make him king (6:14f.). Jesus utterly rejects their response, and accuses them of following him because of the material advantages of the encounter, and not because they had perceived it as a true sign

14. Cf. A. Culpepper, *The Anatomy of the Fourth Gospel. A Study in Literary Design*, Philadelphia: Fortress Press, 1983, 165–79, for a comprehensive survey of Johannine irony and its role in the literary strategy and theological technique of the writer.

of his identity. Thus the subsequent division after Jesus' discourse is not altogether surprising.

The portrayal of popular messianic hopes based on the mosaic-eschatological-prophet expectation is inadequate by Johannine standards, yet it links up with the initial reaction of the Galilean disciples on first discovering Jesus: 'we have found the one whom Moses wrote about in the law' (1:45), and 'Rabbi, you are the Son of God, you are the king of Israel' (1:49). In making these confessions they are, however, encouraged to expect more: 'greater things than these shall you see' (1:50), something that is realised within the narrative in the very next episode, when, we are told by the narrator, that Jesus revealed his glory in the first Cana sign and his disciples believed in him (2:11). From the outset, then, they are totally identified with the point of view of the narrator(s) who have also seen his glory and received of his fullness (1:14,16).

Thus, Galileans are the first to make the transition from popular messianic hopes to full-blown Johannine faith. The expression 'the Galileans received him' (4:44) presumably reflects this response, yet like so much of Johannine language, it is capable of being understood at two distinct levels.[15] On the second occasion the Galilean reception was based on the signs which they saw him accomplish at the festival, but, as noted already, there is no mention of Jesus distrusting them, as was the case with the Jerusalem-based response to the same signs (2:24). Too much should not be read into this absence of negative narratorial comment, however, since soon Jesus makes the highly critical comment: 'Unless you see signs and wonders you will not believe.' Even though this observation does not, we believe, amount to a rejection of the Galileans, it still must be read as a clear warning that signs can function ambivalently in the Johannine perspective, and that Galileans, no less than Judeans, are capable of misinterpreting them. This is the point that is made

15. W.D. Davies, in *The Gospel and the Land*, 326, maintains that if John had intended the Galileans of 4:44 to refer to his own of 1:11 he would have used the same verb, λαμβάνειν, not δέχεσθαι in the second instance. However this argument is perhaps too literalist, and not sufficiently open to the nuances of Johannine thought and the range of positive meanings that the verb δέχεσθαι offered the author.

directly in the opening section of ch. 6, so that the Galilean crowds who seek Jesus for the wrong reasons, and whom the narrator says followed him because they observed (ἐθεώρουν) the signs that he did on the sick (6:2) are soon to be castigated by the main character because they did not see (εἴδετε) the signs (6:26)![16] Signs that are recognised as genuine works of God in Jesus lead to true discipleship, whereas those which are accepted because of their wondrous character only, are not adequate.

Subsequently, we meet another form of Galilean response in the persons of the brothers of Jesus. Rather than follow R.E. Brown in seeing them as ciphers for a form of Jewish Christianity that was unacceptable to the Johannine community,[17] we shall do well to trace their narrative role within the work. They are encountered for the first time after the original Cana miracle, when the narrator tells us: 'After this he descended to Capernaum with his mother, his brothers and his disciples and there they remained only a few days' (2:12). Coming immediately after the mention of the disciples seeing his glory revealed in the Cana story and believing in him, the mention of the brothers is a surprise. They had not been mentioned previously in the narrative, though his mother was among the invited guests at the wedding feast. We cannot then think of them as being among those who saw his glory, and in retrospect their links with Capernaum prepare the way for the negative response which he is to receive in the synagogue there in ch. 6. Nathanael, 'the Israelite in whom there is no guile', as the prototypical disciple, is from Cana in Galilee, not Capernaum (21:2).

The only other appearance of the brothers occurs in ch. 7, as Jesus prepares to go to the feast of Tabernacles. As was already indicated, their attitudes are contrasted with those of Jesus in terms of the proper καιρός for their respective appearances. The contrast can also be expressed in regard to what is hidden (ἐν κρυπτῷ) and what is public (ἐν

16. On the distinction between signs and deeds in the Johannine perspective cf. R.E. Brown, *The Gospel of John*, vol. 1, Anchor Bible, New York: Doubleday, 1966, Appendix 3, 525–32; R. Schnackenburg, *The Gospel according to John*, vol. 1, E.T. London: Burns Oates, 1981, Excursus IV, 515–28.

17. *The Community of the Beloved Disciple*, London: Chapmann, 1979, 73–81.

παρρησίᾳ), and this is applied to the deeds of Jesus. The attitudes in question correspond to the distinction already established between the understanding of Jesus' deeds as works, not as wonders which capture the imagination of the public, without any inner appreciation of their source or intention. Thus the brothers share the point of view of those who persist in a totally superficial understanding of Jesus. In the author's terms they are Ἰουδαῖοι, not Israelites, Judeans, not Galileans. It is not surprising then to find them absent at the cross, when care of the mother is entrusted to a disciple, not a brother, despite the fact that they had been listed in her company earlier (2:12; 19:27).

This reading of the fourth gospel's focus on Galilee has uncovered rather different aspects of our topic from that of the other evangelists. As the Galilean pilgrim who goes to Jerusalem for all the great feasts of the Jews, Jesus is, ironically, a threat to the temple, indeed to all forms of localised worship of the Father (4:23; 11:48). Only the author, and those with whom his vision is shared, including the reader, are in a position to fully appreciate the significance of Jesus' threat in theological terms (1:14,51), yet at the surface level of the plot the Pharisees and the high priests also recognise the danger: 'This man does many signs; if we allow him to continue thus all will believe in him and the Romans will come and destroy our nation and our place' (11:47f.). Their decision helps the movement of the plot to its final denouement, when their 'lifting up' of Jesus turns out to be his exaltation. The pilgrim who subverts the place of pilgrimage and its feasts by fulfilling in his person the symbolism attached to that place and those occasions, is indeed paradoxical. Irony serves the author to explore the deeper theological insights of the vision with which he is grappling, and, as Wayne Booth observes, also invites the reader to ascend to a higher plane of cognition that is not accessible to all.[18] The fact that Galilee enters into the ironic patterns the author seeks to develop shows just how important the memories associated with the region were to early Christian self-

18. *A Rhetoric of Irony*, Chicago, The University Press, 1974, 36.

understanding, even when there is little concern to develop a realistic narrative account of that setting.

Still there is no idealisation of Galileans or Galilee, despite the fact that the hero was a Galilean pilgrim. We saw that Galileans could in the author's view espouse a superficial attitude to Jesus' deeds that was as blinding to the true realities as was Pharisaic legalism, whose pathetic condition is parodied in the trial before Pilate. In their desire to celebrate Passover in an undefiled condition the Jews would not enter the courtyard of the governor (18:28), even as they were about to reject the true Passover lamb (1:29; 19:13-36). In the case of the Galileans it was not legalism that blinded them but their over-enthusiastic and superficial reaction to the deeds of Jesus. It was an attitude that was shared by both the Galilean crowds and the brothers of Jesus alike, thereby aligning them with the Jews and the world, the two great symbols of negative response within the narrative. Equally, however, it could lead to a proper understanding that turns Galileans into Israelites because they can recognise the glory of God in Jesus, thus leading them and others to a mature faith in him (2:11; 4:53; cf. 20:31).

PART TWO

Historical Investigations

CHAPTER FIVE

The Social World of First-Century Galilee

EVEN though the social world of Galilee is embedded, in the sense of not being developed in all its details in the gospels, we were still able to decipher its main outlines as perceived by the various gospel writers. Various aspects were touched on, hinted at or merely presumed in the depiction of episodes and individuals and in the social concerns that are echoed in the main character's utterances. Our task in the present chapter is to evaluate these depictions and assumptions in the light of what can be reconstructed about the real Galilee of the first century, based on the documentary evidence available, including of course the gospels themselves.

Most contemporary analyses of social worlds begin with those elements of the infrastructure that are regarded as all-determining, namely the economic and ecological factors, moving on to other aspects of the superstructure, such as questions about political and legal authority and cultural affinities.[1] Given the recognised interaction of many factors, both infra- and supra-structural in shaping any social system, it is indeed a moot point where precisely one should begin. Provided critical account is taken of the ways in which various aspects of the system do interact and each is allowed its proper role, one's starting-point would seem to be largely a matter of strategy, since it would be naïve to suggest that by starting with the infra-structural factors one was being somehow more objective. In this instance it is proposed to

1. Elliot, 'Social-Scientific Criticism of the New Testament', 17; G. Theissen, 'Zur forschungsgeschichtlichen Einordnung der soziologischen Fragestellung', in *Studien zur Soziologie des Urchristentums*. WUNT 19, Tübingen: J.C.B. Mohr, 1983, 3–34, who defends the approach against the charge that it implies a total acceptance of the Marxist, materialist explanation of early Christianity.

begin, not with economic factors, but with the political situation, precisely because a pre-judgment suggests that this may well have played a vital role in determining the other factors in first-century Galilee.[2] In the course of the present analysis this decision will have to be tested as we proceed, particularly in discussing the economic situation and its overall potential for alienation among the populace at large.

The issues which emerged from our reading of the gospels may be summarised as follows:(1) Political—who controlled life in Galilee? (2) Organisational—within what kind of boundaries did Galileans live their lives? (3) Economic—who owned the resources and what effect did this have on the lives of others within the province? (4) Cultural—what values, assumptions and attitudes determined the Galilean ethos? It is in this order that we propose to discuss the social world of Galilee, always keeping firmly in view the recognition that all these issues are deeply interconnected.

1. Political Realities and Jesus' Galilee

Political rulers impinged rather lightly on the public career of Jesus in Galilee; it was in Jerusalem that the great encounter with secular power occurred, according to all the versions of the story. Both Matthew and Luke are conscious of the importance of the political situation during the infancy of Jesus also. While Luke is interested in locating the event within world history, Matthew indicates that both the paranoid personality of Herod the Great and the contrasting rules of his sons, Archelaus in Judea and Antipas in Galilee, determined the fact that Jesus came to grow up in the latter province. What is significant about this information is the contrast that it presumes between Galilean and Judean social life, which is seen as the direct result of the prevailing political power. This contrast, we maintain, should not be underestimated in judging the social world of Galilee.

We are given one brief insight into Antipas' character in the story of the birthday banquet and the beheading of the

2. As T.F. Carney, *The Shape of the Past. Models and Antiquity*, Lawrence, Kansas: Coronado Press, 1975, notes, in antiquity élites and their governments tended to think about economic matters in terms which were essentially strategical or political (p. 190).

Baptist. Though Luke omits the story he is the most aware of the immediate threat to Jesus that the Herodian presence represents, with the warning from the friendly Pharisees that Herod sought to kill him (13:31). While there may be good reason to suspect this notice as part of the Lucan characterisation of the Pharisees, it is still a highly pertinent question to ask whether or not Jesus, in terms of the strategy to be adopted during his public ministry, had to take account of the antagonism of Herod. The death of the Baptist did have a clear political motivation according to Josephus (*J.A.* 18:116–19), in view of Antipas' broken marriage with the Nabataean princess, which John had criticised.[3] The fact that Antipas was only given the status of tetrarch by Augustus (despite the gospels' use of βασιλεύς) showed a degree of mistrust or at least a query as to his administrative abilities. Clearly, in these precarious circumstances Antipas could not allow political and social subversives to go unhindered throughout his territory. Yet in Luke's account he showed no burning desire to have Jesus removed from the scene when the opportunity finally presented itself at Jerusalem. The gospel evidence alone can scarcely answer our question, therefore.

The most easily documented impact of Antipas' reign on Galilean life is his building projects—the ornamentation of Sepphoris and the founding of Tiberias on the lake-front, probably in the year 19 CE.[4] Sepphoris was to be the ornament of all Galilee according to Josephus, who also tells us that it received the name Αὐτοκράτωρ (*J.A.* 18:27), which probably signifies a degree of independence along the lines of a hellenistic πόλις. Excavations currently in progress will hopefully uncover the full character of this city in the heartland of Galilee, which had been sacked by the Roman Varus in 4 BCE on the death of Herod the Great. Already there seems to be agreement among the excavators that the

3. Cf. H. Hoehner, *Herod Antipas*, S.N.T.S. monographs 17, Cambridge: University Press, 1973, especially 136–46; P. Hollenbach, 'Social Aspects of John the Baptiser's Mission in the Context of Palestinian Judaism', *ANRW* II 19, 1, 850–75, especially 862–4, though somewhat uncritical in its use of the gospel evidence; R. Horsley and J. Hanson, *Bandits Prophets and Messiahs. Popular Movements at the Time of Jesus*, New York: Winston Press, 1985, 180f., with greater attention to the political implications of John's social gospel.

4. Details in Freyne, *Galilee*, 122–34 and notes.

theatre, which is estimated to have seated between four and five thousand people, is Herodian.[5] Later, at the time of the first revolt, the city was unpopular with Galilean peasants. This may have been due, in part at least, to its continued Herodian connections, which caused it to side with the Romans, as its coinage for the year 67 CE with the inscription Εἰρηνοπολις 'city of peace' indicates.[6] Yet, despite this stance and the signs of Greek culture in the material remains, Sepphoris was, and continued to be, a Jewish city.[7]

It is possible to speculate on the reasons that prompted Antipas to build a new capital at the lake-front, naming it after his patron Tiberius. No doubt a combination of personal and strategic factors was at work. Galileans, including 'those in power', that is, presumably, wealthy land-owners, were compelled to join the residents of the new city who were drawn from everywhere. One could attribute their apparent reluctance to religious grounds, since Josephus mentions that Jewish graves had been violated in the building of the city (*J.A.* 18:38), something that is also reflected in later rabbinic legends about the purification of Tiberias.[8] However, at the time of the first revolt, Jews who are described as being most zealous for their ancestral customs were present in the city without any qualms, it would seem. Thus the initial hesitancy of the Galileans can be attributed more plausibly to other factors. The natural rural/urban tensions that one finds everywhere in antiquity would certainly have been accentuated in the case of a new city, many of whose inhabitants would have had no natural links with the hinterland.[9]

5. See E. Meyers, E. Nehud, C.L. Meyers, 'Sepphoris, Ornament of All Galilee', *BA* (1986) 4–19; J. Strange and T. Longstaff, '"Sepphoris" (Sippori). Notes and News' *IEJ* 34 (1984), 51–2 and 269–70.

6. See S. Cohen, *Josephus in Galilee and Rome. His Vita and Development as a Historian.* Leiden: Brill, 197, 7–12, for a detailed discussion of this coinage.

7. See M. Goodman's review of H.A. Harris, *Greek Athletics and the Jews*, Cardiff: University of Wales Press, 1976, in *JJS* 28 (1977) 206f. Goodman challenges Harris's assumption that the stadia of Galilee were intended for use by the locals, suggesting that their purpose was not necessarily for use but for self-advertisement which was typical of the Herodian style. Cf. further his *State and Society in Roman Galilee A.D. 132–212*, Totowa, N.J: Rowman and Allanheld, 1983, 81–4.

8. See L. Levine, 'R. Simeon ben Yohai and the Purification of Tiberias. History and Tradition', *HUCA* 49 (1974) 143–85.

9. On the general question of urban/rural relations in antiquity cf. R. McMullen, *Roman Social Relations 50 B.C. to A.D. 284*, London: Yale University Press, 1974, 28–56.

Galilean peasants would have found it an uncongenial environment, except for those who had lost their land and would have been grateful for Antipas' bequest of plots of lands as well as house (*J.A.* 18:35). The fact that there does not appear to have been many Galileans in that category tells its own story about economic conditions in the province, as we shall see. It is a measure of the sense of alienation that the country people felt for the city that some Galileans joined the destitute classes in Tiberias in destroying Herod's palace in 66 CE. In the case of the Galileans at least it would be extremely difficult to disentangle religious, social and cultural motives for this action.

The Galilean notables, on the other hand, had their own reasons for not wishing to be part of the new city. By agreeing to join Herod's city they were being directly brought within the net of his control. It is tempting to identify these people with those whom Mark describes as the οἱ πρῶτοι τῆς Γαλιλαίας, whom we find celebrating the king's birthday and so beholden to him (Mk 6:21). Besides, Herod the Great had experienced considerable difficulty from Galileans living in the vicinity of Arbela and Sepphoris (*J.W.* 14:395,417,430). Though Josephus seeks to discredit this resistance as coming from brigands, the more likely hypothesis is that they were ousted Hasmonean nobles who had lost their privileged position in the transfer of power from Hasmonean to Herodian government in Galilee.[10] Could it be that Antipas' removal of the seat of his court from Sepphoris to Tiberias was the result of continued opposition from that quarter, since by compelling the Galilean nobles to join him at Tiberias he could more easily control their loyalties?

In the light of this brief discussion of the presence of Herodian political power in Galilee as represented by the two cities, what can be said about the absence of any mention of either in the gospels? It is quite unlikely that Jesus' avoidance of either place was due to religious attitudes, in view of his apparent disregard for the purity laws and his openness to

10. S. Freyne, 'Bandits in Galilee. A Contribution to the Study of Social Conditions in First Century Palestine', in *The Social World of Formative Christianity and Judaism. Essays in Tribute of Howard Clark Kee*, ed. J. Neusner, P. Borgen, E. Frerichs, R. Horsley, Philadelphia: Fortress Press, 1988, 50–69.

gentiles, even to the point of travelling in their territory—something that is well attested in all the narratives. His avoidance of the main Herodian centres of Galilee is best explained, therefore, in the light of a conscious decision not to become directly embroiled in a confrontation with Herodian power.[11] The fate of the Baptist must surely have been a salutary warning (see Mt 14:13). It was possible to conduct an itinerant ministry to the villages, relatively unimpeded, by adopting the strategy of avoiding open confrontation. Insofar as criticism of the Herodian court was called for, Jesus, unlike John, confined himself to a social critique of a more general applicability. 'Those who are clothed in purple' are viewed from a distance that was far-removed from Jesus and his followers in terms of their respective value systems (Mt 11:8; Lk 7:25). The fact that we meet Joanna, the wife of Herod's steward, Chuza, among his retinue (Lk 8:1), suggests that for some of those who inhabited that other world of wealth and power, his words did not fall wholly on rocky ground.

Yet we met Herodians as opponents of Jesus in both Galilee and Jerusalem (Mk 3:6; 12:13). Their precise identity is not certain—actual members of the Herodian family, or more probably, supporters of Herod because of the benefits accruing to them through Herodian rule.[12] Their opposition to Jesus would have been natural in view of the social critique that he mounted against the wealthy. Insofar as one can attribute any plausibility to their joining forces with the Pharisees (Mk 3:6), it is most easily understood if one could assume with Luke that the Galilean Pharisees belonged to the propertied classes in the province, something that we shall examine in detail later. Nor should one underestimate the Herodian influence at Jerusalem, in view of their continued

11. W. Bösen, *Galiläa als Lebensraum und Wirkungsfeld Jesu*, Freiburg im Breisgau: Herder 1985, 69–75, also discusses this question and favours the view that Jesus in all probability preached in Sepphoris but without success and in his opinion this would explain the silence of the gospels. However, the gospels are not silent on unsuccessful ministries to other Galilian cities (see Mt. 11:20–24). The fact that Jesus' parables reflect the social setting of a city such as Sepphoris does not necessarily suggest a ministry there, especially if there are other more compelling reasons for suggesting that he avoided the city.

12. For a discussion of the various points of view and an identification similar to ours cf. Hoehner, *Herod Antipas*, Appendix Ten, 331–42.

interest in the high-priesthood. The failure of Agrippa II's plea to avert the first revolt could, because of the prevailing attitudes among the revolutionary party, be misleading as regards the general picture of Herodian influence at the centre of Judaism throughout the first century. In this regard at least Herod's family continued his policy of controlling the institutions of Judaism and acting as the mediators between Jewish popular feelings and Roman control.[13] Opposition to Jesus as a subversive of Jewish religious institutions rather than as a political subversive *per se* is not, therefore, implausible among Herodian circles in Jerusalem.

We are not sufficiently informed about the extent of Herodian policing at local level in Galilee to judge whether or not a wandering teacher/healer could expect to encounter difficulties away from the more important centres. Our narratives do not suggest that he met with any political opposition in the villages. Opposition came from religious, not secular opponents, and the attempt to discredit him by suggesting that he was in league with evil forces, at least suggests that on religious issues there was a greater freedom of movement and access to people away from the seats of power. The Capernaum centurion (Lk 7:3) is a benefactor of the Jews and is prepared to accept help from a member of their ethnic group, without any question as to the healer's intentions or political ambitions. His role was probably that of a border policeman and not a sign of a strong military presence everywhere in the province. The only other local official we encounter is the synagogue ruler, but his difficulties with the popularity of Jesus are religious rather than political (Lk 13:14).

Neither are we in any position to fill out the picture concerning the administration of justice. Judges, litigants and prisons are all assumed (Mt 5:25–6; Lk 12:52–9), but we are largely in the dark as to how these functioned or who was in charge of them at local level. The probability must be that neither Antipas nor his father before him interfered greatly with the system that had operated since Hasmonean times, which would have combined the use of local elders for minor

13. See R. Horsley, 'High Priests and the Politics of Roman Palestine', *JSJ* 17 (1986) 23–55, especially 38f. Cf. *J.A.* 18:273; *J.W.* 2:193; Philo, *Legatio*, 299.

offences with a more centralised arrangement for major crimes.[14] Sepphoris had been made the seat of one of the five Roman synedria that Gabinius had established in Palestine, thereby developing the administrative and legal processes, but clearly recourse to the supreme sanhedrin in Jerusalem with its special authority for Jews was always possible for litigants, as the case of the Galilean mothers who charged the young Herod with murder shows (*J.A.* 14:167, 170f., 179f.). Josephus would have us believe that he organised Galilee for the administration of justice, but the two accounts (*J.W.* 2:570f. and *Life*, 79) do not easily harmonise. The liklihood is that the former version arises from his desire to present himself as an authoritative and responsible governor to varied readerships, and that the more realistic of the two, that of *Life*, reflects the existing arrangements which he discovered in the province.[15] The incident such as that reported at Lk 12:13 in which Jesus is asked to mediate between two contending brothers on a property issue is, therefore, not symptomatic of a breakdown of law and order. Rather it illustrates the kind of authority that a holy man could achieve within a rural setting, on the basis of respect that had been earned in other spheres of life, from people who had no desire to deal with bureaucracy, Jewish or Roman.

As a client-king, but without the title, Antipas was under constraint by Rome to maintain order and ensure that the tribute was paid annually. In the execution of these tasks he needed to have the support of the local leaders who acted in the role of a provincial aristocracy.[16] It was for this reason, we suggested, that the leading men of Galilee were included as part of his court retinue, together with the great ones (μεγιστᾶνες) and the superior military officers (χιλίαρχοι).[17] That on the whole he succeeded in maintaining the

14. On the question of village administration in the second century, cf. Goodman, *State and Society*, 119–28, and on the legal situation E. Schürer, (revised by G. Vermes, F. Miller, M. Black), *The History of the Jewish People in the Age of Jesus Christ*, 4 vols. Edinburgh: T. and T. Clark, 1973–85, vol. II, 210–18.

15. For a discussion cf. Cohen, *Josephus in Galilee and Rome*, 92 n. 26.

16. See Horsley, 'High Priests and Politics', 27–31.

17. A. N. Sherwin-White, in *Roman Society and Roman law in the New Testament*, Oxford, Clarendon Press, 1963, remarks on this verse that on the basis of the technical terms used we are in the presence of a 'petty Jewish prince under strong Roman influence' (p. 137). For a discussion of the terms and their technical meaning cf. in addition, Hoehner, *Herod Antipas*, 102 n. 3.

proper balance between the Jewish peasantry of his realm and Roman imperial power may be inferred from the length of his tenure; and his deposition, unlike that of his brother Archelaus, was not because of his failure to be a suitable power-broker for Rome, but because of the astuteness and better imperial connections of his nephew, Agrippa I. In the light of this judgment it is improbable that Jesus and his movement posed a serious threat on the political situation in Galilee, or at least that they were perceived in that light. Though mention is made of popular efforts to make Jesus king by force (Jn 6:14f.; cf. Mk 6:45), the absence of any serious reaction from Antipas or his administration must place a question mark over this information. At least if there was such popular acclaim with political intent, Jesus must have succeeded in defusing it rather quickly by portraying his mission in a very different light. In this regard there is a striking contrast between himself and the Baptist, at least as far as Antipas was concerned.[18]

2. The Organisation of Galilean Social Life

The discussion of Jesus' avoidance of Sepphoris and Tiberias already introduced the village culture of Galilee, at least indirectly. It was suggested that Jesus confined his ministry to the villages of Galilee, and on this all the gospels are agreed. Though Luke uses the combination κατὰ πόλιν καὶ κώμην, we have suggested that his use of the term πόλις is rather loose, and Mark is much more precise in distinguishing between village and city (Mk 8:27).[19] Presumably because of his gentile interests, Mark shows a greater awareness of the hellenistic city territories surrounding Galilee—Gadara, Tyre and Sidon, Caesarea Philippi and the Dekapolis (5:1; 7:24, 31; 8:27). There were other cities also in the neighbourhood of Galilee in the first century—Ptolemais/Acco on the coast; Gaba and Scythopolis in the great plain; Qedesh on the northern borders with Tyre and Bethsaida—Julias on the eastern frontier with the territory of Philip.[20] By the first century, then, the old name 'Galilee of the gentiles' could be

18. The question of the basis for popular kingship in Galilee is discussed in detail in ch. 6 below.
19. See Sherwin-White, *Roman Society and Roman Law*, 129.
20. For a detailed discussion of each foundation cf. *Galilee* 101–138.

said to have taken on a new actuality, encircled as the region was with Graeco-Roman cultural centres of varying status, quite apart from the Herodian foundations already discussed.

How is one to evaluate the impact of this administrative arrangement on the internal organisation of Galilean life? Josephus tells us that Galilee was thickly populated with 204 villages and cities in his day of which three are mentioned as the largest cities—Sepphoris, Tiberias and Gabaroth (*Life* 123.235). Elsewhere he speaks of the numerous villages, thickly populated, giving rise to intense cultivation of the soil (*J.W.* 3.42f.). A recent archaeological survey of Galilee and the Golan (1976) claims that there is a surprising lack of ceramic evidence until the second century BCE, and even then the vast majority of the sherds are found in lower Galilee until the second century CE, when there are definite signs of an increased habitation in upper Galilee also, coinciding presumably with the migrations northward after the second revolt.[21] However, this region, which is later named Tetracomia, clearly retained its village structure of habitation, despite the intensive programme of urbanisation in the wake of the two revolts as part of official Roman policy.[22] Aerial photography combined with Talmudic evidence has assisted in corroborating this picture of an essentially rural way of life, with intensive cultivation even at some distance from the centres of habitation and along the terraces and slopes of the hills.[23] Repeatedly in *Life*, Josephus speaks of the Galileans from the

21. See E. Meyers, J. Strange, D. Groh, 'The Meiron Excavation Project: Archaeological Survey in Galilee and the Golan, 1976', *BASOR* 230 (1978) 1–24, especially 18–20. The fluid nature of these conclusions may be discerned from Meyers's more recent remarks in 'Galilean Regionalism: A Reappraisal', in W. Scott Green, ed., *Approaches to Ancient Judaism. vol 5. Studies in Judaism and its Greco-Roman Context*, Brown Judaic Studies 32; Atlanta. Scholars Press, 1985, 115–31.

22. See Goodman, *State and Society in Roman Galilee*, 120; A.M.H. Jones, 'The Urbanisation of Palestine', *JRS* 21 (1933) 265–75.

23. See S. Applebaum, 'Judea as a Roman Province. The Countryside as a Political and Economic Factor', in *ANRW* II, 8, 355–96, especially 361–6. According to him the pressure on land was due to the displacement of Jewish peasants from the territories of the Greek cities after Pompey's intervention. Hence, while there is evidence of evolution from peasant holdings to large estate owners with their centres in villages or at fortified points, the predominant pattern which had been established in Hasmonean times was that of the small holdings, extending far beyond the nucleated village centres. Compare Freyne, *Galilee*, 156–76; Goodman, *State and Society*, 31–6.

land coming to his assistance, and he takes it for granted that these are able to bring supplies for a large army.[24] Equally, the gospels presume that adequate provisions for a sizable crowd can be procured in the surrounding villages (Mk 6:36). Thus literary and archaeological sources combine to confirm a picture of an essentially rural Galilee, whose inhabitants are committed to the peasant way of life and live in villages, though surrounded by a circle of Greek-style cities on the periphery (cf. *Life* 58).

This raises the question of what precisely is the difference between the two types of settlement and how can one draw the line for first-century Galilea? Among Josephus' villages are such places as Capernaum, Bethsaida and Cana, centres of relative prosperity apparently, and designated as cities in the gospels. On the other hand Tarichaeae (Magdala) would appear to warrant inclusion in Josephus' list of Galilean cities in view of the fact that it had walls and a hippodrome (*J.W.* 2:599.606; *Life* 138.), as well as its own territory (*J.W.* 2:252f.; *J.A.* 20:159). Clearly then, the term village can cover a wide range of settlements, and we must look to features other than the purely physical as determinative of their character.[25] In general it can be said that villages are distinguished from cities in antiquity in terms of their internal organisation and political independence—a relative term, of course, in hellenistic times. In this regard the naming of Sepphoris as Αὐτοκράτωρ (J.A. 18:27) is indicative, and Tiberias certainly had a βουλή or council, as well as an assembly of the whole people δῆμος *J.W.* 2:639.641) At Capernaum, despite its thriving character and size we hear of the elders (πρεσβύτεροι) approaching Jesus on an issue concerning the whole community, namely, aiding a gentile benefactor in need (Lk 7:3). This differentiation in terms of internal organisation of the

24. See S. Freyne, 'The Galileans in the Light of Josephus' *Vita*', *NTS* 26 (1980) 397–413, especially 403–5.

25. Goodman, *State and Society*, 27f., believes that Josephus' use of the term πόλις for several places which do not have any constitutional claims to it—Tarichaeae, Chabulon, Gabara, Gischala, e.g.—is a sign of the size and prosperity of many of these Galilean 'villages'. In this regard the Talmudic sources are terminologically more conscious of the variety of types of settlements, with a fourfold distinction—*kefar* (nucleated rural settlement), *'ir* (villa, city), *'ayarah* (village) and *giriah* (estate, village, in relation to a larger centre). Cf. Applebaum, 'Judea as a Roman Province', 362f.

city and village would be typical—the one based on the Greek ideal of democracy, the other reflecting ties of kinship, seniority and wealth.[26] It would generally be assumed also that the population of cities was cosmopolitan in character, whereas that of the village was likely to be more homogenous, and therefore, presumably, more attractive to Jews desirous of preserving a distinctive way of life.[27] Such generalisations are of course very rough indeed, and larger settlements that might technically be described as villages differ little in character from the cities, as can be seen from the material remains of several of the sites that have been excavated in Upper Galilee, albeit dating from a later period.[28]

This discussion raises the further question of the mutual regard in which the inhabitants of cities and villages held each other, particularly in view of our judgment that Jesus' avoidance of the Herodian cities was deliberate. We shall postpone to a later chapter a consideration of whether or not that ministry was supportive of village values and assumptions about life, but clearly any adequate answer must depend on how urban/rural relations functioned in a more general way in first-century Galilee. We have already alluded to these in passing when discussing the foundation of Tiberias. Further evidence of deep-seated tensions comes from Josephus' *Life* where the Galilean country people are portrayed as being hostile to both Sepphoris and Tiberias, in the latter case at least, even before Josephus' arrival in the province (*Life* 177f., 390–92). While it is possible to suggest historical reasons for this antipathy, a more culture-oriented approach could scarcely fail to recognise that the general urban/rural tensions to be found everywhere in antiquity were also operative here, especially in view of the deep-seated rivalry that existed between the two places (*Life* 37f.). It seems safe, then, to draw on what is known of such relations generally in

26. See Mc Mullen, *Roman Social Relations*, 14, 27.

27. Cf. J. Neusner, 'The Experience of the City in Late Antique Judaism', in *Approaches to Ancient Judaism*, vol. 5, ed. W. Scott Green, Atlanta: Scholars Press, 1985, 37–52.

28. Cf. in this regard the excavations ar Meiron, Khirbet Shema and Gush Halav as published by Meyers, Strange and Groh. For a convenient summary, see *Archaeology, The Rabbis and Early Christianity*, London: SCM, 1981, 45f.

antiquity and apply this cross-culturally of the Galilean situation generally, even when the material remains, such as coins and ceramics, suggest steady contacts because of trade and commerce.[29]

Rarely do villagers speak for themselves, at least in writing, and particularly in antiquity. Apart from odd glimpses, we can only infer their view of the situation in the light of the way in which urban dwellers express themselves about the countryside. Clearly they were worlds apart, and everything, from accent, to gait, to dress, helped to accentuate those differences and underline the unequal relationships as far as the peasant was concerned. Consequently, the peasant viewed the city as dangerous and alien, and regarded its inhabitants with suspicion at best, and at worst with hostility. 'Those who are clothed in fine garments are in the house of kings' (Mt 11:8) expresses well the peasant mentality in regard to urban dwellers, as does the expression of wonder at the temple building by the Galilean pilgrims (Mk 13:2). It was not without reason that the peasant regarded the city as a hostile place, since it was the seat of those who controlled their lives socially and economically—the tax and rent collectors and other bureaucrats of the central administration. Despite the many large Jewish colonies in the cities of the empire the Jewish peasant certainly experienced the city as alien, as can be seen from the many references in rabbinic literature which view it as a place that has been set up to extort and oppress.[30] The peasants living in smaller villages were powerless against visitations from the city, unless they resorted to violence or flight. Neither tactic was likely to improve their lot.

Notwithstanding this general picture there is irrefutable

29. In his most recent statement on the matter Meyers calls for a revision of the notion of Upper Galilee being culturally isolated, in view of the ceramic and numismatic evidence from the centres excavated by him and his team ('Galilean Regionalism: A Reappraisal', 123–5). However, in view of earlier statements by the same team that Upper Galilee was sparsely populated until after the second revolt ('The Meiron Excavation Project', 18), it is difficult to see the relevance of this evidence for establishing cultural patterns in the first century.

30. Cf. S. Applebaum, 'Hellenistic Cities of Judea and its Vicinity', in *The Ancient Historian and his Materials, Essays in Honour of C.E. Stevens*, ed. B. Levick, Farnborough, 1975, 59–73; also McMullen *Roman Social Relations*, 34, and Neusner's article cited n. 27 above.

evidence of some movement between the two worlds. This was due to the economic forces which bound the two together in a symbiotic relationship of convenience, however unequal it might be. Because of the difficulties of transportation, the local market was absolutely vital for the peasant for whatever disposable goods he had to offer, and in addition the city provided some essential services, such as the provision of jars and other instruments that were required for even the most basic agricultural production. Villagers with some craft drifted to the larger centres of population, but so too did those who for whatever reason—shortly to be discussed—had lost their property in the countryside. But the city needed the countryside also, mainly in terms of food production, often denuding the peasants of all but the barest necessities of life. This was possible because the urban rich found that investment in land, even to the point of owning a whole village (Lk 14:18), was a way to safeguard their money profitably.[31]

In such instances the new owner's relationship with the villagers might resemble that of a patron and his clients. The owner controlled the affairs of the village, either personally or through appointees and reaped the economic benefits, while the peasants were allowed to remain on their own land after falling into debt through a bad harvest or some other misfortune that upset the very fine balance between being a free, that is a landowning, peasant and a share-cropper or tenant.

Sketchy as this picture is, its main feature can be documented for first-century Galilee. At Tiberias in 66 CE we meet some Galileans who join forces with the destitute classes in destroying Herod's palace (*Life* 66), an episode that can best be explained as illustrative of the rural poor drifting to the nearest urban centre and joining forces with their urban counterparts in an act of social resentment, dressed up in religious disguise. The list of places where disturbances broke out against Jewish inhabitants prior to the first revolt includes several cities in the circle of Galilee (*Life* 24–6), which

31. See in general for the ancient world McMullen, *Roman Social Relations*, 48–51, against the views of Rostovtzeff, who attributes the main source of large wealth to commercial transactions. For Judea in particular, cf. M. Goodman, "The First Jewish Revolt: Social Conflict and the Problem of Debt", *JJS* 33 (1982) 417–26.

inevitably points to the fact that there had been a drift of Jewish peasants from Galilee to those centres over the previous decades.[32] In this respect those Jews of Caesarea Philippi who required oil from native-grown olives and were prepared to pay a high price for it (*Life* 74f.; *J.W.* 2:591f.) suggest that the Galileans in Tiberias were not necessarily typical of all those who left the land.

Even today when peasants go to a city in search of employment they seek out relations or previous acquaintances who can cushion the cultural gap between the two life-styles. In the case of the Jewish peasants religious ties would have helped considerably to strengthen those links between city and country. Archaeological evidence based on coins, pottery and other material remains, confirms this picture of constant interchange between the cities, especially of the coast, and the larger 'villages' of the Jewish hinterland, even in Upper Galilee.[33] Though much of this evidence comes from the late Roman and early Byzantine periods, it still must be regarded as typical of the general relationships in that region for the earlier period also. In addition to the hellenistic cities, there seems to be little doubt that the better land in the territories of the Herodian cities was owned by people who resided either in Sepphoris or Tiberias. The case of Crispus, the brother of Justus of Tiberias, who formerly had been a high administrative officer in the service of Agrippa I and who was away from the city in his estates across the Jordan at the time of Josephus' appointment, may be seen as typical (*Life* 33).

Galileans then did have real, if ambivalent relations with the surrounding city culture, and Jesus' freedom of movement as well as that of the crowds following him from various

32. For details of Jewish communities in these centres cf. Schürer-Vermes-Miller, *A History of the Jewish People*, II, 144–50; Goodman, 'The Problem of Debt', 418.

33. In this regard Meyers, 'Galilean Regionalism: A Reappraisal', 124, endorses my opinion of the influence of Tyre on the upper Galilean hinterland, based on the numismatic evidence, expressed in *Galilee from Alexander the Great to Hadrian*, 114–21. Cf. R. Hanson *Tyrian Influence in the Upper Galilee*, Cambridge, ASOR Monographs, 1980. The recent observations of R. Vale in 'Literary Sources in Archaeological Description. The Case of Galilee, Galilees and Galilean', *JSJ* 18 (1987) 210–28 are a timely reminder that our picture of Galilee and Galileans is in danger of being determined by the literary sources. Another profile with greater emphasis on regional differences emerges if archaeological data are used as a starting-point.

regions, which Mark in particular points to, is wholly plausible, at least in terms of social relations. Many of those who came to Jesus may have been Jewish, or gentiles attracted to the Jewish way of life in fact. McMullen's remark that town and country get along because they had to applies here also. The more troubled situation of the immediate pre-war period, about which we are better informed because of Josephus' direct involvement in the Galilean situation, gave rise to only occasional outbursts of rural aggression against the urban wealthy, and these usually took place in border regions, well away from the cities. This strongly suggests that in less troubled times, as during Antipas' reign with which the gospels are concerned, the relations were on the whole stable, however we explain the hostility towards the Jews that occurred in the hellenistic city territories.[34]

Jerusalem, because of its role as the religious capital, had special links with the Galilean countryside. The religious dimension of these links will be explored in the next chapter, but here it is important to note briefly how they impinged on social relations in Galilee. Attention has already been drawn to the central role of the Jerusalem sanhedrin in terms of the administration of justice, despite the establishment by Gabinius of an aristocratic provincial assembly at Sepphoris. That the control of the Jerusalem council extended, at least potentially, to other areas of life would seem to be presupposed in the appointment by the revolutionary council of Josephus as governor of Galilee and Gamala, and the subsequent attempts to unseat him in favour of a broadly based delegation with a nice mix of aristocratic and plebeian elements. This is all the more significant because part of the territory claimed for Josephus was actually under the jurisdiction of Herod Agrippa II. There is little doubt that in establishing himself with the Galileans over against native 'big men', such as John of Gischala or Justus of Tiberias, Josephus exploited to the full his Jerusalem and priestly

34. Cf. S. Applebaum, 'Jewish Urban Communities and Greek Influences', *Scripta Scripta Classica Israelitica* 5 (1979) 158–77, who attributes the hostilities to the situation that arose at the time of the Hasmonean conquests, and the subsequent appropriation of Jewish lands at the time of Pompey.

connections. Despite the obvious rhetoric of *Life* it must be admitted that in this tactic he was largely successful.[35]

Did the Galileans then regard such involvement in their affairs as normal, even advantageous? During Antipas' reign an annual tribute had to be paid to Rome, and so the Jerusalem authorities were not seen as exerting fiscal pressure on the peasants in regard to secular taxes, as was the case in Judea since Archelaus' deposition. However, many of the wealthy Jews who had acquired land from the Hasmonean or Herodian rulers, would in all probability have been Jerusalemites.[36] Insofar as absentee landlordism was a social phenomenon in Galilee, with all the attendant possibilities of exploitation (Mt 21: 33–45), Jerusalem would have been experienced as a centre of alienation.[37] But, we have seen, this could also operate in the relatively benign form of patron-client relationship. In the case of Jerusalem-based landlords a shared religious world view, even to the point of the tenant having to pay religious dues to the owner in his capacity as a priest, meant that the inherent exploitation was more latent than overt. However, this did not lessen the burden of taxation that the peasant had to carry—religious dues, rent for the use of the land and a contribution towards the annual levy to Rome. The apparent willingness of the Galilean peasants to pay the tithes to Josephus and his colleagues, which they claimed as their due, suggests that Galilee may also have been visited by representatives of the high priests for purposes of collection of dues (cf. Mt 17:24–7). At the same time no violent incident such as that recounted in *J.A.* 20:181, when servants of the high priest appropriated the produce at the threshing floors in Judea, leaving local priests to starve, is specifically reported in Galilee, presumably

35. S. Freyne, 'Galilee-Jerusalem Relations in the Light of Josephus' *Life*', *NTS* 33 (1987) 600–609 has a more detailed discussion of the claims made in this paragraph.

36. Cf. Applebaum's discussion of the social implication of Ecclesiastes 2:4–9 in terms of a new land-propertied class residing in Jerusalem from hellenistic times, 'Jewish Urban Communities', 159–62.

37. Cf. the important study of the social background to this parable in the light of the Zenon papyri by M. Hengel, 'Das Gleichnis von den bösen Weingärtnern (Mc 12:1–12) im Lichte der Zenonpapyri und der rabbinischen Gleichnisse', ZNW 59 (1968) 1–39.

because country priests in the Second Temple period were largely confined to the South.[38]

Because of the political situation, official Jerusalem involvement in Galilean social affairs was probably indirect, certainly during the reign of Antipas. Village life functioned in a relatively undisturbed way, it would seem, despite the pull of the cities and the pressure from central administration, civil and religious. Some indication from our texts, aided by archaeological evidence and cross-cultural comparisons, can help to fill out the picture of the internal workings of a Galilean village, always bearing in mind the huge differences that must have existed between centres with a population of 15,000 people according to Josephus (*J.W.* 3:43) and the more remote hamlets comprising no more than a cluster of dwellings. We meet various village officials in the gospels, as well as on inscriptions, but there is no complete picture of village life. The πρεσβύτεροι or elders is a common form of local administration, both in Palestine and in the Mediterranean world generally (cf. Judith 6:12–16). In addition the village scribe (κωμογραμματεύς) is well documented, and the νομοδιδάσκαλοι of Lk 5:17 may have a corresponding function in a Jewish setting, taking charge of various administrative and legal matters such as boundary determination, overseeing of burials and the like.[39] A recent inscribed lead weight from Sepphoris mentions a certain Simon the ἀγοράνομος, or market inspector, a position that is well attested otherwise.[40] Later rabbinic texts speak of *parnasim* (overseers) and *gabbaim* (collectors) whose official role had to do with the administration of public charities, though there are hints of a wider role for the former.[41] The essentially communal nature of village life would appear to be attested in the form of

38. There were imperial granaries in upper Galilee according to *Life* 71. The silos reported in Sepphoris in the recent excavations there may well have been for a similar purpose of storage, thus explaining in part Galilean animosity towards the place. Applebaum claims that there is now archaeological evidence from Samaria also of fortified grain supply-centres, north of Qarwat beni Hassan, see 'Jewish Urban Communities', 170f.

39. See G. McLean Harper, 'Village Administration in the Roman Province of Syria'. *YCS* 1 (1928) 105–28.

40. Cf. the note by Y. Meshorer, in Meyers, Netzer, Meyers, 'Sepphoris, Ornament of All Galilee', 16. The term is applied to an official of Jerusalem in 2 Macc 3:4.

41. See Goodman, *State and Society*, 121–7.

synagogue building known to us from the pre-70 period, of which that at Gamla is the outstanding example. Its rows of seats on all sides suggest an extreme form of democracy, characteristic of the Jewish rebels, according to the excavator,[42] yet the gospels suggest gatherings of the whole village community for such events as the visit of a wandering healer or the burial of a widow's son (Mk 1:27; Lk 7:12; 13:14). In the synagogue we also meet officials such as the ἀρχισυνάγωγος and the ὑπηρέτης, but it is not clear that these have any other function in the village than that of overseeing the synagogue service.

Yet life within the village confines was far from idyllic. Dwellings were small and clustered together, and generally, living conditions must have been primitive, giving rise to frequent illness and a short life-expectation.[43] Attacks from passing robbers or highwaymen were frequent, explaining the location of some of the more remote settlements—away from the road and high up on the slopes of the hills.[44] Invading

42. Thus Applebaum, 'Jewish Urban Communities', 173f, citing S. Guttman's report of the fisrt season of excavation there (1979). Cf. further, S. Gutmann, 'The Syanagogue at Gamla' and Z. Maoz, 'The Synagogue of Gamla and the Typology of Second Temple Synagogues', in L. Levine ed., *Ancient Synagogues Revealed*, Jerusalem: Israel Exploration Society, 1981, pp. 30–34 and 35–41 respectively. Most recently L. Levine strikes a cautionary note regarding the identfication of the Gamla building as a synagogue as well as a definite typology for pre-70 synagogues, 'The Second Temple Synagogue. The Formative Years', in L. Levine ed., *The Synagogue in Late Antiquity*, Philadelphia: ASSOR Publications 1–31, especially 11f. Cf. also J. Strange, 'Magdala' in *IDB* Supplementary vol., accepting the report of an earlier survey that a square-shaped building (no longer identifiable) represents a similar 'popular' form of synagogue building in Galilee from the pre-70 period; see also J. Strange and H. Sharks, 'Synagogues where Jesus Preached found at Capernaum', *BAR* (1983) 24–31; S. Loffreda, 'Ceramica ellenistico-Romana nel sottosuole della sinagoga di Cafarnao' in G. C. Bottini ed., *Studia Hierosylimitana* III, Jerusalem, 1982, 273–312; V. Corbo, 'Resti della sinagoga del primo secolo a Cafarnao' ibid., 313–57.

43. Archaeological evidence, from Capernaum e.g., suggests single-storey courtyard houses clustered together and made from local basalt stone. But Capernaum was a relatively thriving centre and could not be regarded as typical of more remote hamlets. Equally, the villa excavated by the Meiron team is untypical except for the very higher echelons of society. For a convenient summary of the evidence, literary and archaeological, cf. Goodman, *State and Society*, 27–31; see also B. Bogatti, 'Caphernaum, la ville de Pierre', *La Monde de la Bible*, 27 (1983), 8–16.

44. This is clearly demonstrated by the location of such first-century sites as Sepphoris, Jotapata, Gush Halav and Gamla. According to Meyers, Strange and Groh, 'The Meiron Excavation Project', 5f., there is evidence of a later settlement at Yodefat (Jotapata) down the hill from the fortified town of the first revolt, and there are traces of walls at some sites which date back to the early Roman period, thus corroborating in a general way such literary evidence as Lk 7:12 (Naim); *Life* 45.71 (Gischala), 186ff. (various places in upper and lower Galilee).

armies were also frequent sources of great harassment, as the villagers were compelled to make provisions available, irrespective of their own needs.[45] In this regard Galilee, from early hellenistic times, had more than its fair share of campaigns fought either on its borders or within its territory. As an example of the disruption involved, the case of the village of Chabulon, a border town between Galilee and Ptolemais at the beginning of the first revolt, may be cited. At the approach of the Roman general, Cestius Gallus, the inhabitants all fled, and the soldiers were allowed to pillage all the provisions and ravage the surrounding villages (*J.W.* 2:503f.). Capture meant certain death or slavery.

These hazards of village life do not surface in the gospels, but, as has been stressed frequently, Antipas did bring a definite stability to Galilee and cushioned it from some, at least, of the harsh realities of village existence elsewhere. What we encounter, rather, are the petty squabbles of neighbours who sow weeds among each other's wheat, or small-town animosities leading to retaliation and violence at a local level.[46] Villagers generally shared such communal facilities as wells, olive presses, threshing floors and baking ovens, it would seem, but these could easily give rise to local dissensions rather than fostering community spirit. At a slightly higher level on the social scale, such as among the Galilean fishermen with the hired servants (Mk 1:20), cooperation was possible in order to facilitate profitability from the market for the produce (Lk 5:7).

There was, then, differentiation even within the village, with wealth, however limited, the deciding factor. Reciprocal relationships within the family or with near neighbours arose from common needs and determined the prevailing value system. The golden rule of doing to others as you expected to have done to yourself (Mt 7:12) applied particularly in that situation. All could expect to be in need, given the limited

45. The Hefzibah inscription explicitly mentions freedom from billeting of soldiers as a concession to some of the villages in the neighbourhood of Scythopolis. Cf. Y.H. Landau, 'A Greek Inscription found near Hefzibah', *IEJ* 16 (1966) 56–70, especially lines, 14f., 23–5; Freyne *Galilee*, 179. Cf. Lk 3:14.

46. R. Horley, in 'Ethics and Exegesis "Love your Enemies" and the Doctrine of Non-Violence', *JAAR* 54 (1986) 1–29, gives an excellent analysis of these sayings (Mt 5:39–43), taking account of the actual social circumstances of village life.

resources in great things and in small (Lk 11:5), and the fabric of village life was thus established on a network of interdependent relationships. In such a situation the weak could easily be ignored, and in the case of certain illnesses expelled from the village altogether (Mk 1:40; 5:1f.), even though, as mentioned already, there is some evidence of organised care for the needy, at least in the rabbinic literature. In a word, life in a Galilean village was never easy and sometimes brutal, constantly under pressure from above, usually from the city or city-based people that threatened to deprive the less fortunate of the necessities of life, thus reducing them to penury. Enjoyment was confined to the odd visit of a wandering minstrel or the religious festival. Though fraught with danger, the pilgrimage to Jerusalem must have had a very definite social function for Galilean Jewish peasants, lifting them temporarily out of the narrow confines of village life and bestowing a sense of belonging to something greater (Lk 2:41, 44).

This limited picture of the organisation of Galilean life on a large and small scale must suffice for our present purposes of recovering the social world of Jesus and his movement. We shall postpone to the final chapter discussion of whether his teaching and activity reinforced or challenged the assumptions and values of those who clung tenaciously to this lifestyle. The examination of social relations and organisation has repeatedly suggested that economic realities were all important. We must now attempt to highlight the most significant aspects of these, particularly because so much of Jesus' teaching was explicitly concerned with issues of wealth and poverty.

3. The Economics of Galilee: Resources and their Control

In the introductory chapter dealing with recent studies of the historical Jesus it emerged that the economic situation of Galilee was determinative of the way in which Jesus' role was perceived by different authors. In the present chapter as we have moved from a consideration of political control to social organisation, the same issue has emerged as central. We opted to begin with the political situation because it seemed that the reign of Antipas did bring stability to Galilean life in economic as well as political terms. The social organisation of Galilee suggests that it was controlled by economic factors also—the city over the village and those with property over those without it in the village. In dealing with these issues we have begun to address some of the variables that shape the economic system in any society.[47] We must now attempt to profile all the relevant variables for Galilee more explicitly. It is only when some overall picture of the prevailing situation is in place that it is possible to evaluate whether or not change was occurring, and if so, what forms it took, what its motivations were and how it was likely to affect the population as a whole. As already intimated, those who do take stock of the social world of Galilee in plotting the career of Jesus there, invariably assume that in the first century there was rapid change because so many were so alienated by the prevailing conditions. But the question must be asked whether this estimate is based on an accurate profile of the situation, carefully differentiating Galilean conditions under Antipas from those in Judea under the early procurators, or in Galilee itself immediately prior to the first revolt, when all of Palestine was under direct Roman rule.

How is one to begin to classify the Galilean economic situation? Foremost in importance must surely be its natural, as distinct from its religio-cultural, location as the hinterland of the great Phoenician coastal trading centres of Tyre and Sidon, as well as Ptolemais/Acco. This gave it immediate access to the sea-lanes that were so important for availing of the more extended opportunities for trading which the hellenistic age provided. Equally, caravans of traders and merchants going to the east had to pass through or around Galilee. It seems legitimate to infer that the material evidence from a later period in terms of coins, ceramics and glass-ware, which have been found in the Upper Galilean sites, are indicative of older patterns of contacts through trade, which did not at all signify cultural or religious assimilation.[48]

47. Cf. Carney, *The Shape of the Past*, 137–224 on the study of what may be termed 'economic' in antiquity, especially 154 on the strategy of profiling.

48. Cf. notes 28 and 32 above. Meyers, though misrepresenting my earlier views on Galilean religious loyalty, has drawn renewed attention to the special features of the

On the other hand, the Herodian centres as well as the cities of the Dekapolis had helped in the development of a redistributive economy for Galilee itself, giving rise to storehouses, market-places, a scribal bureaucracy and large estates. While these economic developments were taking place the old, reciprocal form of exchange continued in the villages and is clearly echoed in the sayings of Jesus also (Mt 7:2).[49] Thus we can say initially that the economic situation of Galilee was highly complex, and accordingly there were bound to be conflicting norms and values there also.

The development from one type of economy to another naturally gave rise to greater specialisation. As early as the third century BCE we learn from the Zenon papyri of intensive cultivation of the vine, the sinking of proper wells and the provision of other important facilities at Beth Anat in Galilee, reflecting the increased technical advances that are associated with hellenistic culture generally. The salting of fish at Tarichaeae and the production of glass at Tel Anafa are other examples from the region of such early developments.[50] These in turn gave rise to greater production and increased opportunities for wealth, arising from the possibilities for marketing, both local and international. Yet the absence of fine wares or other items of luxury from the remains of the earlier period, suggests that these advances had only a limited effect on living standards generally then. The emergence of a native ceramic industry that was able to successfully imitate imported styles cannot be documented for the first century apparently, and we must not be too ready to transpose backwards to the pre-70 period developments that belong to

synagogue buildings in Upper Galilee, especially the absence of such mosaics and other ornamentation as are to be found in those of the rift and the Bethshan valley, and which points to a conservative or 'orthodox' point of view among the Upper Galileans, as a way of 'maintaining identity', see 'Galilean Regionalism: A Reappraisal', 126.

49. Carney, in *The Shape of the Past*, 141, lists the four types of exchange that have been postulated for antiquity and later mentions Syria in particular as the place where market economies were to thrive (p.197).

50. For details see Freyne, *Galilee*, 170–76.

the late Roman or even early Byzantine periods.[51]

These possibilities for development were offset by the family units which operated on values other than those of a business firm—values that concerned status, patronage, pursuit of luxury and the like in the case of the large landowners. Those who were less well off in terms of the primary resource of land were motivated by loyalty to ancestral values and maintenance of their subsistence situation for themselves and their families rather than any burning desire to exploit resources to their full economic potential.[52] In such a prevailing situation there is a real danger that resources will be depleted rather than developed. Insofar as we are aware, Antipas, or indeed any of those who controlled affairs in the province before or after him, made no effort to restructure Galilean life so that its natural potential in terms of land and water could be fully exploited.[53]

Herod the Great was much more likely than his son, Antipas, to have thought in those terms, and his project of settling emigré Jews from Babylonia in northern Transjordan, leaving them free of taxation, may be seen as an enlightened piece of development that paid off richly almost a hundred years later when we hear of their descendants as wealthy and loyal Herodian subjects at the outbreak of the first revolt (*Life* 54–61). Yet establishment of the port of Caesarea and the developments in Samaria, which from recent archaeological evidence was rural as well as urban, strongly suggest that any centralised land-policy that might have been

51. According to Meyers, 'Galilean Regionalism as a Factor in Historical Reconstruction', *BASOR* 221 (1976), 95–101, especially 97, so-called Galilean bowls with everted lips, as well as globular cooking pots, basins with a folded rim and *terra sigillata* bowls are to be found in Upper Galilee and the Golan, from the second century CE at least, thus suggesting a continuity of material culture between the regions, and marking them off culturally from the south. Yet, apparently, imported fine glass ware is later, thus suggesting an improvement in the economic conditions from the late Roman and early Byzantine periods, see Meyers, Strange, Groh, 'The Meiron Excavation Project', especially 10–16. The absence of blown glass at Tel Anafa in the earlier period has also been noted by G. Weinberg, 'Hellenistic Glass from Tel Anafa', *Journal of Glass Studies*, 12 (1970) 17–27.

52. T. Shanin, 'The Nature and Logic of Peasant Economics', *JPS* 1 (1974) 186–204; Carney, *The Shape of the Past*, 198–200.

53. On the fertility of Galilee cf. *J.W.* 3:42.516–21 and Pliny, *Nat. Hist.* V. 15. 70–72. Apart from grain and fish, olives and grapes are also frequently mentioned in the ancient sources.

implemented, occurred in the south rather than in Galilee.[54] Certainly, the settlement of the Babylonian Jews as well as the founding of Gaba, 'the city of cavalry', on the borders of Galilee (*J.A.* 15:294; *J.W.* 3:36), was for defensive rather than agricultural purposes, as can be gleaned from the village style of life in the former case and the apportioning of lots of land rather than the establishment of large estates in the latter. The fact that Upper Galilee was still relatively sparsely populated in the period is itself indicative. The peasant strike, which involved the refusal of Galilean as well as other Jews to sow the fields at the time of Gaius Caligula's planned desecration of the temple, was, therefore, seen as disastrous by the Herodian aristocracy at Tiberias. They were aware that payment of the tribute, and the consequent maintenance of their own privileged position was, paradoxically, dependent on the peasantry being able to deliver the required produce, thus making payment of the tribute possible. (*J.A.* 18:273–8).

There seems to be no good reason, therefore, to abandon the conclusions arrived at by historical analysis in my earlier study, and now corroborated by Goodman's investigation of the second-century evidence, namely, that Jewish peasants continued to own small holdings of land in Galilee, live their lives in villages along fairly traditional lines and be moderately productive in terms of local markets for the most part.[55] When we speak of the dominant class in Galilee being peasant, it is such as these we have in mind, while recognising of course that there were others there at both ends of the land-owning spectrum—owners of large estates (often absentee) and tenants, share-croppers and day labourers, who previously may have been owners themselves.

Along the lake-front one finds greater signs of more intense production. The salted fish industry at Tarichaeae, which made the export of fish possible on a far wider scale, is the outstanding example. Other towns in the area, notably

54. According to S. Applebaum, 'Jewish Urban Communities', 176, the incidence of field towers in western Samaria after the Hasmonean conquests suggests agricultural intensification in that region. At the same time he notes that the securing of hereditary proprietorship of land which occurred under Nehemiah (Neh 10:32), and which may have been eroded in Ptolemaic and Seleucid times, was one of the motivating factors of the Maccabean resistance.

55. *Galilee*, 156–70; *State and Society*, 31–40.

Capernaum and Bethsaida, would appear to have been engaged in the same industry. This is reflected in the gospels also, where we hear that the fishermen, Andrew and Peter, were from Bethsaida, and the latter seems to have taken up residence at Capernaum.[56] For the rest, the clearest indications we have are of the grain industry. Apart from the silos of Sepphoris suggested by archaeology, we hear from the literary sources of imperial granaries in Upper Galilee and at Besara on the borders between Galilee and the great plain (*Life* 71.118f.). In all probability, however, these were repositories for the collection of the tribute paid in kind, or belonged to the royal estates in the great plain, and did not signify any widescale development of the agri-business throughout the province. At all events the wealth that resulted from this more productive side of the economy was not likely to have been redistributed or ploughed back into further development, least of all for improving the lot of the small-holder, or others at the lower end of the social scale. Building projects such as those at Sepphoris or Tiberias would certainly have provided some work for people who had been squeezed off the land because of pressures of various kinds. But these were limited in scope, had other alienating aspects for the Jewish peasants, unlike work on the temple in Jerusalem, and in the case of the unskilled they would have meant subsistence wages only.

Poverty then was a basic fact of life. As far as the gospels are concerned it is in Jerusalem that we meet the clearest examples of the urban poor—the widow's mite in the temple treasury (Mk 12:41–4); the blind, like Bar-Timaeus, begging at Jericho or in Jerusalem itself (Jn 9:1; Mk 10:46; Ac 3:1–2), or those poor on whom the cost of a jar of ointment could well have been spent (Mk 14:4f). True, Josephus does mention the destitute classes explicitly at Tiberias (*Life* 66). As already mentioned, the poor drifted naturally to the cities, as well as the more skilled. Yet poverty undoubtedly existed in the rural areas also. In this regard Luke's picture of the limited goods economy of the village seems altogether realis-

56. For recent discussions of the location and character of both sites cf. V. Tzaferis, 'New Archaeological Evidence on Ancient Capernaum', *BA* 46 (1983) 198–204; B. Pixner, 'Searching for the New Testament Site of Bethsaida', *BA* 48 (1985) 207–16.

tic, even if we must be careful not to extrapolate from certain 'typical' parable characters to a description of the total situation. This is by no means monochromic, even in terms of the parables. There are single family farms, large holdings and absentee landlords as well as slaves, day labourers, the destitute and hired servants represented in the gospel stories. The variegated picture is similar to what we can infer from the other literary sources, especially Josephus and the Mishnah/Tosefta. The extent to which 'wealth-levelling mechanisms', such as the biblical injunction of caring for the poor and the poor man's tithe operated, is difficult to assess, in the absence of any direct evidence.[57] The gospel of Luke assumed that those who controlled the wealth, namely the Pharisees, were interested only in sharing with those from whom they could expect to receive in return, and if the historical Pharisees are to be identified with the townspeople, following Josephus, then there must be a general assumption of verisimilitude for the Lucan portrayal. These would be the traders, artisans and others engaged in the service economies of the towns—the direct product of hellenistic culture in Palestine itself.[58] On the other hand the patron-client style relationship of the wealthy land-owner and his peasant tenants, which was of course open to exploitation of the worst kind, could also function in a relatively benign fashion for the dislocated peasant, prepared to be a share-cropper or lessee, especially when this operated within the context of a shared symbolic world.

It is now time to ask whether or not this Galilean economy had within it those alienating forces as far as the majority of Galileans are concerned, which are so often assumed to have been operative in the background to Jesus' ministry. Here attention must be drawn to the conclusions arrived at in the previous study of Galilee, namely, that the province was not at the time of the first revolt seething with disaffection and in

57. Cf. the important study from a sociological point of view of B. Lang, 'The Social Organisation of Peasant Poverty in Biblical Israel', reprinted in B. Lang ed., *Anthropological Approaches to the Old Testament*, London: SPCK, 83–99.

58. E. Rivkin, 'The Internal City. Judaism and Urbanisation', JSSR 5 (1966) 225–40, has some highly stimulating suggestions on the social location of the Pharisees, even if the picture is drawn in too general terms, without sufficient attention to all the sources. Cf. ch. 6 below.

a state of revolutionary turmoil.[59] This conclusion was arrived at, by an examination of, among other indicators, the way in which the actual campaign was conducted in Galilee. With the call-to-arms going out from the revolutionary council in Jerusalem—surely then, if ever—we should be able to discern Galilean political feelings and attitudes towards oppressors and those who were seen as their collaborators. When, however, the Josephan militaristic rhetoric, especially in *J.W.* is acknowledged for what it is,[60] we are left with a situation of relative unpreparedness for revolt, revolt that was confined to a few centres that quickly capitulated at the approach of the Romans and a peasantry that was frightened, confused, and with little interest in a revolutionary struggle (*J.W.* 4:84). In view of the close relationship between nationalistic aspirations and economic hardship, as these manifested themselves openly in Judea in the same period,[61] those who still seek to defend a revolutionary ethos for Galilee thirty years earlier must certainly, it would appear, re-examine their assumptions and conclusions.

Yet, this conclusion, telling as it would appear to be, should not be used to foreclose the discussion of the changing economic situation in Galilee. For one thing the demise of the 'zealot-hypothesis' as an umbrella theory to explain all instances of nationalist or social unrest throughout the first century means that each episode has to be examined in regard to its aims, methods and motivations in a much more nuanced way than before. One does not have to be involved in a nationalist struggle in order to feel socially dislocated, because of perceived or real exploitation. Factors other than those which led to the coalescence of religious and social forces for change in Judea may well have been operative in a more hidden, but nonetheless real way in Galilee. Since the situation at any time of rapid social change is highly complex

59. Among the more notable proponents of this view, but based on very different premises, may be cited M. Hengel, *Die Zeloten* AGSU 1, 2nd edn Leiden: Brill, 1976, arguing from the religious motivation of Jewish nationalism, and H. Kreissig, *Die Sozialen Zusammenhänge des Judaischen Krieges*, Berlin, 1970, from a marxist-leninist perspective.

60. Cf. Cohen, *Josephus in Galilee*, especially 91–100.

61. Cf. *Galilee*, 229–34; D. Rhoads, *Israel in Revolution, 6–74 c.e.. A Political History based on the Writings of Flavius Josephus*, Philadelphia. Fortress Press, 1976, 72–6, 80–82.

and consequently, much more difficult to capture, we do not propose here to construct an elaborate model for measuring all aspects of the changes. Instead it is intended to focus on one particular probe-zone which suggests itself on the basis of our sources, namely the incidence of social banditry in Galilee, which can serve as a test of the profile which has been offered.[62]

Social Banditry in Galilee. The recent studies of banditry point to the strong social component of the phenomenon, as a spontaneous reaction of the deprived and alienated against the rich and powerful.[63] Instead of treating all the Josephan references to λησταί in first-century Palestine as part of his vilificatory tactics against the Zealots, Richard Horsley in particular has called for a reappraisal of the situation in terms of social banditry, a sociological model that displays the following traits: a general situation of socio-economic oppression that makes the peasantry vulnerable and marginalised; the bandits enjoy the support of the village people since they attempt to right their wrongs by violent reprisals against their oppressors; villagers and bandits share a common set of values and religious assumptions which justify their actions by appealing to a divine justice that is hoped for.[64]

If such a theory were applicable to first century Galilee it would clearly have serious implications for the profile which has just been given of the economic situation there. At least it would have to be seen as a pointer to the collapse of the prevailing stability, which we have assumed for the reign of Antipas at least. Yet according to Horsley social banditry had already manifested itself in Galilee from the time of the young Herod's governorship of the province in 48 BCE, and continued right up to the outbreak of the first revolt in 66 CE. In a separate study I have examined all the references to banditry

62. Our method of procedure at this point has been influenced by Carney, *Models of the Past*, 152–65 and 332–42. A probe-zone is defined as an area in which change is critical, and on the basis of recent sociological study of the phenomenon, social banditry would certainly come within that category.

63. Cf. in particular the studies of E. Hobsbawn, especially his *Bandits*, 3rd rev. edn, New York: Pantheon Books, 1981.

64. R. A. Horsley, 'Josephus and the Bandits', *JSJ* 10 (1979) 37–63 and 'Ancient Jewish Banditry and the Revolt against Rome', *CBQ* 43 (1981) 409–32. Cf. Hengel, *Die Zeloten*, 42–5 and 319–22.

in Galilee mentioned by Josephus from the point of view of Horsley's categories.[65] There are indeed examples of banditry in Galilee as well as in Judea, but the category 'social banditry' as defined by him is much more applicable to Judea than to Galilee in the same period. Rather than repeat that analysis here it seems more appropriate to examine how well those characteristics of the phenomenon that are pertinent to the situation under discussion—the economic conditions of Galilee during Antipas' reign—are in fact applicable to conditions there.

Undoubtedly there was social and economic exploitation of peasants in Galilee, as indeed everywhere else in the Roman empire of the first century.[66] In profiling the socio-economic situation, however, Horsley begins from the position of a peasantry that had been reduced to penury—concerned about 'what it would eat and how it would be clothed' (Mt 6:25–33; 33; Lk 12:12) and proceeds to paint a rather bleak picture indeed, based on a double taxation system that exhausted up to 40 per cent of the peasants' produce. In addition, he lists the hardships that were the direct result of the Hasmonean/ Herodian struggles for power, Herod's reign with his heavy demands on resources because of his lavish building projects and natural disasters such as famines and earthquakes, as all contributing to the beleagured situation of the first-century Jewish peasant.[67] Banditry was the inevitable outcome of this situation.

Our profile differs from this, not so much in denying that any or all of these factors were present in first-century Palestine, as in querying their impact on Galilee before or during the reign of Antipas. The absence of any direct warning about banditry in the recorded sayings of Jesus, as distinct from that attributed to John the Baptist in a Judean context (Lk 3:14; cf. *Life* 72f.), may just be one straw in the

65. 'Bandits in Galilee'; in particular I differ from Horsley's evaluation of the troubles at the time of Herod, which, in my opinion, are better explained in terms of the ousted Hasmonean aristocracy's attempt to recoup its position rather than as signs of social banditry on behalf of the peasants.

66. See McMullen, *Roman Social Relations*, 28–56; P. Garnsey, 'Peasants in Ancient Roman Society', *JPS* 2 (1975) 222–35.

67. Cf. his most recent and explicit account of the situation (in collaboration with J. Hanson) in *Bandits, Prophets, and Messiahs*. 52–62.

wind. But even if we are to accept that there was an increase in banditry in the years when Galilee came under direct Roman rule (44 CE, presumably), its incidence there is not at all as frequent as Horsley's profile suggests. Most noteworthy, perhaps, is the absence of any reference to the *sicarii*, whose presence in the Judean countryside from the time of Felix onwards is specially commented on by Josephus as a sign of the increase of banditry (*J.W.* 2:238.254). More significant, however, is the fact that the two other characteristics—common cause with the peasants and a shared world-view that looks for divine vengeance against the oppressors—cannot be verified in the Galilean context. The bandits' loyalties are mixed. On the one hand the group from the borders of Ptolemais, led by the arch-brigand, Jesus, are prepared to aid Sepphoris against the Galileans and Josephus, while others from Upper Galilee are engaged in harassing the country people (*Life* 77f., 206; *J.W.* 4:84). It is noteworthy in fact that all actual cases of banditry in Galilee are located in border regions—Dabaritta, Ptolemais, Gischala—just where one would expect to find them, close to the major caravan routes and well away from the centres of policing. The only real display of religious zealotry that occurred in Galilee and which would appear to fit the category of social banditry was that of Jesus, son of Saphias in Tiberias, yet he is never designated a brigand by Josephus. True, John of Gischala is designated leader of a Galilean brigand troup in Jerusalem after the collapse of the northern campaign, but this description is undoubtedly part of the vilification of John, which is such a feature of *J.W*, and is not at all to be found in *Life*, where the similarity of aims and background with Josephus is recognised, despite the jealousy on other grounds between the two men. (*J.W.* 2:584–94; 4:106–11; *Life* 43f., 72f.).[68]

We shall have to conclude then that social banditry was not at all a dominant feature of Galilean life in the first century. Those incidents of brigandage that do occur are more scattered and less characteristic of the prevailing situation that Horsley's account would suggest. This is not to claim the absence of oppression, as our earlier profile of Galilean village

68. See U. Rappaport 'John of Gischala in Galilee', in *Jerusalem Cathedra*, 3, ed. L. Levine, Jerusalem, 1983, 46–57.

life makes clear, but rather to claim that on the basis of this particular probe, certain factors had cushioned the worst excesses of the oppression in the Galilean setting, and therefore had made the peasantry as a whole more unwilling to become embroiled in a religiously motivated struggle of violent proportions in order to right their wrongs. Perhaps, then, the concern of Jesus' audience with food and raimant are not symptons of a peasantry totally denuded, but rather reflect attitudes and values that the gospels generally associate with the relatively affluent, as we have seen.

In attempting to assess possible changes within the overall economic system and their likely impact on the different social strata within the province, one must, as Gerd Theissen has noted, look for signs of mobility—movements upwards and downwards on the social scale.[69] Social brigandage, we have suggested, could be one very clear sign of a downward movement for many, as increased pressure came to bear on those at the bottom end of the Galilean social ladder, causing them to engage actively in acts of pillaging against their perceived oppressors. One could argue that though Horsley's model does not fit the Galilean conditions well, there were, nevertheless, *some* signs of disaffection in the region, manifesting themselves in acts of brigandage and thereby pointing to changes taking place within the economic balance. Yet, even if this conclusion is accepted, such changes must be placed in the larger context of Palestinian social relations generally. There is widespread agreement that those relations had been deteriorating during the second period of procuratorial rule (45–66 CE), and Galilee could not have remained totally insulated from such changes. Yet there can be no doubt that there was a sharp contrast between Galilee and Judea, both in terms of the oppression and the response to it. The destruction of the ἀρχεῖα, the official record of debts, was one of the first acts of the Jerusalem rebels, but in Galilee, we hear of no similar gesture of protest, even though there were such records as Sepphoris, a place which was unpopular with the Galileans for other reasons (*Life* 30). Does this mean that Luke's picture of the prevalence of

69. See *Sociology of Early Palestinian Christianity*, 40.

debt—a picture that is quite plausible in itself for any peasant society in antiquity—reflects better the Judean rather than the Galilean conditions, even as late as 66 CE?[70]

In coming to a final assessment of the economic situation, there is a hidden factor operative, namely people's motivation. In the end it seems to be the most plausible general explanation for Galilean peasant attitudes. Religious loyalty towards those who controlled the symbolic centre in Jerusalem is not an adequate explanation, in view of the bitter dissensions that emerged among the warring factions in Judea and the violence that erupted in Jerusalem during the first revolt. These displayed deep-seated and long-standing tensions that could now be brought out in the open. It is tempting to suggest that Jesus' condemnation of such thriving centres as Capernaum, Chorazain and Bethsaida, all situated in close proximity to each other and enjoying both the fruits of the fertile plain of Gennesar and the fish industry from the lake, was the result of their rejection of his radical demands. These would represent a direct threat to the comfortable life-style of the inhabitants of such towns and the religious values that supported it.

One of the variables in any economic system is the amount of increased technology that is introduced and the consequent specialisation of production. In Palestine generally this was directly related to the influence exerted on the ethos by the hellenistic culture. An examination of the Galilean situation from this perspective should, therefore, help further in clarifying the economic issues and serve as a final probe in regard to the changing values and attitudes, with their impact on the economy generally and its likely development.

4. Culture—The Galilean Ethos and the Gospels

As described by Mark, Galilee, though Jewish, was a place whence the Jewish teacher/healer Jesus and his retinue could travel with ease to gentile territory and be received there. Likewise people from other regions could visit Galilee freely, it would seem. In one instance at least a non-Jewish person, Syro-Phoenician by birth, but described as 'Ἑλληνίς—that

70. See Goodman, 'The First Jewish Revolt: Social Conflict and the Problem of Debt', 418f.

is, with Greek cultural affiliations, was the beneficiary of an encounter with the healer. Thus, even though some boundaries between the Jewish and Greek culture are recognised, they are not regarded as insurmountable. Matthew used the Isaian passage that speaks of 'Galilee of the gentiles' as a proof-text for the legitimacy of Galilee as a place of messianic visitation, whereas Luke seeks to confine Jesus' movement to Galilee, deliberately, it would seem, but without precluding people from the Phoenician coast coming to hear him. In John the Greeks who wish to approach Jesus do so through a disciple with a Greek name, Philip, who came from Bethsaida, a townlet that had been raised to the status of a city by the Herodian half-brother of Antipas, also called Philip, giving it the added name Julias in honour of the emperor's wife.

In their different ways, then, all the gospels presume gentile contacts and associations for Galilee, and these have been exploited in the telling of the story of Jesus. It is indeed posible to recognise in this emphasis a reflection of the later gentile mission of the church, but that should not preclude a more detailed exploration of the actual situation in Galilee in Jesus' own day, since there is ample literary and archaeological evidence to indicate a general verisimilitude for the picture. In the past this non-Jewish association of Galilee has been exploited by the History of Religions approach to Jesus and his environment, even to the extreme of suggesting that because he was a Galilean, Jesus was not a Jew.[71] However, our understanding of the interpenetration of Jewish and hellenistic cultures has been greatly developed by the studies of Tcherikover, Bickermann, Hengel and Stern, just to mention the more influential. New data from archaeology is constantly calling for a reappraisal of the situation, highlighting just how complex the relationship in fact was at every level—political, economic, cultural in the broad sense and religious. There is an increasing consensus emerging from all this discussion which emphasises that 'the little tradition' does not have to be the loser in such an encounter, but that both great and little traditions alike are deeply affected by it.

71. This was the conclusion of Walter Grundmann's study, *Jesus der Galiläer' und das Judentum*, Leipzig, 1941. But cf. W. Bauer, "Jesus der Galiläer", in *Festschrift für Adolf Jülicher*, Tübingen, 1928.

This complex situation becomes even more difficult to assess as one moves away from the cities and their immediate territories to the smaller and more remote villages. How far did the 'new ways' emanating from élites penetrate, especially in view of the urban/rural tensions already discussed? Obviously it is impossible to discuss all aspects of the question here. What is called for is an approach to the issues that will help to profile the situation in Jesus' day, free as far as possible from certain in-built biases about what the categories 'Jewish' and 'hellenistic' involve.

The first question to be addressed is that of the ethnic strands in first-century Galilee, since there had been several administrative changes over the previous centuries—Ptolemaic, Seleucid, Hasmonean, Herodian—and the gospels assume that the population which Jesus addressed was Jewish, to the point that when non-Jews are encountered they are explicitly adverted to. For our purposes the impact of the Hasmonean conquests is crucial, since the accepted point of view has been that there was a re-judaisation of the north as part of the reconquest of traditional Jewish territory. This theory is based on Timagenes' report, which Josephus repeats, that Alexander Jannaeus had forcibly circumcised the Iturean people (*J.A.* 13:318f.). Whatever credence is to be given to this notice, it can certainly not be taken to mean that the Galileans we meet in the literary sources of the second century were from an ethnic background that only a hundred years previously was non-Jewish.[72]

This question, then, must be separated from another, though related one, namely, that concerning the density of Galilean population. Josephus certainly seeks to convey the impression of a thickly populated province at the time of the first revolt, but on the basis of the archaeological evidence of the admittedly highly provisional survey of the Meiron team, it appears that upper Galilee was sparsely populated until

72. The popularity of this position owes much to its espousal by E. Schürer, *Geschichte des Jüdischen Volkes in Zeitalter Jesu Christi*, 3 vols, reprint, Hildesheim: Olms, 1971, I, 275f. and II, 9–12. It is repeated without any question in the revised Schürer, Vermes, Miller, II, 7–10, despite the fact that, as S. Klein pointed out long ago, the Galileans are never once described as half-Jews either by Josephus or in the Tannaitic literature, unlike the Idumeans who were also forcibly circumcised at the same time, *Galiläa vor der Makkabäerzeit bis 67*, Berlin, 1928, 17–21.

after the second revolt, so that Josephus must have been referring to lower Galilee, the scene of his own operations for the most part. But according to the Meiron survey even in lower Galilee there was a sharp upsurge in the population in the wake of the Hasmonean conquests, suggesting that the whole region was not thickly populated earlier.[73] If this is the correct history of the settlement of Galilee, it would mean that my overall conclusion in the earlier study that the population of Galilee in the second century BCE belonged to old Israelite stock requires modification, but not drastic revision.[74] Some of them were of old Israelite stock, who, for whatever reason, had maintained their loyalty to the Jerusalem temple (Tobit 1:6–8). While some of these were deported to Jerusalem by Simon the Maccabee at the onset of Antiochus' persecution (1 Macc 5:15–20), the population in Galilee increased considerably later in the same century, presumably through a colonisation policy of the successful Hasmoneans, partly in the form of large estates, but also in terms of smaller foundations, in which the land was divided up in allotments with individual owners.[75] Whatever colonisation did take place certainly did not change the balance of the ethnic strands from Jewish to non-Jewish, even though an openness to the technical aspects of hellenism would have to be presumed from what we know of the Hasmonean rulers themselves. One would have to assume the introduction of some Greek influences into the population with the advent of Herodian rule, as in Palestine generally, but the likelihood is that these would be found among the new administrative and technical class that emerged in both Sepphoris and Tiberias.

73. Meyers, Strange, Groh, 'The Meiron Excavation Project', 16–22.

74. Freyne, *Galilee*, 23–26.

75. Cf. Applebaum, 'Jewish Urban Communities', 174f., and 'Judea as a Roman Province', *ANRW* II, 8, 355–61, on what he describes as Hasmonean 'internal colonisation'. The strategically located town of Simonias in western lower Galilee (*Life* 115), probably to be identified with biblical Shimron, is, he suggests, one example of a site that was resettled in hellenistic times, according to pottery remains, and the Greek form of its name may be derived from the last of the Maccabean brothers.

All the indications are that these were of essentially Jewish rather than gentile stock.

The evidence emanating from the material remains must be correlated with this general picture, yet the argument is, of necessity, partly circular in that some pre-existing picture of the situation is required to interpret the archaeological data also. Nevertheless, very clear advances are being made. There seems to be good reason for distinguishing between upper Galilee/Golan on the one hand and lower Galilee on the other, based on the evidence of epigraphy, ceramics and architectural style.[76] Such differentiation would correspond with what can be gleaned from the literary sources and what we would expect from our knowledge of roads and other means of broader communication. Even when we exclude such obvious centres of wider contacts as Sepphoris and Tiberias, the other lower Galilean centres such as Capernaum, Bethsaida and Tarichaeae were large enough and sufficiently cosmopolitan due to trade to have broader cultural horizons. Besides, the lake transport allowed for easy access to the whole region of the Dekapolis, just as the gospels portray the situation.

While these general considerations are significant, it remains to evaluate their impact on Galilean life generally—the attitudes and assumptions that constituted the ethos there. One way of attempting a meaningful answer to this question is to relate them to the various levels of the social spectrum already discussed. At one end of that spectrum are the peasants, in terms of the small land-owners, tenants and day labourers, living in the more remote settlements, for whom almost certainly Aramaic was the lingua franca. However, in view of its broad use in the whole Syrian region, language alone would not isolate them from wider contacts in the region, even at Tyre, since the evidence from inscriptions and other indicators suggests that a pattern of *diglossia*, and

76. This has been claimed repeatedly in the various publications of the Meiron team. Cf. e.g. *Archaeology, the Rabbis and Early Christianity*, 42.

possibly *triglossia* (Hebrew, Aramaic and Greek), operated.[77] What would have isolated these people more was their links to the soil in terms of day-to-day drudgery and all-seasons cultivation in order to procure the necessities of life and meet their various obligations. Consequently, trading and other contacts would of necessity have been local, apart from the pilgrimage with its strong ethno-centric effects. At the other end of the spectrum were people like Justus of Tiberias, Jewish by birth and religious persuasion, working in the Herodian bureaucracy and described by Josephus as 'not unversed in Greek education' (*Life* 40). As a Herodian, Justus was typical of a small but influential group in Galilee, of whom Chuza, the ἐπιτρόπος of Antipas, would be one example from the earlier period (Lk 8:3). The popularity and, therefore, the impact for cultural change of such men on the population as a whole would inevitably be minimal because of their position, something that the case of Justus amply illustrates.

In between these two extremes were any number of lesser officials—scribes, tax-collectors, military officers and the like. The friendly centurion of Capernaum suggests that such characters could in fact play a genuine bridging role between the two cultures. Besides, there are the inhabitants of the larger 'villages', whose trading and other contacts might be expected to create a climate of tolerance between Jew and Greek. However, the highly complex character of the situation can be gauged from the case of Tarichaeae. Its Greek name that is indicative of its involvement in the fish trade, as

77. Meyers, in 'Galilean Regionalism: A Reappraisal', accuses me of simplifying the linguistic situation, to the point of claiming that Greek was the lingua franca of all Galilee (119). This is a misrepresentation of my discussion, *Galilee*, 141, and Meyers makes no attempt to answer the question there posed: how far changes in language patterns can be taken as indicators of changes at a deeper level in terms of attitudes and values? Granted that because of experiences in my own culture I may have overstressed the ideological implications of both Greek and Hebrew—the Bar Cochba correspondence should have alerted me to the many inconsistencies that can occur in such matters—I am still not convinced that inscriptions alone, often from a much later period, can give us an accurate profile of linguistic practices generally. Why is there a Targumic tradition emanating from Galilee, if Hebrew was in fact a widely spoken language there in the first century? Cf. further, M. McNamara, 'The Spoken Aramaic of First Century Palestine', *PIBA* 2 (1977) 95–138; C. Rabin and G. Mussies, articles in *Compendia*, II, 1007–64.

well as the fact that there was a hippodrome there (*Life* 138), might be thought to point to a thoroughly Greek ethos. Yet it was in this very place that we meet the most glaring act of xenophobia in pre-revolt Galilee—the demand for expulsion of the noblemen refugees from Trachonitis unless they underwent circumcision (*Life* 112f.).

The example of Tarichaeae cautions against any easy conclusions about cultural openness, therefore. Those who might seek to extrapolate from the lower Galilean setting of Jesus' ministry to a more 'open' attitude on his part, need to be reminded that cultural links at one level do not necessarily mean adoption of the values and assumptions of the larger culture at other, more intimate levels of life. The ancient world operated very much in terms of élites who, despite the more democratic outlook created by the diffusion of the Greek πόλις, still lived for each other to the exclusion of the vast majority of the population. Peasants on the other hand, and it is this that constituted them as peasants, did not live independent lives, but were controlled by forces from without. Jewish peasants in Galilee had their own religious sanctions, as we shall presently see, but they were peasants nonetheless, with all the in-built restrictions that that fact of life imposed. The realisation that they were living in a limited goods society in which basic commodoties were in short supply and high demand tended to make them even more suspicious of forces outside the village, and created a reluctance to share a common life-view or life-style with those outsiders. If in fact Jesus avoided the Herodian cities, Sepphoris and Tiberias, which for all their Jewishness were alien centres as far as peasant Jews were concerned—as well as the cities, but not the villages of the surrounding territories, as Mark suggests—the assumption that his message was inspired by the universalist outlook of the Greek world would seem to be a priori less likely.

Thus, while Galilee can in general terms be said to be open to the heterogenetic factors of the Greek cities and their network of influences, one must await much more precise data before deciding that the whole Jewish population there was equally affected by all those factors. There are many examples of a pluralistic environment functioning in reverse, creating sub-cultures that seek to withhold themselves from full participation in the larger ethos.

There are in fact some indications that this is precisely what happened to Jewish communities living in the territories of the Greek cities in the whole of Palestine, and in the environs of Galilee in particular. On the eve of the first revolt, Josephus tells us, there was an outbreak of hostilities against the Jewish inhabitants of those cities and their territories. The fate of the Jews of Scythopolis was particularly disturbing in that many of them were massacred, even though they had refused to join their co-religionists in other parts of the country in the reprisals that the Jews were mounting (*J.W* 2:468; *Life* 27).[78] Presumably in the preceding decades those Jews had been able to practise their religious observances, thereby maintaining a separate cultural identity also, while benefiting from the greater economic possibilities of the urban environment. The story of the Jews of Caesarea Philippi who were prepared to pay even exorbitant prices for oil from olives grown in Galilee illustrates both the religio-cultural separatism and the economic prosperity (*Life* 74; *J.W.* 2:591f.).

It may well be that these hostilities were caused by the increased nationalism that seems to have affected Palestinian Jews generally in the immediate pre-war period, and that therefore they are untypical of relations earlier in the same century. The incidents at Tarichaeae and Scythopolis were exceptions on both sides, it could be argued. Yet the probability is that underlying both situations more deep-seated factors were at work, that can be dated to the mutual animosity that was generated between Jew and Greek by the Hasmonean treatment of the Greek cities during the wars of conquest, and subsequently after their restoration to an independent status by the Romans.[79] The Syrian mercenaries in the Roman army were particularly hostile to the Jews according to *J.A.* 19:364–6. Thus a long-established pattern of animosity and mutual recriminations was at work, often

78. G. Fuks, 'The Jews of Hellenistic and Roman Scythopolis', *JJS* 33 (1982) 407–16.

79. U. Rappaport, 'Jewish-Pagan Relations and the Revolt against Rome in 66–70 c.e.', in *The Jerusalem Cathedra*, I, ed. L. Levine, Jerusalem, 1981, 81–95.

undoubtedly beneath the surface so that it was possible for commercial and other contacts to be established. The fact that Jewish villages can be attested for the territory of the Greek city of Hippos in the Dekapolis, shows that Jews could and did participate in aspects of life other than the religious in both urban and rural settings of the Greek cities. Yet the underlying problem, both religious and social in character, remained and was likely to flare up at the slightest provocation, only for more 'normal' relations to be restored again. The reign of Antipas must be seen as one such period of relative normalcy in this regard, and hence the picture which Mark has drawn of easy movement between Galilee and its gentile environment is more likely for the time of Jesus than for that of writing the gospel some thirty years later, when relations were at an unsurpassed low ebb.

Conclusion

This survey of Galilean social life shows how interconnected the political, social, economic and cultural aspects really were. In evaluating the gospel pictures it must be said that despite their lack of detail or concern with describing the whole system, there is an essential faithfulness to the situation as it can be more adequately described from literary and archaeological sources. What has emerged is a dominantly village and peasant ethos which forms a viable sub-culture in the heartland of Galilee, despite pressure from various quarters, most notably from the élites who formed the Herodian aristocracy within Antipas' territory, and the Jerusalem priestly ascendancy with both religious and secular claims on their allegiance. In addition, the larger cultural context of the Greek world as this was mediated to Galilee and Galileans was an ambivalent experience. While it certainly offered greater opportunities for economic advancement through the development of markets and other services, it also generated a hostile environment in which their 'little tradition' was in constant danger of being submerged or destroyed entirely. Our next chapter will examine this aspect of Galilean life, exploring the manner in which the social world just described influenced the reception of the Jewish symbolic world-view in that setting.

CHAPTER SIX

Galilean Religious Affiliations in the First Century

DIVERSITY has been recognised as one of the hallmarks of pre-70 Jewish religion, and most discussion has been concentrated on Josephus' four philosophies as illustrative of this phenomenon. In some recent studies more attention has been given to the social circumstances that gave rise to the various parties and the ways in which their particular interpretations of the received symbols of Jewish faith resulted in the creation of new symbolic worlds that were meaningful for their adherents.[1] The gospels give only a limited view of this diversity with their references to Pharisees and Sadducees, scribes and chief priests, but without any mention of the Essenes and only a passing possible reference to the Zealots (Lk 6:15).[2] Often also various groupings that at best are unlikely, in the light of our other knowledge of the situation, are mentioned as forming an alliance against Jesus.

In the present chapter we are concerned to explore this question of diversity, not directly in terms of parties, but rather on a regional basis, given the differentiation between Galilean and Judean social life that emerged in our previous discussion. Since social worlds and symbol systems interact, each shaping and being shaped by the other, it is legitimate to ask what particular understanding of Jewish faith and practice emerged in Galilee, and how the internal differences in the social world there affected the overall picture. It is not

1. S. Isenberg, 'Power through Temple and Torah in Greco-Roman Palestine', in J. Neusner, ed., *Christianity, Judaism, and Other Greco-Roman Cults. Studies for Morton Smith at Sixty*, Part Two, Leiden: Brill. 1975, 24–53; H. Kippenberg, *Religion und Klassenbildung im Antiken Judäa*, Göttingen: Vandenhoeck und Ruprecht, 1978.

2. On the significance of ζηλωτής as replacement for Mark's Καναναῖος, cf. Fitzmyer, *The Gospel according to Luke I-IX*, 619.

suggested that the Galileans emerged as a separate religious party alongside the others,[3] but rather we seek to address the question that our texts raise, but do not answer in any satisfactory way, namely, what did the average Galilean peasant—the dominant strand in the population, we have maintained—think of their Jewish belief and how did she/he give practical expression to it?

If the gospels do not give us a very full picture of Galilean religious loyalties, our other literary sources are often as tantalisingly vague. Hence the difficulty in building up a reliable profile of the 'average' Galilean, and the repetition of the stock stereotypes. In order to advance the discussion we shall have to proceed by inference therefore, asking in a deductive fashion how various symbols functioned, or were likely to have functioned in that environment, often using as our yardstick the more intensified expressions to be found in the various philosophies.[4] Three symbols were absolutely central for all religious Jews of the period—those of temple, torah and land— even though a concentration on one or other element of this triad to the point of subordinating the other two, could and did produce a new configuration, 'a new Judaism', to cite Neusner, that found expression in one or other of the parties already mentioned. One way of measuring Galilean religious affiliations then, would be to seek to determine the support for the different parties in Galilee. Yet apart from the problem of accurate information, already mentioned, such an approach would not adequately uncover the affiliations and motivations of the average Galilean, but only of the adherents of a particular party, likely to have been only a minority of the population at best. In addition, the argument would be largely one of silence. The gospels do not mention Sadducees in Galilee, not to speak of Galilean Essenes!

3. The effort of S. Zeitlin, in 'Who were the Galileans? New Light on Josephus' Activities in Galilee', *JQR* 64(1974) 189–203, to establish this on the basis of *Life* cannot be regarded as successful; cf. Freyne, 'The Galileans In the Light of Josephus' *Vita*'.

4. In this we are following the suggestion of J. Neusner, *Major Trends in Formative Judaism*, third series, *The Three Stages in the Formation of Judaism*, Brown Judaic Studies 99, Chico: Scholars Press, 1985, 9–34, who rightly stresses the continuum between ordinary Jewish piety in the first century and the particular emphases, about which we are often better informed.

An alternative approach is to attempt to identify Galilean attachment to the three symbols in question, evaluating that attachment in terms of its likely relationship to the social world just described. Inevitably, discussion of the acceptance or rejection of the different points of view of the various philosophies will need to be raised in this approach also. Yet, by addressing directly the question of the reception of the symbols in a particular social world there is the advantage of casting the net more widely, with the possibility of judging how various strata of the population identified with different symbols. Jacob Neusner[5] has neatly identified each symbol with an ideal type—the priest, the scribe and the freedom fighter/messianist—and attention to the possible social role of each in the Galilean context should further help to focus the discussion and prepare for the task of our final chapter, the consideration of the social and religious role of Jesus and his movement in Galilee.

1. Galileans and the Temple

In terms of the ritual expression of their beliefs the temple was undoubtedly the focal point for all Jews in the pre-70 period. Fidelity to the pilgrimage obligations, the loyal discharge of the half-shekel offering and the sense of outrage at the very threat of its defilement are all highly indicative of the emotional involvement with this centre by those who would regard themselves as Yahweh-worshippers.[6] Its destruction by the Babylonians and subsequent rebuilding in the Persian period had accentuated that attachment, as exilic and post-exilic prophets and psalmists extolled its praises in oracles and songs that were repeatedly sung and commented on through the subsequent centuries. The defilement by Antiochus Epiphanes and the fact that Pompey had dared to enter the holy place a hundred years later only heightened the

5. Apart from the work cited in note 4 above, cf. his *Judaism in the Beginning of Christianity*, SPCK, 1985.

6. Apart from the standard introductory works such as *Compendia Rerum Judaicarum ad Novum Testamentum*, vol. 2 and Schürer-Vermes-Miller, *The History of the Jewish People*, vol. 2, cf. in particular S. Safrai, *Die Wallfahrt im Zeitalter des Zweiten Tempels*, German trans. Neukirchen-Vluyn: Neukirchener Verlag, 1981.

sensitivity of all devout Jews about any threat to the sacred centre of their life, as the incident about the statue of Gaius Caligula, already referred to, makes abundantly clear. Herod the Great with his astute political sense had spared no effort in lavishly refurbishing it, thereby placating those Jews who resented his ousting of the Hasmonean restorers, while at the same time providing work for the Jerusalem populace. Nevertheless, the more sensitive elements of the Jewish people were less than impressed by Herod's generosity, as is shown by the incident of the two Pharisaic teachers who resisted with their lives the erection of the hated golden eagle symbol at the entrance to the temple, (*J.W.* 1:648–53: *J.A.* 17:149–154). Throughout the whole procuratorial period the temple repeatedly became the flashpoint of Jewish nationalist aspirations, often involving Galileans also, and culminating in the 'take-over' of the temple by the lesser clergy in 66 CE as the final throwing down of the gauntlet to the Romans.[7]

In the light of this brief sketch it is easy to recognise that the Jerusalem temple, as the cult centre of the Jews, was capable of generating 'powerful, pervasive, and long-lasting moods and motivations', to cite Clifford Geertz' well-known definition of religion as a cultural system.[8] So long-lasting in fact were the moods that long after the destruction of 70 CE and the failure to have it rebuilt seventy years later, the Tannaitic sages who framed the Mishnaic system and the Amoraic ones who commented on it, still saw the temple as the centre of Israel's symbolic life. The former built their system on the Utopian statement that the temple with its sacrifices, offerings and festivals was still intact,[9] and for the latter the temple was, according to their speculation, the very centre of the created cosmos. [10]

The centrality of the temple had also given Jerusalem a pre-eminent, even mythological character in Jewish thought,

7. See C. Roth, 'The Debate on the Loyal Sacrifices', *HTR* 53(1960) 93–7.

8. Reprinted in his *The Interpretation of Cultures*, New York: Harper Torchbooks, 1973, 87–125, here 94.

9. See J. Neusner, *Judaism. The Evidence of the Mishnah*, Chicago: University Press, 1981, especially 225–9, 230–31, 248–50.

10. See P. Schäfer, 'Tempel und Schöpfung. Zur Interpretation einer Heiligtumstraditionen in der Rabbinischen Literatur', reprinted in his *Studien zur Geschichte und Theologie des Rabbinischen Judentums*, AGJU 15, Leiden: Brill, 1975, 122–33.

dating back to the Zion traditions at least.[11] In political terms it was a 'temple city', with the whole of the territory occupied by Jews, including of course Galilee, its sacred land. In purely economic terms the city lived off and by the temple with its income and revenue heavily dependent on the pilgrimage traffic and the inflow of various gifts from all over the inhabited world, including the half-shekel offering, paid in Tyrian currency.[12] The need for suitable animals and other forms of offerings meant that markets of various kinds were developed, thus providing a natural outlet for the produce of the land in the immediate vicinity. Yet these two aspects of Jerusalem's control—the political and the economic—were embedded in its religious identity as the holy city, the city of David and Solomon. Not merely did it house the temple, the dwelling place of God with Israel, it was also the seat of learning and wisdom, inhabited by priests and sages who could command respect from all Jews for their holiness or their knowledge of sacred lore.

Any threat to Jerusalem or its religious legitimacy was inevitably treated with immediate hostility. The case of Jesus ben Hananiah, reported by Josephus, illustrates admirably the sensitivity of the Jewish religious aristocracy to any suggestion that divine favour might be withdrawn from the city. Just four years before the outbreak of the first revolt, this 'simple peasant from the lower classes' came to Jerusalem, performing symbolic gestures that were reminiscent of such Old Testament prophets as Amos and Jeremiah, and in the temple began to utter prophecies of doom against Jerusalem, the temple and the people. Despite being chastised by both the aristocracy and the Roman governor, he continued his dirge of woe on Jerusalem, especially during festivals, until at last he was killed by a stone thrown from one of the Roman missile-engines encircling Jerusalem (*J.W.* 6:300–309).[13]

11. G. von Rad, *Theology of the Old Testament*, 2 vols., E.T. London: Oliver and Boyd, 1965, 2, 175. The relation between the Sinai and Zion traditions has been explored in a creative way recently by J.D. Levenson, *Sinai and Zion*, New York: Winston Press, 1985.

12. Details in J. Jeremias, *Jerusalem at the Time of Jesus*, E.T. London: SCM, 1969, 31–54.

13. Cf. Horsley, *Bandits, Prophets, Messiahs*, 172f.

The story is certainly not unlike that of Jesus the Galilean, at least superficially. In all the Synoptic accounts the plot is centred on a journey to Jerusalem for the feast of Passover, and in the fourth gospel for other feasts as well, notably those to do with the feast of Tabernacles (chs. 7–8) and the feast of Dedication (ch. 10). Though later theological reflection on 'the way' of Jesus, the exodus motif and the replacement and/or fulfilment of Jewish festival expectations can all be discerned in these accounts as presently narrated, there is also a realism apparent in terms of the actual pilgrimage experience: Luke's account of the Samaritan opposition to the Galilean pilgrims; families travelling together to protect and support each other on the journey; country peasants experiencing a sense of awe in urban surroundings and being recognised by their accents; the withdrawal to a nearby village for overnight accommodation because of the festival crowds. In addition, John is familiar with temple topography (Solomon's portico) and the temple ceremonial (light and water associated with the feast of Tabernacles). Clearly then there is a genuine intention to present Jesus and his retinue as Galilean pilgrims, even though there is no mention of his sacrificing (except in the infancy narratives of Luke, with their conscious Old Testament colouring of the characters), or the bringing of tithes or other signs of full participation in the temple ritual (apart from belated payment of the half-shekel offering, Mt 17:24–7).

One could interpret this silence as signs of protest, at least, emanating in Galilee, especially in the light of Jesus' symbolic overturning of the tables of the money changers, and the prohibition in Mark against carrying of vessels in the temple courtyard, actions whose subversive nature has been highlighted by several commentators, most notably E.P. Sanders, in the light of what he calls Jesus' 'restoration eschatology'.[14] Alternatively, one could suspect that the silence about offering sacrifice is due to the early Christian understanding of Jesus as the new sacrifice for sin (Mk 10:45; 14:24). Obviously, the issue of Jesus and the temple is a central one in the light of our texts and will be discussed in detail in the

14. *Jesus and Judaism*, 61–76.

next chapter. Here we must seek to put the question into the larger perspective of Galilean attachment to the temple generally, since this expressed itself not just on the occasion of the pilgrimage, central though that experience was, but also in Galilee itself. Acceptance of the temple system as a whole gave the Galilean land-owning peasants what, again in Geertz's terms, can be described as a fusion of ethos and world view, 'by giving a set of social values what they most need to be coercive, an appearance of objectivity'.[15] In regarding the conditions of life as imposed by the very structure of the cosmos itself, and not as variables that could be changed by human agency, the peasant is more conditioned to accept his lot as natural, despite its oppressive aspects when viewed from a different perspective. The incident of the peasant strike, which was centred in Galilee and was motivated by concern for the sacredness of the temple, is ample proof if such be needed, that social consequences of the most dire kind could be accepted with equanimity for the sake of deeply held religious convictions.

There were alternative religious options open to the Galilean peasant in his immediate surroundings and from within the Israelite tradition itself. As a way of testing Galilean loyalty to Jerusalem and its temple we can look for signs of support among them, either for the Samaritan cult centre on Mt. Gerazim, or the ancient site of Dan, which apparently functioned in some sense even in hellenistic times.

The hostility of the Samaritans towards the Jewish pilgrims from Galilee, mentioned by Luke (9:26) and reflected also in John, can be readily corroborated from Josephus (*J.A.* 20:123; *J.W.* 2:237). Hence there appears to have been no likelihood that Galilean Jews would have been tempted to worship at Mt Gerazim. There is some evidence that the cult of the God of Mt Gerazim had spread beyond the immediate confines of Samaria into the Beth Shean valley, and more recently still, evidence of its presence on the island of Delos has surfaced.[16] Doubtless, its spread was attributable to its thoroughly hellenised character since the days of Antiochus

15. 'Ethos, World View and the Analysis of Sacred Symbols', in *The Interpretation of Cultures*, 129–41, here 131.

16. See A.T. Kraabel, 'New Evidence of the Samaritan Diaspora has been Found on Delos', *BA* 47(1984) 44–6.

IV (2 Macc 6:2), something that can also be recognised later in the links of Simonian gnosticism with Samaria.[17] In all probability it was this syncretistic, if not downright pagan character of the cult, allied to other factors, both cultural and social, which had been operative for a long time, that made Samaria an unattractive cult centre for Galilean Jews, some of whom at least would have shared the Hasmonean hostility towards the place because of their southern provenance. The thorough-going hellenised character of nearby Samaria/Sebaste increased further the cultural and social gap between the two communities, despite the shared Mosaic patrimony of the Pentateuch. It is paradoxical that this shared foundation myth could only bridge the social gap between Galileans and Samaritans within certain strands of the Jesus-movement that had apparently rejected the religious claims of Jerusalem,[18] whereas for others in the same movement of a more Jewish orientation, Samaritans did not even belong to the lost sheep of the house of Israel (Mt 10:5), despite their own claims on the Delos inscription to be 'the Israelites in Delos who make offerings to the sanctuary (ἱερὸν) Argarazein'. In Jesus' own day to have praised a Samaritan in a Galilean Jewish context for befriending somebody on the temple way, was to make a highly provocative statement that ran counter to all their experiences.

What of Dan? Here was an old cultic centre that had been specially activated to attract the northern Israelites away from Jerusalem (1Kgs 12:26–32). Had it too, lost its appeal in the changed circumstances of hellenistic times? The recently published bi-lingual, dedicatory inscription: ΘΕΩΙ ΤΩ ΕΝ ΔΑΝΟΙΣ, 'to the God who is in Dan', with what appears to be an Aramaic translation,[19] suggests that it must still have

17. See Freyne, *Galilee*, 274f.; R. Coggins, *Samaritans and Jews. The Origins of Samaritanism Reconsidered*, Oxford: Blackwell, 1975.

18. See the successful mission of the hellenist Philip in Samaria, following Stephen's martyrdom because of his attack on the temple, Ac 8:4–8. For a convenient discussion cf. E. Schillebeeckx, *The Christ. The Experience of Jesus as Lord*, 343–9, and further, O. Cullmann, *The Johannine Circle*, E.T. London: SCM, 1976.

19. According to A. Biran, 'To the God who is in Dan', in A. Biran, ed., *Temples and High Places in Biblical Times*, Jerusalem: Nelson Glueck School of Biblical Archaeology, 1981, 142–151, who has been conducting the excavations at Dan, the inscription was found close to the area which the excavators have identified as the *bamah*, containing several structures suggesting cultic activity, below a Roman floor and above a hellenistic one.

retained its character as a cult centre, and, one could reasonably claim, some appeal also for Galilean Jews. The temptation to read more into this piece of evidence is natural, given the circumstances and the associations of the place in earlier, Israelite times. The maker of the vow is called Zoilos, a Greek, not a Jewish, name, but names alone are highly unreliable indicators of cultural or religious affiliation in that epoch. The fact that the God is unnamed may point to Yahweh, since Amos refers to the God in Dan, but without giving this God a name (Amos 8:14); however altars to unnamed gods are found in pagan contexts also. Finally, the plural ΕΝ ΔΑΝΟΙΣ could mean 'among the Danites', but there is no evidence elsewhere that inhabitants of the region considered themselves to be descendants of the ancient tribe. Josephus, with his casual mention of 'the temple of the golden calf', as he describes the region where the Jordan rises (*J.W.* 4:3), would seem to suggest that pagan worship in that region could be thought of in terms of ancient Israelite idolatry, though no such temple has been found there. Even if we were to agree with Biran that Zoilos was a Jew, he is scarcely representative of Galilean Jews generally, the vast majority of whom lived in lower Galilee in this period. Even those living in upper Galilee, and therefore in close proximity to Dan, would scarcely be attracted to a syncretistic cult centre (a statue of Aphrodite has also been found close by, according to the excavator) in view of their cultural conservatism, as this manifested itself later.

There is evidence of both public and private worship of various pagan deities within the region in Roman times, yet it is surely not coincidental that all the inscriptional evidence that so far has come to light is from the territories of the surrounding cities.[20] In many instances these are merely older semitic deities in Greek dress, and hence Jewish attitudes towards them and their adherents would have formed part of the ongoing distrust of the hellenistic environment of which we spoke in the previous chapter.[21]

20. Details in Freyne, *Galilee*, 266–75.

21. Cf. J. Teixidor, *The Pagan God. Popular Religion in the Greco-Roman Near East*, N. Jersey: Princeton University Press, 1977; D. Flusser, 'Paganism in Palestine', in *Compendia*, 2, 1065–1100.

There was one particular hellenistic deity that could conceivably have been attractive to country Jews, especially in Galilee, namely Dionysus, the wine god, whose association with Beth Shean/Scythopolis is documented in both literary and archaeological sources.[22] Morton Smith has argued that the cult of the wine god was indigenous to Syria-Palestine for a very long time, Dionysus being identified with Yahweh by some Jews, and seen by others of a more syncretistic disposition as the *interpretatio graeca* of Yahweh. Still others, namely followers of Jesus, contrasted him with the true vine, Yahweh's logos.[23] Of particular significance for Galilee is Smith's reconstruction of a wine-making festival at Sidon, in which Dionysus' gift of the wine to the Sidonians was celebrated, according to a report from Achilles Tatius, a pagan writer, whom Smith seeks to date to the second century CE. Other links existed between Galilee and the Phoenician coast, as we have seen, and the question should be asked whether Galilean Jews would have found anything incompatible with their Yahweh-worship in such celebrations, particularly since according to Josephus (*J.A.* 15:395; *J.W.* 5:210) and Tacitus (*Histories* V,5) there were representations of vines with huge grape-clusters over the gate of the Jerusalem temple, and many drew the inference that the Jews worshipped Dionysus, according to Tacitus.

In the light of that information, coupled with the traditional celebration associated with the feast of Tabernacles, itself originally a grape-harvest festival, it would come as no surprise to find traces of Jewish participation in local wine-festivals, without necessarily any sense of compromising their Yahweh worship.[24] But we have no direct evidence of any

22. B. Lifshitz, 'Scythopolis. L'histoire, les institutions, et les cultes de la ville à l'époque hellénistique et impériale' in *ANRW* II, 8, 262–94, especially 275f.; Freyne, *Galilee*, 270; E. Meyers, E. Netzer, C. Meyers, 'The Mosaics of Ancient Sepphoris', *BA* 50 (1987) 223–31. The Dionysus mosaic now uncovered points to aristocratic circles (whether Jewish or pagan).

23. 'On the Wine God in Palestine. Gen 18, Jn 2 and Achilles Tatius', in *Salo M. Baron Jubilee Volume*, Jerusalem, 1975, English Section 815–29.

24. G. Porton, in 'The Grape Cluster in Jewish Literature and Art of Late Antiquity', *JJS* 27(1976) 147–58, shows how it is well attested in the literature of the Second Temple period as well as that on synagogue art, but that there were debates about it in rabbinic circles, probably due to the fact that it had become an important symbol on the coins of Bar Cochba.

such involvement, and evidence from later periods shows that in the matter of synagogue art and archictecture, pagan motifs and style could be adapted to serve a Jewish religious culture that was intensely resistant to any easy syncretism, more particularly in areas such as upper Galilee, where commercial links might have suggested the very opposite.[25] The Jews of Caesarea whose desire for native oil we have already discussed, are equally good examples of a similar resistance in the first century also.

If, therefore, the result of this probe must be that there is little current evidence that the other attractions of hellenism had coroded the basic loyalty of Galilean Jews for Jerusalem and its temple, what can be said of the influence of this particular attachment on their lives within the province? How well, for example, did the pilgrimage function as a way of overcoming the undoubted urban/rural tensions at the economic and social levels that we have already encountered? In attempting to answer such questions as this, anthropological considerations on the function of pilgrimage can, perhaps, point in the right direction. Victor Turner has drawn attention to two aspects of pilgrimages that at first sight appear promising, namely their similarity both to tribal initiation rites and to rituals of affliction.[26] The pilgrim, like the initiate, enters a new and deeper spiritual world by embarking on a journey from familiar surroundings to the holy place, where eventually the divine is encountered in visible, tangible signs of its presence. In the case of the pilgrimage the communal experience adds to the sense of belonging to a new and different world also. On the other hand the hardships associated with the pilgrimage and the dangers inherent in the journey are readily accepted by the pilgrim as a way of being rid of personal or familial evils, such as illness or mischance, that are usually perceived as divine punishment for moral transgressions, even when the curative aspects of the pilgrimage are not always highlighted.

Galileans certainly encountered dangers in making the

25. Goodman, *State and Society*, 84–7; Meyers, 'Galilean Regionalism: A Reappraisal', 126f.

26. See V. Turner, *Image and Pilgrimage in Christian Culture. Anthropological Perspectives*, Oxford: Blackwell, 1978.

pilgrimage to Jerusalem, not just those inherent in travel in antiquity generally (cf. Lk 10:30; 22:35–7), but more particularly from the Samaritans for religious reasons, as already noted. Besides the increased Roman presence in the city at the time of the festival had its own dangers, as some Galilean pilgrims had learned to their cost (Lk 13:1). We have already suggested that there were social benefits inherent in the pilgrimage journey for those from more remote areas, for whom it offered a break with the narrow confines of the village. But what of the bonding with the urban Jews? There is evidence, at least from later rabbinic sources, that concern with the strict observance of the purity laws could be relaxed somewhat on the occasion of the great festivals.[27] Thus a greater sense of belonging to the priestly people, the holy nation, was undoubtedly engendered, and yet the bringing of the agricultural gifts or their equivalent for the priests, as well as the elaborate ceremonials, reinforced the hierarchical structuring of Israel that the temple and its system mirrored, with all the social consequences that were involved.

Dissatisfaction with the temple and its priesthood, as well as debates about its legitimacy, were a constant feature of Second Temple Judaism, with the Essenes providing the most openly critical stance.[28] In view of such currents it is quite remarkable how stable the office of the high priest remained throughout the first century, being in the virtual control of just a few families. Despite evidence of tension between them from time to time, and signs of popular unrest, these families were able to maintain a fine sense of balance among themselves, in order not to undermine the office itself and its relations with the Roman provincial government.[29] One literary expression of criticism of the Jerusalem priests is found in the Enochic corpus and has particular importance

27. See A. Oppenheimer, *The Am Ha-Aretz. A Study in the Social History of the Jewish People in the Hellenistic Roman Period,* Leiden: Brill, 1977, 156–60.

28. See P. Davies, 'The Ideology of the Temple in the Damascus Document', *JJS* 33(1982) 287–301; J. Murphy-O'Connor, 'The Damascus Document Revisited' in K.H. Richards, ed., *Society of Biblical Literature Papers,* no. 25, Atlanta: Scholars Press, 1986, 369–83, especially, 376–9.

29. R. Horsley, in 'High Priests and Politics of Roman Palestine', *JSJ* 17(1986) 23–55, examines their role against the backdrop of provincial Roman aristocracies.

for our discussion of Galilean attitudes.[30] The author/seer relates a vision in a cultic setting which he received in upper Galilee (1 Enoch 14:18–22). This occurs in a context that is extremely critical of the existing temple priesthood, especially for their sexual aberrations, suggesting strong idolatrous overtones (15:3–4). Similarly, the *Testament of Levi* locates the call by heavenly vision of the patriarch Levi to the high-priesthood in the same region (chs. 2–7). Both accounts must be read as criticisms of the Jerusalem priesthood, and the northern setting at least raises the question of whether these might not reflect wider Galilean criticisms of the priesthood, because of social oppression or other perceived failures. If our earlier suggestion that some of the wealthy absentee landlords were Jerusalem priestly aristocrats has any foundation, such criticism would be very natural. Lohmeyer and others have spoken of an apocalyptic mood in Galilee, but without offering any precise social base for it, but more recently the suggestion has been made that a rather different apocalyptic tradition to that represented by the *hasîdîm* (and Daniel) is to be found in Enoch, emanating from disaffected elements of the peasantry, thus suggesting a link with Jesus.[31] The gospels certainly presume such a mood among the audiences of Jesus, with his frequent use of apocalyptic images and language, yet The Book of Daniel is represented in this repertoire at least as frequently as is 1 Enoch.

It is notoriously difficult to pin down apocalyptic images to precise locations in view of the cosmic symbolism of the literature and its mythological associations. Mount Hermon had very old resonances in Hebrew literature as a place of religious significance (Ps 29; 42; 49, e.g.), and in view of the prominence of the Enochic corpus as well as *The Testaments* at Qumran, it seems more likely that this criticism of the Jerusalem priesthood had emanated among disaffected Jerusalem priests themselves, among whom the origins of Qum-

30. See G. Nickelsburg, 'Enoch, Levi, and Peter: Recipients of Revelation in Upper Galilee', *JBL* 100(1981) 575–600.

31. M. Barker, 'Some Reflections on the Enoch Myth', *JSOT* 15(1980) 7–29; R. Murray, 'Jews, Hebrews, Christians: Some Needed Distinctions', *NT* 24(1982) 194–20, and 'Disaffected Judaism and Early Christianity: Some Predisposing Factors', in '*To See Ourselves as Others See Us*', 263–81.

ran Essenism are to be located. [32] Mount Hermon could then have been chosen as the polar opposite to Mount Zion without the suggestion that the authors or their circles lived in the region, any more than did Matthew, who chose to oppose the mountain in Galilee to that in Jerusalem, as a way of contrasting the true Israel with the faithless. We do not hear of Galilean priests until the later rabbinic sources, and it is likely that there were very few actually resident in the province until after 70, or more probably after 135 CE. Accordingly, the priest and his altar were viewed from a distance in Galilee, a Jerusalem and Judean rather than a local phenomenon, and in this the gospel narratives appear to be altogether reliable witnesses to the actual situation.

Despite this reluctance to follow Nickelsburg in locating a visionary tradition in upper Galilee—at least to the point of its having any major impact on the population at large—there was, however, a country-based criticism of the temple, apocalyptic in tone and emanating from the lower classes, as the example of Jesus ben Hananiah, already cited indicates. We do not know, of course, where Jesus came from, simply that he was ἀπὸ τῆς χώρας, from the land. But so too was Jesus of Nazareth, and in view of the similar features of both their appearances in Jerusalem, the question should be asked whether Galilean country conditions might not have fostered such criticism of Jerusalem, its temple and people. Josephus' *Life* can help us somewhat in measuring the actual attachment to priests and temple in Galilee at the time of Jesus ben Hananiah's protest, thus providing a framework for an answer to the question. As part of their policy of containing the revolt, the Jerusalem aristocracy appointed somebody of their own ilk who was of priestly lineage, as were his two companions, to control of Galilee. Josephus makes the point that the Galileans willingly gave them 'the tithes that were

32. Nickelsburg, 'Enoch, Levi and Peter', 587, recognises that the presence of 1 Enoch in the Qumran library provides a context in which the Enochic criticism would have been at home, but in his view the polemic is older, and because of the precise geograpahic data from upper Galilee it reflects a visionary tradition of northern Galilean provenance, which may well have been continued in later Jewish and Christian usage. More recently he has attempted to strengthen the links with upper Galilee by taking Damascus in CD to refer to the actual city, and not exile in Babylonia, see 'I Enoch and Qumran Origins: The State of the Question and Some Prospects for Answers', in *SBL Seminar Papers* (1986) 341–60, especially 352f.

their due', thus underlining the fact that he used his priestly origins to reinforce his position within the province. Some local 'big men' such as John of Gischala and Justus of Tiberias resented the appointment and tried, unsuccessfully, to dislodge Josephus, even with an appeal to Jerusalem. The only response was a delegation of Jerusalemites, constituted in such a way as to win the widest possible support among the people of Galilee, and with the priestly and aristocratic elements dominating once again.

Even when Josephus' picture of the Galileans' loyalty to himself is judged to be overdone, as part of his attempt to discredit Justus of Tiberias, we are still left with the very definite impression that Galilean loyalty to Jerusalem and its priesthood can be presumed on the part of those who control that centre. In chiding Justus and his class in Tiberias, Josephus writes of Sepphoris' refusal to support 'the temple that is common to us all', despite the unpopularity of this and other pro-Roman actions, in contrast to Tiberias, which had in fact revolted (*Life* 348f.). Thus, appeal to the temple and its symbolic significance for Galileans would appear to have been part of the strategy of Josephus and those who sent him to Galilee.[33] The refusal of the people of Sepphoris to become involved in defence of the temple, was not due to any lack of support for its religious significance, but was, rather, part of their pacifism in regard to the revolt from the very beginning. Thus, on the basis of this evidence, we can say that, however we classify the movement of Jesus of Nazareth, Galilee would not appear to provide the proper social setting for a rural protest against either Jerusalem or its temple, any more than it provided the context for an Essene-style, apocalyptically based criticism of the existing priesthood and their conduct.

2. Galileans and the Land

We are then left with the conclusion that the inhabitants of first-century Galilee continued to find the Jerusalem temple and the religious system based on it a meaningful expression of their beliefs and life-experiences. How can we best interpret this finding, surprising as some might find it, in

33. Freyne, 'Galilee-Jerusalem Relations', 606f.

view of the demands that such loyalty made on the strained resources of the peasants in particular, as we have seen? One possible answer is that the temple symbolised and guaranteed their attachment to the land, the fruits of which had to be shared with the temple personnel according to Pentateuchal law. Since the Israelite system, at least from the time of the Deuteronomic reform,[34] combined temple and land in a continuous, differentiated sacred space, one way of testing our tentative answer to the question of Galilean loyalty to the temple is to examine their attachment to the symbol of the land also.

With the restoration after the exile in Babylonia, temple and land, now in reality just a tiny temple-state in the Persian period, were further linked by Nehemiah's reform of the tithing laws (Neh 10:36–38; 12:44; 18:26). Further adjustments to this system occurred in the hellenistic period, it would seem,[35] yet the idea of bringing a representative sample of the gifts of the land to the central sanctuary remained unchallenged in principle right up to the destruction in 70 CE. The story of the Galilean Tobit, who 'alone of all his kinsmen of the tribe of Naphtali', made the annual pilgrimage to Jerusalem with the prescribed offerings, may be taken as illustrative rather than as factual for our purposes. (Tobit 1:5–8). Indeed when the temple was destroyed and the second century sages addressed the question of how Israel might be reconstituted as the holy people, one whole division, that of Agriculture (*Zeraim*) was dedicated to exploring the legal implications of the production of food and the agricultural offerings for the small, land-owning householder, to whom the document as a whole was addressed.[36]

34. For a discussion of the theme of the land in the Bible cf. W.D. Davies, *The Gospel and the Land*, especially 15–35; W. Zimmerli, 'The Land in the Pre-Exilic and Early Post-Exilic Prophets', in *Understanding the Word. Essays in Honor of B.W. Anderson*, ed. J.T. Butler, E.W. Conrad, B.C. Ollenburger, *JSOT Supplement Series* 37, Sheffield 1985, 247–64.

35. Freyne, *Galilee*, 282f. and 303 nn. 74–8.

36. Neusner, in *Judaism*, 53f., 79–87, 126–32, 172–80, explores the development of the law from that which was the concern of a sect (before the wars) to a period of transition (between the wars), to its final stage addressing all Israel in its land (after the wars). Cf. also Appendix I, 287–300, where the results of Neusner's students' studies of the development of the various tractates are summarised. Cf. further, A.J. Avery-Peck, *Mishnah's Division of Agriculture. A History and Theology of Seder Zeraim*, Brown Judaic Series 79, Chico: Scholars Press, 1985.

According to Jacob Neusner the generative principle of this division, which itself is to be seen as a work of legal imagination, was the problem of how the faithful Israelites were to give expression to the belief that Yahweh was the owner of the land and that they were his lessees. In view of the fact that the division as a whole has been deemed by Alan Avery-Peck not to show any great continuity with the pre-70 legislation, but to be largely the work of the Yavneans and Ushans, we may well conjecture that the end-product was part of a defiant response of the sages to the loss of land-ownership, which we know to have been the direct result of the two wars (*J.W.* 7:216). The implication of the absence of any developed body of general law prior to the wars must surely be that, prior to that period, the majority of the population living on the land took the agricultural regulations seriously as these had developed in hellenistic and Roman times. The report of Josephus already referred to (*J.A.* 20:181.205–207), which relates how the servants of the high priests forcibly collected their dues in the villages, is less a sign of dissatisfaction with the religious demands which the symbol of the land made than an indication of the growing tensions prior to the first revolt between the lesser, local clergy living in the Judean countryside and the Jerusalem-based high priests. Similarily, if the letter, dealing with the discharge of certain agricultural obligations, from the Jerusalem sages to the men of various regions, including Galilee, has any historical significance for the pre-70 period, unlikely though that supposition is,[37] it too could scarcely be interpreted to mean a general laxity in this regard, but should be read rather as a determination of the due date for discharge of

37. For details cf. Freyne, *Galilee*, 302 n.73. The letter attributed to R. Simeon ben Gamaliel and R. Johanan ben Zakkai and addressed to the men of Upper and Lower Galilee, reads: 'Let it be known to you that the fourth year has arrived, but still the sacred produce has not been removed. And now make haste and bring the olive heaps, for they hinder the confession (cf. Dt 26:13). And it is not we who have begun to write to you, but our fathers to your fathers' (T. Sanh 2:2; y Ma'as Sch 5:56b). However, attribution to the Jamnian leaders by later sources is no guarantee of authenticity, since it reflects the appeal to the authority of past tradition, as in the conclusion to this letter. In all probability, then, this letter, and a similar one dealing with the fruit of fourth year trees, reflects much later conditions and disputes in Galilee.

the offerings in question, owing to varying climatic conditions in various regions.

There is, then, a strand of Jewish practice which can be deduced from the Second Temple period and which indicates how the symbolism of the land functioned effectively for many country people, including Galileans. Setting aside the tithes of what the land produced and ensuring that the first-fruits were brought to Jerusalem made severe demands, both economic and physical. Yet they also served as a reminder of Yahweh's presence as the source of gracious goodness in a more generalised way in the land, and as pledges of his faithfulness. The Hasmonean wars of conquest had extended the boundaries of the land to their proper, that is their Davidic limits, including Galilee within their ambit, and the forced judaisation of Itureans and Idumeans to the north and south shows that there was a definite religious intention to the conquest also. Control of the land meant that there could no longer be any defilement of the holy place—'that freed from our enemies, we might serve him in holiness and justice before him all our days' (Lk 1:56). It is against this background of a theocratic state and in the immediate context of a Roman take-over that first-century Jewish nationalism was spawned. This was to adopt a much more militant, even ideological stance, leading ultimately to the two revolts. While both of these undoubtedly had a political and social dimension, they were from the Jewish perspective holy wars of liberation, freeing the land from those foreigners who controlled it against God's will for his land, and from those natives who collaborated with such foreigners.[38]

According to Josephus, Judas the Galilean, a Jerusalem-based σοφιστής, was the instigator of such revolutionary ideas in 6 CE, calling on his fellow countrymen to refuse to participate in the Roman census and to call no man lord except God (*J.W.* 2:118; *J.A.* 18:3–9.23–25). Because of his Galilean origins (though his campaign was directed solely to Judea, the territory of the deposed Archelaus) and due to his

38. Despite the fact that M. Hengel's fundamental study, *Die Zeloten*, can be criticised for an over-synthetic picture of the Zealots, it is one of the work's great merits to stress the essentially religious dimension of the first revolt, something that the coins in particular corroborate.

presumed identity with Judas, son of Hezekiah, who ten years earlier had led a revolt at Sepphoris, there is a general assumption among the scholarly community that first-century Galilee was the hot-bed of Jewish revolutionary ideas. This view of the social situation in the province has then often served as the backdrop for evaluating Jesus' zealotism, or alternatively, his pacifism![39] A critical assessment of these views with special reference to Galilee can certainly assist in assessing religious attitudes in the province, particularly as these expressed themselves in relation to the symbol of the land. The Zealot construct, in terms of a single party that inspired the various manifestations of social and political unrest, has increasingly lost ground among the scholarly community in recent times,[40] yet several of those various manifestations did have religious significance in terms of the symbol of the land, and two in particular call for some comment—prophetic movements of liberation and popular messianic demonstrations.

Mention has already been made of Jesus, son of Hananiah, the peasant country prophet of an oracular type, who met his death while daring to prophesy the destruction of the temple and the city. But there were other types of prophetic manifestations also, which involved crowds of people from the countryside following a designated leader, whose symbolic actions resembled those of Moses and Josua from the stories of exodus and conquest of the land.[41] There was the Samaritan prophet who was about to lead a great crowd to Mt Gerazim, there to recover the sacred vessels that Moses had hidden, only to be intercepted by Pilate with considerable loss of life (*J.A.* 18:85–87). Again there was Theudas who led many of the Judean country people, taking their possessions with them, to the desert, with the promise of a miraculous

39. Contrast S.G.F. Brandon, *Jesus and the Zealots*, Manchester, 1967, and J.H. Yoder, *The Politics of Jesus*, Grand Rapids: Eerdmanns, 1972.

40. M. Smith's criticism, 'Zealots and *Sicarii*. Their Origin and Relation', *HTR* 64(1971) 1–19, has prompted more detailed studies such as D. Rhoads, *Israel in Revolution 6–74 c.e.*, and most recently, R. Horsley, 'The Zealots. Their Origin, Relationship and Importance in the Jewish Revolt', *NT* 28(1986) 159–92.

41. R. Horsley, 'Like one of the Prophets of Old: Two Types of Popular Prophets at the Time of Jesus', *CBQ* 46(1984) 471–95; 'Popular Messianic Movements at the Time of Jesus. Their Principal Features and Social Origins', *JSNT* 26(1986) 3–27; *Bandits, Prophets and Messiahs*, 135-89.

crossing of the Jordan—an exodus-style movement in reverse—only to have himself beheaded by the governor Fadus, and the most able-bodied of his followers slaughtered (*J.A.* 20:97–8; Ac 5:36). Finally, there is the case of the returned Egyptian prophet who led crowds of common people (from the countryside, according to *J.W.*) to the Mount of Olives in order to demonstrate how the walls of Jerusalem would fall, Jericho-like, at his command, but again the governor, Felix, moved in quickly with his troops, killing four hundred of the prophet's followers, even though he himself escaped (*J.A.* 20:169–71; *J.W.* 2:261–6; Ac 21:38).

Despite Josephus' rather disparaging account of all these episodes, it is not difficult to recognise a common pattern. There is no evidence of any militaristic intention, and hence these movements cannot be said to share the ideology of violence as espoused by the *sicarii* and the Zealots later. All three seem to expect a miraculous divine intervention, suggesting a heightened apocalyptic environment, and the followers of all three movements, not just the leaders, were ruthlessly dealt with by different Roman governors. Since they all originated in the country, Horsley claims that they are clear signs of the impoverished condition of the peasantry as a whole,[42] a position we do not fully share with regard to Galilee, in view of the discussion in the last chapter. Yet, two aspects are important for the present discussion. None of the movements in question occured in or near Galilee, nor, insofar as we are informed, did any Galileans participate. Secondly, the exodus/conquest motifs from Israel's past strongly suggest that the symbolism of the land may well have played a heightened role, at least in the case of the Egyptian, whose hopes were modelled on Josua's, but whose ire, significantly, was directed against Jerusalem.

On the basis of this evidence, we shall have to conclude that, unless the Jesus movement can be seen as a similar Galilean phenomenon, there is no other instance of a mass movement of Galileans that would fit such a category, or suggest that the memory of the conquest of the land played a significant role in the collective memory there in the first

42. *Bandits, Prophets, Messiahs*, 52–63; 'Popular Prophetic Movements', 12–14.

century, to the point of arousing apocalyptic expectations of an eminent deliverance. We shall leave final judgment on the Jesus movement until the next chapter, but it is appropriate at this juncture to point to the absence of any Roman intervention against him, either directly or on their behalf by Antipas. When eventually Rome did become involved, no attempt was made against any of Jesus' followers. Once again, the difference between conditions in Galilee and those prevailing under the procurators in Judea surface as being of vital significance to the inhabitants of both regions and their perception of their own situation in religious terms.

What of popular messianic manifestations? Again Horsley's analysis in terms of differentiation of social background, religious motivation and strategy is both helpful and challenging.[43] He argues that in the first century, alongside the royal Davidic messianism of the literate élites another form of hope in kingship resurfaced that had its roots in a more charismatic form of leadership, was popular, even revolutionary in its support-base and conditional on the king maintaining the egalitarian social values of the mosaic covenant. Even more significant for our purposes perhaps, is its northern provenance, as mainifested in the election of certain kings by such northern prophets as Elijah and Elisha, as well as the criticism of the official Davidic line by Jeremiah.[44] Horsley seeks to categorise the popular risings under Judas, son of Hezekiah, at Sepphoris in Galilee, that of Simon in Perea and Athronges in Idumea as examples of such popular movements, all of whom are said 'to aspire to kingship', βασιλεία, by leading popular revolts against the military and other strongholds that had been established by Herod the Great, at the time of his death (*J.A.* 17:271–85). Once again we shall postpone the question of how far Judas' action might be seen as a suitable analogue for Jesus' role in Galilee, simply noting the absence of any violent action on the part of Jesus—indeed, his avoidance of such places as Sepphoris entirely—or any moves

43. *Bandits, Prophets and Messiahs*, 110–17; 'Popular Messianic Movements', *CBQ* 46(1984) 471–95.

44. For this part of his analysis, Horsley is indebted to F.M. Cross, *Canaanite Myth and Hebrew Epic*, Cambridge, Mass.: Harvard University Press, 1973, 220f., 230.

against him by political authority, such as happened in the case of Judas, with the sacking of Sepphoris by Varus.

Insofar as such popular messianic movements could be said to be based in the country, and therefore concerned with land rights of the peasantry, the question arises as to whether the Judas episode fits into such a category, thus witnessing to a Galilean-based movement for a more equitable sharing of the land? Earlier, in discussing the incidence of social banditry in Galilee, we disagreed with Horsley's assessment of the economic situation of the peasantry, and equally in this instance we do not believe that the social basis of Judas' revolt was that of a disaffected peasantry, but rather the remnants of an ousted aristocracy that continued its efforts to restore Hasmonean control at the expense of the Herodians.[45] It may well be that Jesus who came from Nazareth, only four kilometres from Sepphoris, as Horsley reminds us, was at the centre of such a popular messianic movement, as Jn 6:14f. suggests, but the point here is, that if that is in fact the most appropriate designation of his role, it should not be based on the understanding that the armed revolt of Judas, son of Hezekiah, thirty years earlier, provides a suitable analogue for him.

A final probe of Galilean attitudes towards the land can be conducted in the light of the situation immediately prior to the first revolt. Various movements of protest surfaced in the period—seven groups in all are listed by Josephus for Jerusalem during the revolt—each with their different social and religious orientation. Yet a concern with 'the land' seems to have been common to all of them, especially its ownership and its purity in terms of its freedom from alien influences. We have met Jesus, son of Saphias in Tiberias more than once, and it is he rather than John of Gischala, who best represented the most radical expressions of these sentiments

45. See Freyne, *Galilee*, 214–16; Horsley, in 'Popular Messianic Movements', sees my suggestion about Judas espousing some recognisable form of kingship as based on the false supposition that 'the peasantry had no messianic ideas of their own, and were incapable of producing their own leadership' (483, n.32). But the question must surely be where are the peasantry likely to look for their leaders and in what role would they be likely to cast them? It certainly seems difficult to see the Judas episode as an example of Horsley's popular kingship in view of Josephus' explicit reference to the indiscriminate plundering in which Judas was engaged.

in a Galilean context, despite John's involvement in Jerusalem later.[46] On one occasion Jesus was able to arouse popular feeling against Josephus, even among the Galileans, by associating himself with claims that he was about to hand over the country χώρα to the Romans. Brandishing the law of Moses, he called on the people to abandon Josephus for his betrayal of their country's laws. (*Life* 129–35). It is difficult to decide whether χώρα here is being used in the religious sense we have been discussing, but the probability is that this is the case, even if Josephus is not specific on what particular laws would have been violated. Yet the fact that the Galileans 'from the land' readily support Josephus with tithes and other provisions counterbalances this more radicalised view of the sacredness of the land, which corresponds with other more radical expressions in Tiberias in this period.[47] This, we have claimed, suggests a less radical, but nonetheless religious view of the land and its produce, because of Josephus' priestly background and his appointment to Galilee by the Jerusalem council.

In exploring the nature of Galilean attachment to the land as symbolic of Yahweh's care for Israel, we have looked in particular for signs of Neusner's apocalyptic/messianist ideal type as a pointer to real feelings and attitudes towards the land within the province. The results on the whole have been meagre and scarcely support the view that the land functioned there as evocative of heightened, apocalyptic expectations, similar to other parts of the country. Rather, land and temple were important to Galilean peasant Jews, not as a call to radical action because of their deprivation, but as confirmatory of their position as small landowners blessed by nature, that is by the God of Israel, who resided in the Jerusalem temple. The importance of this conclusion for the overall argument of this study cannot be over-emphasised.

3. Galileans and the Torah

One of the stereotypes from studies about Galilee has been the claim that the Galileans were not fully observant in regard

46. Cf. U. Rappaport, 'John of Gischala: From Galilee to Jerusalem', *JJS* 33(1982) 479-90, especially 488f., on John's break with the moderates, due to their failure to support his claims in Galilee against Josephus.

47. Freyne, 'The Galileans', especially 403–5.

to torah. The real question, however, has to be, as Jacob Neusner pointed out in his review of my previous study, with whose version of what constituted *halakah* are they considered to be out of line?[48] Once the inhabitants of Galilee are classified as Jewish, the question of their torah-observance has already been answered in a general way, as the discussion of their attitude to the related symbols of temple and land in the present chapter has demonstrated. Torah, in the sense of the Pentateuch, the official account of Israel's election and constitution in the land by Yahweh's gracious goodness, with all the attendant responsibilities that were involved, is the most basic of the three symbols we are discussing—at once the foundation-myth and a description of a way of life. The torah-narrative tells how temple and land came to be central for Israel, and the stipulations regarding each are laid down in the legal sections of the document. Since, however, there had been major developments in regard to what should constitute torah in the narrower sense of 'God's will for Israel' during the second temple period, our present task is to determine how far these different understandings and developments had found their way to Galilee and under whose aegis? This question becomes critical in view of the determining role of social factors in shaping those different approaches to torah, alluded to at the outset of the present chapter. Furthermore, the gospel narratives also press the question, since they all presuppose opposition to Jesus within the province stemming from those whom we know to have had a special interest in the issue, namely, the scribes and Pharisees.

Two initial observations are called for before directly addressing the questions just posed. It would be generally agreed among N.T. scholars today that the debates and tensions between church and synagogue in the post-70 period had a fundamental influence on the formation of our gospels.[49] Since the scribes and Pharisees of Jesus' day were the fore-runners of those who refashioned Judaism after 70, there must be a general assumption which, to be sure, is open to

48. *JR* (1982) 429f; reprinted in a lengthier version as 'Galilee in the Time of Hillel: A Review', in *Formative Judaism. Religious, Historical and Literary Studies*, Brown Judaic Studies 37, Chico: Scholars Press, 1982, 65–70.

49. S. Freyne, 'Vilifying the Other and Defining the Self. Matthew's and John's Anti-Jewish polemic in Focus', in '*To See Ourselves as Others See Us*', 117–44.

refutation, that their narrative portrayal in the gospels will be polemically coloured, thus giving a false, or at least, a one-sided view of the situation in Jesus' day. Thus, the distorting influence of later controversies on the judgment as to the actual opponents that Jesus was likely to have encountered in Galilee needs to be carefully monitored.

There is a second distorting factor, however. By concentrating on the point of view of the literate groups, the Pharisees and Essenes in particular, we run the risk of misjudging the overall situation in another way. Though obviously influential, Josephus says that the Pharisees numbered no more than 6,000, and the Essenes were probably fewer still. The intensification of certain aspects of Jewish faith and practice that we associate with these various groups might lead to the assumption that these determined the total Jewish religious ethos. 'People of the land' may well have become a pejorative religious term later in rabbinic circles, but that should not lead us to the erroneous conclusion that the country Jews were unconcerned about the essentials of Jewish faith, as we have seen.[50] As always the silent majority leave very few traces of their views, and we are left to infer these from scattered pieces of evidence, literary as well as material potsherds, that may with sufficiently judicious juggling be shaped into a plausible pattern for that time and place.

In proposing the model of ideal types as a way of mapping the various strands of early Judaism, Neusner has listed the sage with the torah scroll alongside the priest and his altar and the freedom fighter with the coin of liberation. The discussion of the way these latter two might have functioned in Galilee has not been able to uncover any significant evidence for either—none at all in the case of the priest, and with no dominating frequency in the case of the freedom fighter. The scribe, however, had a wider range and a different social role in terms of the needs of the whole community. Already in the

50. In the light of Neusner's overall approach to the rabbinic corpus, I can no longer concur with Oppenheimer's conclusions that the issues surrounding the *ammey ha'arez* are much earlier than the actual texts, as I did in *Galilee*, 308 and 327 (cf. p.336 n.7). His concern with the social issues behind such disputes is laudable; but post-Neusner, the historical significance of rabbinic statements can no longer be judged independently of the intention of the document as a whole and its social setting. Cf. further, Goodman, 102–4.

second century BCE in the person of the Jerusalem sage, Jesus ben Sirach, one can see how torah-learning and demotic wisdom—the direct result of the universalist spirit of the hellenistic age—could be combined in a thoroughly Jewish framework that is deeply conscious of the special election of Israel.[51] As a class the scribes had continued to grow in importance, and those who belonged to the Pharisaic party, in addition to their professional and advisory role in the various administrations, were also involved in fashioning a way of life for the pious Jew, even away from the temple and the land. Yet Jerusalem was their centre and the seat of their authority, where, it seems, they vied with the priestly aristocracy in terms of social importance, as the arbiters of what constituted the proper way of life for Jews, even in cultic matters.

Given this social role for all of Judaism, it is not surprising to find representatives of the scribal class in Galilee also. In this regard the gospel picture would appear to be both realistic and reliable, but because of the shadow of subsequent controversies over these accounts, we shall do well first to examine the other evidence for both scribal teaching and Pharisaic presence within the province.[52] In truth, however, it is not possible to name more than a handful of native Galilean teachers from our documentary sources. Apart from Jesus of Nazareth, there is Judas the Galilean, who is described by Josephus as a σοφιστής, having close ties with the Pharisees (*J.W.* 2:118), Eleazar who came from Galilee and taught at the court of Izates, the king of Adiabne, 'a man with the reputation for being extremely strict when it came to interpreting ancestral laws' (*J.A.* 20:43), and Yose, the Galilean, whom we meet among the Yavnean scribes.[53] What is

51. M. Hengel, *Judentum und Hellenismus*, 252–72; J.T. Sanders, *Ben Sira and Demotic Wisdom*, *SBLMS* 28, Chico: Scholars Press, 1983.

52. The tendency in the Synoptic tradition, particularly in Matthew, to combine scribes and Pharisees is generally recognised as a very definite result of the later polemics, though Luke has preserved the distinction accurately, Lk 11:37,45. Cf. *Galilee*, 306f. and 335 n.2.

53. According to J. Lightstone, 'Yose the Galilean in Mishnah-Tosefta and the History of Early Rabbinic Judaism', *JJS* 31(1980) 37–45, the traditions preserved in his name stand outside the mainstream concerns of other Yavneans, thus attesting to the diversity of interests that were fused then. However, Lightstone does not have any suggestions as to why such a peripheral tradition was preserved, and the question of its possible links with Galilee does not even arise.

noteworthy about all of these is that they are to be found teaching outside Galilee itself, but at important centres such as among the Babylonian exiles or at the centre of scribism, be it Jerusalem or Yavneh.

Viewed in this light, Jesus' teaching in Jerusalem is not at all incongruous, even if it has been charged with deeper theological meaning by the evangelists. Yet this attraction to the centre should not be mistaken for a lack of interest in teachers by the Galilean populace. The anecdote of Johanan ben Zakkai's condemnation of Galilee because of his own poor reception during 20 years spent at Arav (*y Shabb* 16, 15d), is now seen by Neusner, not as biographical in any sense, but as reflecting a search for an earlier precedent to the Ushan teachers' move from the south to Galilee in the mid-second century CE.[54] It therefore must be taken to reflect much later views about Galileans and their attitude to torah. The case of the Babylonian Jew, Zamaris, whom Herod planted in Batanea, is much closer to our concern for first-century attitudes, and according to Josephus, people flocked to him from every quarter because of his interpretation of the laws (*J.A.* 17:26–31). Unfortunately, the information is no more specific, but it surely is not without some relevance for Galilean country Jews, in view of the contacts between the two regions, suggested by both material remains and literary sources.

These examples are too few, too scattered and too diverse in their underlying attitudes to give grounds for any conclusions on the social role of the scribe in Galilee. A more promising approach, therefore might be to examine the evidence for the role of the synagogue there in the period that interests us, especially since the gospels assume that it was a firmly established institution for the province, not merely as a house of prayer and scripture reading (*beth tefillîm*, Lk 4:16–30) but also as a place where scribal teaching was disseminated

54. Compare his recent statement, 'The History of a Biogrpahy. Yohanan ben Zakkai in the Canonical Literature of Formative Judaism', in *Formative Judaism. Religious, Historical and Literary Studies*, 5th series, Brown Judaic Studies, 91, Chico: Scholars Press, 1985, 79–86, with his earlier, *Development of a Legend. Studies in the Traditions concerning Yohanan ben Zakkai*, Leiden: Brill, 1970.

(*beth midrash*, Mk 1:22.39).[55] It should be remembered that despite the democratisation of educational as well as other aspects of life in hellenistic times as indeed is also the case today many would claim, the society's educational system served mostly to preserve the position and priorities of its dominant social class.[56] If the priest and his altar was confined to Jerusalem, and so had to depend on loyalty to the system which they controlled to bring the people to them, the scribe with his torah scroll operated under no such constraints, and the synagogue, as the alternative holy place of the future, was a natural focal point for his activity, even while the temple still stood.

The archaeological evidence for pre-70 synagogues is still disappointingly meagre. Yet there are *some* Galilean remains, most notably from Gamla, which for reasons already discussed can serve as typical of Galilee for our purposes also.[57] As mentioned already, the suggestion has been made that its seating arrangement—rows of tiered steps or seats around the four walls—points to the egalitarian nationalism of the immediate pre-war period, but this inference is not at all obvious, though the presence of a *miqva*, or ritual bath in close proximity suggests that it may have been used only for religious purposes, thus anticipating the Galilean synagogues of a much later time. These would certainly include education, or study of the torah, though later separate rooms for study are found, with the increased sacralisation of the main synagogue room itself, including the *bema* and torah-shrine as permanent features. According to *Life* 277 the synagogue at Tiberias was used for a community meeting, and this would almost certainly have been a feature of its social function in the pre-70 period generally. Thus we do not have to postulate a building as elaborate as that of Gamla, or presumably even Capernaum, to accept the gospel picture

55. The absence of any explicit reference to prayer as part of the synagogue worship in the pre-70 Theodotus inscription from Jerusalem, has been noted by L. Levine, in 'The Second Temple Synagogue', p.17, as striking. In the gospels and Acts the temple is mentioned as a place of prayer, but not the synagogue explicitly. Cf. also L. Hoffman, *The Canonisation of the Synagogue Service*, Notre Dame: University Press, 1979, who is not able to adduce any clear evidence for the prayers of the synagogue liturgy during Second Temple times.

56. Carney, *Models of the Past*, 107.

57. Cf. ch. 5 above, nn. 42 and 51.

that communal places of meeting, whether large houses or alley ways even, were widely diffused in Galilee in Jesus' day, and were multi-purpose in function, including meetings of the whole village on the Sabbath.

It is also widely accepted that together with the synagogue, the home was central to the educational system of Judaism, insofar as knowledge of torah was absolutely fundamental to the Jewish way of life, and therefore taken seriously as part of parental responsibility. The home also was the place of celebration of marriages, funerals and circumcisions. Yet public reading and interpretation of the written torah can be documented from a very early stage (cf. Neh 8:8). Apart from the general acceptance of the torah as God's word for his people, consultation of the sacred text at times of national and local crisis was as essential for Jews as was consultation of omens and oracles by pagan people (see 1 Macc 3:46–48). The figure of Jesus of Tiberias with a copy of the law of Moses in his hand as he attempted to incite his fellow-citizens against Josephus, is indicative in this regard. Thus Luke's depiction of Jesus' visit to the Nazareth synagogue is a precious insight into the inner workings of such a gathering in the Second Temple period, particularly in regard to the centrality of the scriptural reading, even when Lucan stylisation of the form and content of the story can be recognised.[58]

The Aramaic paraphrase that was made for the benefit of those who could not properly understand 'the holy tongue' is particularly important in terms of the reception of the torah among the ordinary people. In the light of Bruce Chilton's comparative studies of the Isaiah Targum and the Jesus-sayings' tradition this could prove to be a most fruitful source of our understanding of popular attitudes outside those circles that were particularly concerned with developing their own distinctive halachah. However, as is well known, the

58. B. Chilton, in *God in Strength. Jesus' Announcement of the Kingdom*, Freistadt: Verlag F. Plöchl, 1979, 123–78; and also in 'Announcement in Nazara', in R.T. France and D. Wenham, eds., *Gospel Perspectives*, II, Sheffield: JSOT Press, 1981, acknowledges the adaptation of the scene to the Diaspora setting as in Ac 13:13–42, yet claims that it can be used as a pointer to Palestinian synagogue practice. It could be suggested that Galilean synagogues, as least at the larger centres, did not differ appreciably from those in the Diaspora. This of course would not include Nazareth.

problem of Targum dating is one on which experts in the field are sharply divided,[59] but Chilton's statement on the matter is nuanced: on the basis of language and theme, Jesus is familiar with the interpretative tradition which is preserved in the Isaiah Targum and he presumes his hearers' familiarity with that tradition.[60] In the next chapter we shall return to this suggestion, but for our present purposes it is sufficient to note that the process of making the sacred text known and applying its message to various life-situations of the common people was a central function of the reading of the law and the prophets in the synagogue, quite independently of the more formal schooling that later came to be associated with that institution. We cannot say who precisely performed the role of *meturgamen* or interpreter in the earlier period. Obviously it had to be somebody of both learning and social stature, and in this regard Jesus' criticism of the scribes and Pharisees who seek seats of honour in the synagogue and salutations in the market-place, strongly suggests that they were prime contenders for the role, at least in certain circumstances. However, the fact that the rabbis developed their own schools in the Yavnean and Ushan periods and do not appear to have controlled the synagogues in the second century,[61] though obviously highly influential in those circles, is a strong indication that earlier, at least in Galilee, the synagogues had their own distinctive personnel, other than the scribes and Pharisees. Such local functionaries as the synagogue-leader (ἀρχισυνάγωγος), the ruler (ἄρχων), the elders (πρεσβύτεροι) and the village scribe (κωμογραμματεύς) are known to us from both inscriptional and literary sources, including

59. M. McNamara, in *Targum and Testament,* Shannon, Irish University Press, 1972, and more recently *Palestinian Judaism and the New Testament*, Wilmington, Del., 1983, 205–53, adopts a conservative approach on the matter, believing that the Palestinian Targum to the Pentateuch, especially as represented in Codex Neofiti, is old and therefore can be used for comparative study of the N.T. He has been sharply criticised by, among others, Jacob Neusner and Joseph Fitzmyer.

60. *A Galilean Rabbi and His Bible, Jesus' Use of the Interpreted Bible of His Time*, Wilmington, Del.: Glazier, 1984, 148.

61. On the developing role and unique status of the Rabbi, as embodying torah in the later period, cf. J. Neusner, *Midrash in Context*, Philadelphia: Fortress, 1984, However, he still recognises the validity of his earlier study, 'Studies in the *Taqqanoth* of Yavneh', *HTR* 63(1970) 183–98, dealing with the influence of the historical Yohanan on the liturgical decrees passed at Yavneh as well as with the synagogue service in the light of the destruction of the temple.

the gospels, and any of these, because of their position of influence, wealth or learning could naturally be expected to fill the role of interpreter also.[62]

The extension of the Jewish school to areas outside Jerusalem must be seen against the larger context of the hellenistic spirit, in its positive as well as its negative impact on Judaism. In this regard it must be remembered that part of Antiochus' reform was the establishment of a gymnasium along Greek lines at Jerusalem, and it is scarcely surprising that there is a heavy emphasis on study and schools in the literature emanating from the Essenes and Pharisees, both groups emerging as a direct result of the religious resistance to the hellenistic reform. The centrality of study for the Qumranic Essenes is easily documented, both from the archaeology of the site and their literature (1Q S 6:6–8, e.g.), and Josephus tells us of their concern to educate the young (*J.W.* 2:159, cf. 120). That there were differing Pharisaic halachic positions from an early stage would also be generally accepted, however difficult it may now be to recover anything of the historical Hillel, not to mention Shammai. One can readily recognise later *Tendenzen* in the Talmudic reports that it was the early Pharisaic teachers, Simeon ben Shetah and Josua ben Gamla, who established the schools throughout Israel (y Ket 32c; b Bab Bat 21a), yet when we look for other possible agents of such a development it would be difficult to suggest an alternative, unless one is to attribute it to the Hasmonean judaising concerns more generally.

Apart from the gospels, Josephus is our best, indeed our only guide to the impact that these developments had had on Galilean life in the first century, even if we must beware of his alleged pro-Pharisaic tendencies in both *J.A.* and *Life*.[63] Even

62. The ἀρχισυνάγωγος is known from the first century Theodotos inscription from Jerusalem as well as from numerous others throughout late antiquity (cf. Lk 8:49; 13:1). For a review of the evidence cf. B.J. Brooten, *Women Leaders in Ancient Synagogues*, Brown Judaic Series 36, 1982. The κωμογραμματεῦς is also known from the Vienna and many other papyri and inscriptions. Josephus (*J.A.* 16:203), shows that the role was known in Palestine also in Herodian times.

63. Considerable differences of opinion continue among scholars as to the role of the Pharisaic movement, depending on the significance that is attached to Josephus' accounts in his different works. J. Neusner, following Morton Smith, is sceptical of both *J.A.* and *Life* and therefore maintains his earlier description based on *J.W.* that from the mid-first century b.c. they had been transformed 'from politics to piety'. Any historical gleanings that can be got from either the gospels or rabbinic sources

when due allowance is made for such a possibility, it is quite remarkable that a delegation sent from Jerusalem, partly at least at the instigation of a leading Pharisaic scribe, Simeon ben Gamaliel, was singularly unsuccessful in unseating Josephus. According to his account the delegation of four included three Pharisees, two from the popular party and one aristocrat, along with a member from a priestly background (*Life* 197f.). The Pharisees were chosen to convince the Galileans that they were better informed about the ancestral laws than was Josephus, and Jesus of Tiberias called for their acceptance, not merely because of their noble origins but because of their understanding (σύνεσις, *Life* 278).

Let us presume for now that there is some basis for this report of the delegation's composition, since it is difficult to see how such information could have served to extol the Pharisees in Roman eyes, especially in view of the outcome. It points to the fact that the Pharisees did not have wide popular appeal in Galilee despite John of Gischala's contacts with Simeon. Admittedly, there are some examples from the same period of what might be considered rigorist, Galilean attitudes on matters of Jewish piety—all of which we have encountered earlier in discussing the social world: the insistence on circumcision for the gentile noblemen from Trachonitis, the destruction of Herod's palace with its animal representations and the desire of the Jewish residents of Caesarea Philippi to use only native oil. Of these, only the latter could clearly be said to have affinity to specific sectarian halachic concerns, whereas the other two episodes are, we saw, best explained as being due to the social tensions of the time, despite the religious guise.[64]

confirm the picture of the Pharisees as a party concerned with table-fellowship and dietary laws, see 'Three Pictures of the Pharisees: A Reprise', in *Formative Judaism* (Fifth Series) 51–78. Sanders on the other hand is less critical of Josephus, while allowing for some exaggeration in his later works, and takes the Pharisees to be 'lay experts in the law', as Josephus affirms in *J.W.* (2:162) as well as in *J.A.* and *Life*, (in *Jesus and Judaism*, 388f., n.59 and 194–8.) Both positions will now have to take account of the approach and conclusions of D. Schwartz, 'Josephus and Nicolaus on the Pharisees', *JSJ* 14(1983) 157–71, who adopts a source-critical approach, and finds that, if anything, there is a suppression of information about the Pharisees in *J.W.*, whereas material, possibly damaging to the Pharisees, is in fact included in *J.A.*

64. See J. Baumgarten, 'The Essene Avoidance of Oil and the Laws of Purity', *RQ* 6(1967) 184–92.

Our probe for non-gospel evidence of specific concerns with halachic matters and disputes in Galilee, as these are known to us from the sectarian literature, has had largely negative results. In a separate excursus it is proposed to show that no historical significance for our period can be safely attributed to those references to the Galileans in rabbinic literature. It may well be that an argument from silence is all that is possible, since it was hoped to mount a profile of the (largely) silent majority. Before opting for such a conclusion, however, some discussion of the gospel evidence itself is called for, in the light of the social world already described and the general concern with torah-knowledge, as this has been outlined in the previous pages. In view of the scepticism that is often encountered with regard to the gospels' portrayal of things Jewish, it is at least worth while reminding ourselves with Geza Vermes that perhaps the N.T. itself is out best guide to matters of Palestinian Judaism in the first century.[65]

According to the author of the Fourth Gospel, it was the Jerusalem Pharisaic point of view that to be Galilean was to be ignorant of the law, and therefore accursed (7:49.51). What, if any, substance is there to such a characterisation, even recognising its deeply ironic thrust within the work as a whole?[66] The only other comparable piece of evidence is the attribution to Johanan ben Zakkai already discussed. Otherwise Galileans are portrayed as observing the Sabbath (*J.A.* 13:337; *Life* 158; *J.W.* 2:634), faithful to the pilgrimage, concerned about defilement of the temple, paying their tithes, and some, at least, as being opposed to uncircumcised gentiles in their midst (*Life* 112f., 148–54). In this last instance the Jerusalem priestly aristocrat with Pharisaic associations, Josephus, calls those who were concerned 'Ιυδαῖοι, not the usual Γαλιλαῖοι, and this could well be a slip that reveals the true Jerusalem attitude towards Galileans, matched by the reference at Jn 6:52, namely, that only some Galileans were genuinely concerned with the religious identity of Jewish life. Undoubtedly, there were social divisions between Jerusale-

65. See 'Jewish Literature and New Testament Exegesis: Reflections on Methodology', in *Jesus and the World of Judaism*, 74–88.

66. See Culpepper, *The Anatomy of the Fourth Gospel*, 169–80, especially, 178f.; Freyne, 'Vilifying the Other and Defining the Self', 123–8.

mites and Galileans, and these social tensions, which were everywhere in antiquity, may well have manifested themselves in a sense of religious superiority and disparagement of the ignorance of the country folk in a culture that was essentially religious. In the case of the Galileans, however, there was the added ingredient from the Jerusalem perspective of being suspect by living in the environs of pagan culture and of being cut off from the Jerusalem centre by the Samaritan territory, which was viewed as both socially and religiously hostile. Rather than accepting the statement about the Galileans' ignorance of the law as part of a widespread point of view in the first century, therefore, it would seem better to see it in the light of this background.

Admittedly, the Fourth Gospel shows definite signs of hostile interaction with what can loosely be described as Yavnean Judaism with its emphasis on study and the law.[67] Hence the attitude expressed may be seen as the beginning of an invective against Galileans that finds its ultimate expression in the saying attributed to Johanan much later. In that event it would be fair to assume that the success of 'the Galileans', that is, those who were followers of Jesua ha-Nozri, by the end of the first century CE may well have contributed to the attempt to disparage Galileans made by the Jewish authorities with whom the Johannine Christians had contacts that were far from friendly. However, this conclusion, based on a very changed situation to that which obtained some seventy years earlier, would seem to preclude any such attitudes towards Galileans being formulated at the time of Jesus, even when Galileans were noticeable by their accents in Jerusalem.

Mark, followed by Matthew, has scribes coming from Jerusalem to challenge the authority of Jesus and his disciples' non-observance of the hand-washing regulations (3:22; 7:1). Though there may have been local scribes whose social function was wider than that of torah-teachers, of whom Luke's νομοδιδάκαλοι from every village of Galilee (5:17) could possibly be an example, there is little doubt that Jerusalem was the centre of scribal as well as priestly

67. See S. Pancaro, *The Law in the Fourth Gospel*, Leiden: Brill 1975; J.L. Martyn, *History and Theology in the Fourth Gospel*, rev. edn, Nashville, 1979.

authority as long as the temple was standing. Isaiah and Micah had spoken of the law going forth from Mt Zion, as well as the nations streaming there on pilgrimage (Is 2:2f; Mi 4:4–6). According to Ben Sirach, wisdom, identified with the law, had chosen Mt Zion as her dwelling-place, and the scribe, as the expounder of wisdom, has a role that is urban and court-centred, based on the Solomonic and Ancient Near Eastern origins of wisdom generally (Sir 24; 39:1–11). It has been suggested earlier that Jerusalem scribism, viewed as a professional class, was interested in propagating the study of torah throughout the country already in the Hasmonean period, often no doubt, vying with local teachers and interpreters. Their teaching about the advent of Elijah was known to the Galilean disciples according to Mk 9:11, reflecting their desire to foster conversion to their way of life through arousing expectation of the imminent return of this northern-based prophet who would re-establish the tribes of Jacob (Sir 48:1–12). And even if we must dispense with the anecdote of Yohanan residing in Arav for forty years, the case of Saul of Tarsus, an eager student of torah at Jerusalem, receiving letters of commendation from the sanhedrin in order to go and persecute 'those of this way' at Damascus (Ac 9:1), is a good example of torah-zeal emanating from Jerusalem. Finally there is the composition of the delegation already referred to which was sent from Jerusalem to unseat Josephus, with the underlying assumption both in Jerusalem and in Galilee that the former place was the centre of 'accurate knowledge and strict interpretation of our laws'.

In the light of such evidence there seems every reason to accept Mark's picture, since control of the various media of education, including the synagogue, was a vital element in their struggle for power with the priestly aristocracy. Indeed, their ability to convince the country people to be faithful to pilgrimage and offerings played into the hands of the more aloof priestly aristocrats and served as the real power-broker between these two potential rivals at the centre of power—the priest and his altar and the scribe with his torah-scroll.

It was Luke who gave the most complete picture of the Pharisees in the Galilean setting, combining religious separatism with economic power to establish an élitist control which Jesus challenged. How realistic is such a picture for first-century Galilee? Is it rather one that has been constructed on the basis of Luke's Diaspora experience in order to paint a suitable picture for Jesus' social gospel? Since the ancients did not have economic theories or concepts for analysing the workings of their economies, the choice of typical characters is perfectly understandable. Earlier, when dealing with the social world we suggested that such characters and attitudes could fit well into a 'limited goods' setting, especially if we accept Josephus' placing of the Pharisees among the townspeople (*J.A.* 18:15).[68] John of Gischala, religiously committed, but commercially entrepreneurial, would fit the picture well, even though the sources merely indicate his friendship with the Pharisee, Simon, without, however, saying that he himself was a Pharisee.

Not all Galilean villages were tiny hamlets, and the material conditions of some, at least, could not have differed very much from those of the urban middle and upper classes, despite an overall ethos that was more homogenous, and therefore, more conservative. There was, we have maintained, differentiation in social terms, even within the village. Mark's hybrid, κωμοπόλις, may well be an attempt to capture the character of such places as Capernaum, Corozain and Bethsaida, all situated within close proximity to each other and with their status determined by the produce of both the plain and the lake of Gennesar. They would have been natural settings for Luke's Pharisees and they are also the places upbraided by Jesus for their rejection of his ministry, with its radical implications in the name of a new understanding of God's will for those with possessions, as we shall see. It was in the more 'urban' settings that the rigorist attitudes also surfaced in the immediate pre-war period, but these were not

68. This is one of those allegedly pro-Pharisaic passages in *J.A.* which is regarded as a product of the situation in the nineties, by Smith, Neusner and others. However, Schwartz's source-critical analysis does not allow for such an easy dismissal of its contents. Granted the intention to paint an acceptable picture of the Pharisees, even Neusner's sect, concerned with table-fellowship and dietary laws, would seem to belong to an urban rather than a rural environment. For the suggestion of a plausible social world for the Pharisees, cf. E. Rivkin, 'The Internal City: Judaism and Urbanisation', *JSSR* 5(1966) 225–40, even when his analysis of the rabbinic sources is less than convincing in terms of Neusner's methodology.

typical of Galileans generally, it seemed, and in view of the urban/rural tensions that operated generally the reasons were social as well as religious.

The torah-symbol, that is the written scroll which was believed to contain God's word to Moses for his people, like those of land and temple, does not therefore seem to have generated the same amount of competing viewpoints in Galilee as in Jerusalem. This conclusion, based on a sifting of the available evidence and an attempt at a critical correlation of religious beliefs and social circumstances, helps to confirm further our earlier, tentative conclusions. We have been able to suggest an appropriate context for Jesus' disputes with the scribes and Pharisees within the province, without having to postulate that either he or the Galileans were lax, or unrepentant members of the *am ha aretz* or that Galilee was torn by halachic disputes, based on different understandings of the written torah and its demands. As peasants, the Galileans were more concerned with the harvest than with the holy war (*J.W.* 4:84), and it is not surprising that traces of Essenic influence are singularly lacking from any of the discussions and debates represented by Jesus' sayings. While Jerusalem scribism was able to ensure that the basic demands of the written torah, especially those relating to the central sanctuary, were carried out, their wishes corresponded on the whole with the peasants' aspirations. Yet because of social as well as economic factors operating in that milieu, Pharisaism, as an intensification of those basic demands, had little attraction for those same peasants. Their later characterisation as ignorant of the law, stemming from rabbinic circles, may not have aided us in reconstructing first-century attitudes, but it does point to the ongoing problems, based on those same social and cultural factors, that the successors of the scribes and Pharisees were to encounter, when eventually, rural Galilee was no longer just a mission territory for them, but their actual homeland.

Conclusion. The priest and his altar was in distant Jerusalem. The freedom-fighter with his messianic/apocalyptic hopes and his coins inscribed 'for the liberation of Zion' was a product more of Jerusalem and Judean religious, social and political conditions than of those obtaining in Galilee, even though the province did not escape the ravages of war which their programme ultimately involved for the whole nation. The scribe with his torah-scroll, and his devotees, the Pharisees, were to some extent the indirect result of an alien bureaucracy, now judaised, who proposed a way of life that was as impractical as it was unattractive to peasants. Is there then any place for a new religious movement in this conservative, essentially rural Galilee? To answer that question adequately we shall have to critically assess the message and ministry of Jesus in that setting and among those people, since it is his movement alone that appears to break the mould there, and has given for ever a new meaning to the epithet Galilean.

That there were those, even among the immediate family of Jesus, who were searching for other ways can be seen from the example of his brother James, known in later tradition as the *sadiq*, that is, as one dedicated to a particular form of Jewish piety that had its roots in the apocalyptic-hasidic viewpoint.[69] His devotion took him to Jerusalem and its temple, and eventually into the Jesus movement there, but as a restraining voice. Hence, 'those inhabitants of the city who were considered the most fair-minded, and were strict in the observance of the laws', (Josephan for the Pharisees) were deeply offended at his execution by the high priest Ananus (*J.A.* 20:199–203)—another Galilean whose challenge to the temple aristocracy, modest as it was, could not be tolerated. Yet ultimately it is for Galilean rather than Jerusalem attitudes that he is an important figure. Were there others like him in Galilee? Speculation about Elijah's return seems to have been in the air, and in John's portrayal Galileans who later joined Jesus' permanent retinue, had been in Judea as disciples of the Baptist. Are they stirrings of a general discontent or individuals who escaped the net of religious, economic and social conservatism?

Excursus: The Galileans in the Rabbinic Literature

Jacob Neusner's review of my previous study of Galilee

69. See M. Hengel, 'Jakobus der herrnbrüder—der erste Päpst?' in *Glaube und Eschatologie. Festschrift für W.G. Kümmel*, Tübingen: J.C.B. Mohr, 1985, 71–104.

concentrated particularly on my efforts to use rabbinic sources in reconstructing Galilean religious attitudes. Since then he himself has considerably developed his methodological presuppositions and spelled these out much more clearly than in his earlier writings, which were available to me when engaged in my previous study of Galilee. He now sees that the primary task is to describe the different Judaisms that are represented in the various writings which make up the rabbinic corpus, distinguishing each in terms of the statement it seeks to make within the changing social and religious setting of late antiquity. It is a truly pioneering programme that has not always been enthusiastically received, but which cannot be ignored by anyone concerned with the critical study of Judaism.

Christian scholars need particularly to examine their approaches, since in the past many who have been adept in applying form and redactional methods to the study of biblical texts have been quite content to accept uncritically a synthetic view of Judaism gleaned from sources that are quite disparate both in time of compilation and geographic setting. One does not have to agree with all of Neusner's conclusions in order to take seriously his scholarly agenda and enter into critical dialogue with it. This means in our case evaluating the individual pieces of evidence relating to Galilee in the light of the overall concerns of the work in which they occur. When such an analysis has been completed it may well be that because of correspondences with other pieces of evidence from the pre-70 period earlier traditions in the rabbinic writings may also be detected, traditions which Neusner freely admits are contained in the documents in question, but which he is reluctant to evaluate in terms of their documentary value for the earlier period.

On examination, almost all the references to Galilee and Galileans in the earliest document, the Mishnah, would appear to be illustrative of what in Neusner's view are the basic concerns of the framers of the completed document. These were the removal of grey areas of the law, the exclusion of middle ground and the resolution of doubtful cases—an agenda that was the direct result of the application of a legal imagination to the crisis besetting Jewish religious faith in the wake of the Bar Cochba war.[70]

Several references have to do with differences in weights and measures between Judea and Galilee (Ket 5:9; Kel 2:2; Hull 11:2; Ter 10:8). In these instances it is clearly in the interest of all concerned with careful observance to know what precise amounts they are liable for, and thus have all doubts removed. Equally, different local customs in regard to marriage and passover ritual are used to work out the intricacies of the laws in question about the times for discharging certain obligations (Ket 4:12; Pes 4:5). Traditional divisions can be brought into play by the use of the formula 'Three countries are distinguished concerning...Judea, Galilee and Beyond the Jordan', in discussing the extent to which a particular law is binding and whether or not recognised territorial limits change the obligations in question (Gitt 7:7; Shebb 9:2; Ket 13:10; Bab Bat 3:2; cf. Bab Kam 10:9; Pes 4:5).

The destruction of Galilee is seen as one of the signs of the evil times before the coming of the Messiah, who, however, is not assigned any redemptive role, since it is deeds of piety in accordance with the ideal of the sages that will ensure participation in the world to come (Sot 9:15)[71] Galilean apathy towards the teaching of the sages would appear to lie behind this particular reference to Galilee then. (cf. Yad 4:8).

In the interpretation of vows their binding effect is determined by the intention of those who made them, and this can be inferred on the basis of assumptions of what the inhabitants of different regions mean in using certain terms. The Galileans (at least for purposes of working out the implications of this principle) are presumed by R. Judah to be less well informed than the Judeans on the specific details of certain temple offerings, and hence their vows were presumed to be less specific (Ned 2:4). Finally, in a discussion on the applicability of vows concerning the assignment of one's share of public property, the same R. Judah, in what looks

70. Neusner, *Judaism, The Evidence of the Mishnah*, ch. 6.

71. See J. Neusner, *Messiah in Context. Israel's History and Destiny in Formative Judaism*, Philadelphia: Fortress Press, 1984, 25–31.

like an independent addition, asserts that the Galileans need not assign their portion, since this had already been done for them by their forefathers (Ned 5:5).

If one were to press further and ask how far any of this evidence might or might not be used in documenting pre-70 conditions in Galilee, it would be necessary to face an almost insurmountable task, given the ahistorical nature of the document as a whole and its predominant concerns. To say, for example, that the Mishnah is familiar with the threefold division of Jewish territory, dating back to Pompey's dismantling of the Hasmonean state is not to claim anything of particular moment. Similarly, local customs can be presumed without any great danger of distortion. But what is one to make of R. Judah's statements that Galileans are ignorant of or not responsible for certain matters pertaining to the temple (Ned 2:4; 5:5), in view of the fact that elsewhere they are said to agree with Jerusalem teaching against that of Judea generally (Ket 4:12). Both references are attributed to R. Judah (not the Prince), a contemporary of R. Meir, and in the second instance (Ned 5:5) the reference to the Galileans is attached to the discussion in quite a secondary fashion.[72] Were the comments prompted by genuine information about the Galileans and the temple, however acquired? Or are they simply hypothetical examples to sort out the legal implications of the principles under discussion? Or do they reflect experiences in Galilee of second-century rabbis? The indications are that the observations in question are the result of one or both of these latter possibilities. Nothing can be gleaned from them in terms of pre-70 attitudes.

If, then, the foundation document of Judaism shows little or no concern with historical realities in Galilee of an earlier period, one must be even more sceptical of the later Talmudic references to specific aspects of Galilean life. Goodman's study, *State and Society in Roman Galilee* has shown interesting correspondences between the rabbinic documents' presumed social worlds and that which can be inferred from the archaeology of Galilee and other literary sources, but there is the problem of demonstrating whether or not the world of

72. See J. Neusner, *A History of the Mishnaic Law of Women,* Part Three, Leiden: Brill, 1980, 48.

these documents (Mishnah, Tosefta, Yerushalmi, in particular) is in fact Galilee, even if one assumes that they were produced within the province from the second to the fourth century CE[73]

It is, however, possible to suggest some broad tendencies in the documents in question in their specific references to Galilee and Galileans, related to the conditions that are known to have existed at the time of their compilation. Yerushalmi contains Johanan ben Zakkai's famous dictum concerning Galilee's lack of concern with torah and the prediction of its ultimate destruction (y Shabb 16:15d). Yet balancing this negative evaluation is the declaration that the Galileans prefer honour rather than money, in contrast to the Judeans (y Ket 4:29b). The Babylonian Talmud develops considerably the characterisation of the Galileans as ignorant of torah, sharply distinguishing between the *haberim* in the province and the *am ha-aretz*. (b Hag 24b; b Nid 6a). They are quarrelsome (b Ned 48a) and ignorant (b Ned 18b/19a). Their distinctive accent, known already to the gospel writers, disqualifies them from reading aloud in the synagogue worship, and their general laxity in matters of torah learning is contrasted with Judean concerns in the same matter (b Erub 53a/b; see b Meg 24b). Even Galilean sages can be pilloried, such as Yose because he spoke to a strange woman in public (b Erub 53b), or the Galilean who dared to expound on the chariot in Babylon and was struck dead (b Shabb 80b). Proximity to the land of the Cutheans (Samaritans) is deemed to make the Galileans suspect in matters of purity (b Hag 24b), and Judeans and Galileans are said to be in constant conflict (b Bab Bat 38a/b).

These, and other examples, would seem to point to struggles for control between the sages on the one hand and the more general practice of Jewish belief in Galilee on the other, such as that associated with the great synagogues, e.g. The question of who determined the religious ethos of these is still an open one, as Neusner recognises.[74] We have, then, learned from Neusner's criticism and avoided using these

73. See P. Schäfer's review of Goodman's study, *JJS* 37(1976) 108.
74. See his *Judaism in Society, The Evidence of Yerushalmi. Towards the Natural History of a Religion*, Chicago: University Press, 1983, 151–69.

references to Galilee and Galileans for purposes of understanding the Jewish world of Galilee in the first century. Yet when all that is conceded, it has to be acknowledged that some of the patterns that developed, in a highly rabbinic way to be sure, reflect, however dimly, conditions we know to have existed in the first century already. The Mishnah and its apologists/commentators were not concerned with history, as Neusner's brilliant analysis of the generative principles underlying these works has shown. Yet, by that same standard, the contrast with the early Christian writings—their narrative form and concern with locality—is all the more striking.

CHAPTER SEVEN

Jesus and His Movement In Galilee

THE outline of Jesus' ministry in Galilee is the same in all the gospels—a ministry of healing *and* teaching that is essentially itinerant in character, though some more permanent association with either Cana or Capernaum is suggested; enthusiastic crowds from every quarter, not just Galilee itself, come to him and he is sympathetic to their needs; from the beginning he is accompanied by a small band of permanent followers, later to be symbolically designated 'the Twelve'; opposition from within the province is religious rather than political in tone, even though the Herodians are mentioned in conjunction with the Pharisees; yet Jerusalem is the main source of opposition and it is there that Jesus ultimately meets his fate, while predicting vindication for himself and his followers in apocalyptic terms.

The historian is faced with many difficulties in attempting to assess this picture against the backdrop of the social world already described and the stability of attachment to the basic symbols of temple, land and torah among Galilean peasants that was established in the last chapter. If the social and religious situation was as we have described it, then it is difficult to see how a charismatic/prophetic ministry, such as that which Jesus conducted, had any significant role to play there. One might postulate that insofar as the hellenistic ethos had corroded some of the more stable and conservative values of peasant life, dissatisfaction was inherent in the situation, and the Jesus movement would have had fertile ground on which to work. But Jesus' ministry was to the village culture of Galilee rather than to the more urbanised community, as far as we can tell, even if it seems to have been conducted in lower Galilee for the most part. A failed propagandist for hellenism would scarcely do justice to the evidence, even if such a picture of Jesus would please those who still espouse the older History of Religions approaches to his ministry. Our survey of the way in which protest movements of various kinds emerged and took root in first-century Palestine has not suggested that Galilee was a prominent breeding ground for any of these either. Given its similarity, at least superficially with several of these movements, we could of course claim that it is the Jesus movement itself which supplies the missing link for Galilee. However, initial similarities do not always turn out to be as helpful as might appear at first sight. One essential ingredient seems to be lacking for the Galilean situation, namely, a disaffected peasantry, something that must be emphasised against Horsley (and others), illuminating as several of his studies are. Besides, the absence of any political moves, either by Antipas against Jesus, or by the Romans against his followers, suggests that ultimately comparisons with some of these other protest movements break down at another vital point. As the cases of the Baptist and others make clear, there was no place sufficiently remote from the central political authorities, if a genuine threat to the social order was perceived to be present. On the best assessment of the evidence, it was the Jerusalem aristocracy, priestly and lay, who had the most interest in having Jesus dispatched.[1]

We shall certainly have to explore the similarities with other movements more thoroughly, since Galilee was, after all, a region within a larger whole, whose political and social life was largely determined by adherence to a symbol system that was shared with inhabitants of other parts of the country. It would be foolhardy, therefore, to exclude a priori the possibility of similar movements recurring within the whole catchment area of the shared symbols, irrespective of regional differences at the social level. After all, religious systems do not always function to reinforce social differences, but can also assist in transcending them. Since, however, the conclu-

1. For a discussion cf. the various articles on the trial of Jesus in *Jesus and the Politics of His day*, ed. E. Bammel and C.F.D. Moule, Cambridge: Univ. Press, 1984; O. Betz, 'Probleme des Prozesses Jesu', in *ANRW* II, 25.1, 565–647.

sions so far reached point to differences at the social level we shall do well not to begin with an attempt to find a plausible social world for the Jesus movement similar to those which are suggested by the other protest movements, but instead to concentrate on an evaluation of its impact on the religious symbol-system itself. This is certainly the strategy suggested by our approach so far, with the gospels, rather than any modern, theoretical framework dictating the agenda for us. In the absence of any clearly articulated political moves against Jesus in Galilee, the opposition from those who controlled the religious system in Jerusalem becomes all the more significant, suggesting that it was they, rather than those who were in charge of the social and eco-systems (insofar as these three can be differentiated, of course), who felt the real threat of his challenge.

In adopting such an approach there is no intention of reverting to the point of view of previous studies of the historical Jesus, with their abstract theological concerns. The theory of religious symbols with which we have been operating is broadly functional, in that full recognition has been given to their interplay with social factors, as the argument of the previous two chapters clearly indicates. Indeed, by viewing the Jesus movement in terms of its attempt to reframe the religious symbols that were operative in Second Temple Judaism in a Galilean setting, we shall have some criterion for evaluating its likely social role there also, and possibly even arriving at a realistic estimate of its successes and failures. One of the real problems facing the historian of the Jesus movement who takes account of social factors is to explain the apparent 'disappearance' of the Galilean crowds.[2] Did Jesus deceive them by playing on their expectations, only to fail to deliver in the end? Gerd Theissen's sociological study, so full of insightful suggestions, has to admit that the Jesus movement failed to contain the latent aggression within first-century, Palestinian Jewish society, which had been caused by exploitation in the social and economic areas and which, in

2. See F. Mussner, 'Gab es eine Galiläische Krise?', in *Orientierung an Jesus. Zur Theolgie der Synoptiker. Für Josef Schmid.* ed. P. Hoffmann, N. Brox and W. Pesch, Freiburg: Herder, 1973, 238–52.

Theissen's view, Jesus had sought to address.[3] Yet this picture is open to the criticism of being reductionist also, insofar as it assumes that the aims of the Jesus movement were essentially social rather than religious in character, even allowing for the deep impact that all religious changes had on the social fabric of that society. We cannot, therefore, entirely avoid the hermeneutical circle involved in the interplay of social, economic and religious factors in discussing the Jesus movement in Galilee. The challenge is to remain constantly critical in judging the plausibility of any overall picture, irrespective of our starting-point. Hopefully, the groundwork for such a critical assessment has been laid in the previous chapters. We shall repeatedly draw on the findings there, while being open to the need for revision in the light of new considerations that may be prompted by viewing the situation through the prism of the Jesus movement itself, rather than through its reconstructed social or religious setting.

The historian must constantly pay attention to the data—all the data—available, irrespective of how disparate the pieces may appear to be and how resistant they are to being fitted into a plausible pattern. In the opening chapter it was noted that several recent studies of Jesus opted for either his works or his words, to the virtual exclusion of the other dimension. It was often difficult to discover why certain choices had been made, since the latent biases were not always made clear, and were not sufficiently reflected upon, it would seem. In this study we shall take seriously the fact that Jesus both taught and did certain actions that were seen by his contemporaries as works of power (δυνάμεις), to the point that opponents did not challenge the fact of the deeds, but the source of the power by which they had been accomplished. It is this very combination of deeds and words that makes it so difficult to fit Jesus neatly into any of the roles that can be documented—teacher, oracular prophet, prophet of liberation, aspirant to popular kingship; man of deeds (*hasîd*) despite the clear similarities with all of them, and even though

3. *Sociology of Early Palestinian Christianity*, 111–19.

he is sometimes hailed in one or other of those roles by his audience.[4]

We do not know whether Judas the Galilean performed mighty deeds as well as being a teacher, and we have only a hint of what his teaching was. Theudas, Athronges and the returned Egyptian may have been teachers as well as hoping for mighty deeds of liberation. There is no record of Jesus son of Hananiah's mighty deeds, but only his prophecies of woe. Only a few very general sayings are attributed to Hanina ben Dosa, and we know nothing of the social assumptions of Judas son of Hezekiah, though he aspired to kingship. John the Baptist preached an apocalyptic message of repentance but performed no miracles.

Despite the reworking of his words, as well as the creation of new sayings similar to those which he did utter, and notwithstanding the theological, apologetic and missionary concerns at work in the accounts of the deeds attributed to Jesus, there is unimpeachable evidence of a tradition of words and works going back to the Galilean ministry, that in all probability began to be collected very soon after his death, if we are to credit the findings of source and tradition criticism of the gospels.[5] To choose to ignore or downplay one or other aspect would appear to be foolhardy, if the intention is to understand Jesus in his setting. Of course it is possible to be hypercritical to the point of claiming that these two aspects do not cohere very well, since, it is claimed, it is possible to detect signs in the later tradition of bringing these aspects together so that deeds and words are made to form a single

4. Διδάσκαλος is the most frequent, occurring as an appellation for Jesus 12 times each in Mt and Mk, 17 times in Lk and 8 times in Jn. Προφήτης is less frequent. Of the instances in which Jesus or others think of him in this role, 6 occur in Mt, 3 in Mk, 7 in Lk and 6 in Jn. 'Ο Χριστός, by itself is the least frequent apart from the Fourth Gospel, occuring 7 times in Mt, twice in Mk, 6 times in Lk, but 12 times in Jn.

5. Despite many recent attempts to dispense with Q, especially by those who seek to revive the Griesbach hypothesis, the theory of early collections of the sayings of Jesus which are in some way represented in our gospels of Mt and Lk, still seems to me to be a far better option than the alternatives. For recent discussion of both Sayings and Signs source(s) cf. the publications of the Jesus Seminar group organised by R. Funk, *Forum*, especially, 2,3 and 2,4. The idea of scholars voting on the authenticity or otherwise of sayings of Jesus smacks of a neo-liberal historicism, yet many of the studies are a serious contribution to the ongoing debate about the historical Jesus, and will be specifically referred to in subsequent notes.

unified picture.[6] Yet when viewed in the light of socio-rhetorical patterns in antiquity, the combination of deeds and words as well as the recognition of their intimate relationship in the lives of holy men/prophets/teachers, is both common and well-attested in Jewish and hellenistic circles alike.[7] To suggest that it is not significant for understanding the career of Jesus in Galilee would be to ignore the important social implications of such a combination.

1. Jesus and the Temple

One of the charges brought against Jesus before the high priest which merited death was the claim that he would destroy the temple and build another 'not made with hands' (Mk 14:58). The recent publication of the Temple Scroll from Qumran, probably dating from almost 100 years prior to the career of Jesus, has given a new urgency to understanding this charge against Jesus in the context of Second Temple Judaism as a whole.[8] The Jerusalem priestly authorities had every right to be concerned about attacks on their temple from religious dissidents, though in the case of the Temple Scroll a new physical temple could replace the existing, defiled one, at least as an interim measure.[9] But what of the charge against Jesus? The gospels claim that it was a false one, understandably, but, on the assumption that there is never smoke without a fire, the matter needs to be examined more thoroughly, and

6. Sanders, *Jesus and Judaism*, 134–41.

7. A.B. Kolenkow, 'Relationship Between Miracle and Prophecy in the Greco-Roman World and Early Christianity', in *ANRW* II, 23.2, 1470–1506; V. Robbins, *Jesus as Teacher*, 114. Kolenkow makes the important point that in determining the authenticity or otherwise of an individual miracle-worker, an ascetical life-style was very important, since in the popular mind only 'divine' people would not seek their own benefit. In turn, power to do miracles was attributed to such people because of their asceticism.

8. See M. Hengel, J. Charlesworth and D. Mendels, 'The Polemical Character of 'On Kingship' in the Temple Scroll. An Attempt at Dating 11Q Temple', *JJS* 37(1986) 28–38.

9. D. Juel, in *Messiah and Temple*, SBL Dissertation Series 31, Missoula: Scholars Press, 1977, especially 169–209, sees the charge of Jesus as destroyer of the existing temple arising from within early Christian experience rather than from standard Jewish messianic expectation. On the other hand in the light of the publication of the Temple Scroll, D. Schwartz, in 'The Three Temples of 4 Q Florilegium', *RQ* 10(1979) 83–91, opposes the community-temple theory and argues for the belief in the rebuilding of an actual temple by God as part of the sect's expectation, according to this midrash on 2 Sm 7:10.13. Cf. Y. Yadin, *The Temple Scroll*, E.T. Jerusalem, IES Publications, 1984, 3 vols, I, 210ff., on the implications of column 29 of that scroll.

provides a suitable point of entry to a discussion of Jesus and the symbolic significance of the temple.

The misnamed 'cleansing of the temple' episode immediately comes to mind, and its implications have been thoroughly investigated by Sanders, who sees it as an attack on the very sacrificial system so central to the temple.[10] When viewed in the light of what he calls 'restoration eschatology', it clearly had implications for both Jesus and Judaism. However, without calling into question either the implications of the episode or the eschatological framework for interpreting its deeper significance, its impact was mainly felt in Jerusalem, and when taken in isolation it can only be seen as a prophetic gesture, pointing to a wider horizon of criticism. The impact in Galilee of a stance that is critical of the temple is our chief concern, and more specifically those elements of Jesus' career there that could be seen as directly addressed to the temple and its symbolism.

Among the recorded sayings is the repetition of the Hosean 'I desire mercy not sacrifice' (Hos 6:6; Mt 9:13; 12:7), but even if this were regarded as authentic rather than Matthean redaction, it could scarcely be seen as an attack on the temple, unless it were linked with a positive refusal by Jesus to offer sacrifice and the propagation of such ideas among Galileans. We have noted the gospels' silence about his offering of sacrifices or bringing of tithes, but this is scarcely decisive in view of the later theological concerns. If Sanders's case that Jesus' unconditional forgiveness of sinners is one of the most shocking dimensions of his ministry, is to be upheld, then its implications for the sacrifical system in terms of the *yôm kippûr* ritual need to be spelled out. Surely a consistent policy of fraternising with such people and declaring that thereby their sins were forgiven—a repeated feature of the Galilean ministry—must be seen as undermining one of the most important aspects of the temple's significance. In the ritual of the Day of Atonement, the sociological significance of the phrase 'redemptive media', meaning the processes whereby a community discharges its contractual obligations

10. *Jesus and Judaism*, 61–76; for a convenient summary of various earlier opinions with critical comment, cf. Davies, *The Temple and the Land*, 349–52, nn.45 and 46.

through the performance of certain symbolic actions, joins with its theological meaning—the at-one-ing of Israel with its God.[11] To suggest to those who were in charge of such a ritual that it was no longer necessary was tantamount to undermining the sociological as well as the theological foundations of the group, since the sinners in question were, according to Sanders, not those who merely failed to observe certain purity regulations as defined by sectarian halachic practices, but rather 'the evil ones' of apocalyptic literature—murderers, idolators and those whose actions were destructive of the group's very identity.[12]

Yet there seems to be no good reason for denying that Jesus went to Jerusalem as a Galilean pilgrim, and he assumes that others should go there also to offer their gifts. Their doing so is not criticised; they are simply asked to be reconciled to their brother first, thus highlighting the deeper social dimensions that were involved in the pilgrimage to the central sanctuary (Mt 5:23f.). Pilgrimage to the temple can also be used as an image on which to build a parable, since this was part of common experience (Lk 18:10–14). Are we then faced with a highly ambivalent, even contradictory situation—a recognition of the temple's *de facto* status, and yet an implicit statement of its redundancy in terms of the God-man relationship? Searching the recorded sayings and controversies brings no greater clarity to this situation and there is no report of any confrontation with the priests on the matter of the temple before the final trial scene. Matthew does have the Christologically based declaration 'something greater than the temple is here', added to the more general example of David's violation of the temple in a human crisis, but interestingly, that is in the context of a dispute with Pharisees, not priests (Mt 12:1–10). Similarly, Luke's sympathetic portrayal of Jesus in the temple highlights his encounters with scribes, not priests, but we shall postpone until a later section our evaluation of that situation.

11. K. Burridge, *New Heaven, New Earth*, New York: Shocken, 1969, 6f.

12. *Jesus and Judaism*, 176–209, and his 'Jesus and the Sinners', *JSNT* 19(1983) 5–36; for a brief but perceptive response cf. N.H. Young, 'Jesus and the Sinners: Some Queries' *JSNT* 24(1985) 73–5.

What of the deeds of Jesus in a Galilean setting? Do they suggest any criticism of the temple and its symbolism? It is perhaps significant that a critical attitude towards the temple is more explicit in those two gospels that concentrate on the deeds of Jesus and their symbolic significance, namely, those of Mark and John. The latter actually links the 'greater things' that the diciples will see (clearly, the signs of Jesus) with the fulfilment of Jacob's dream, in which the lines of communication between heaven and earth were established at the suitably named Beth El, 'the house of God' (Jn 1:51; Gn 28:12). For Mark the deeds of Jesus are a sign of his authority and wisdom (1:27; 6:2). Since the temple symbolised divine presence and the communication between heaven and earth that was the centre of Israel's religious experience, it would appear important to follow the lead of these two evangelists' theologically-inspired portraits and explore the possibility that the deeds of Jesus were perceived as a threat to the temple and its symbolism. Mark, it seems, has deliberately excluded mighty deeds in the Jerusalem setting, thus building their significance into the larger Galilee-Jerusalem tensions of his work.

Despite the advances made by such recent studies from a sociological point of view as those of Gerd Theissen and Howard Clark Kee, we still lack a study of the miracle tradition that could be described as fully satisfactory.[13] Indeed a survey of recent opinions on the miracles suggests that there are as many different points of view among the moderns as the ancients—everything from magic to the millennium. The miracle *stories* certainly functioned as propagandist within the context of early Christian mission, as Theissen's study in particular has shown, and as such ancients as the pagan Celsus acknowledge (*Conta Celsum* 8:47). But what of the miracles themselves, how did they impinge on their actual environment, and, in terms of the particular focus of our investigation here, how did their performance relate to the control which the functionaries of

13. See G. Theissen, *The Miracle Stories of the Early Christian Tradition*, E.T., T. and T. Clark, Edinburgh, 1975; Howard Clark Kee, *Miracle in the Early Christian World. A Study in Sociohistorical Method*, New Haven and London: Yale University Press, 1983. Cf. the review of recent writing on the miracles by William R. Schoedel and Bruce Malina, 'Miracle or Magic?' *RSR* 12(1986) 31–42.

the central sanctuary at Jerusalem sought to maintain over the populace at large?

In order to gain some fairly firm foothold on this very swampy terrain, we shall do well to begin with the Beelzebul charge, not because we agree with Morton Smith that the views of outsiders are more reliable than those of insiders, but because in this instance the blatantly vilificatory intentions of the charge in terms of ancient rhetoric points to the fact that as perceived from the centre, these mighty deeds were not just dangerous, they were subversive, and their purveyor needed to be 'destroyed'.[14] We would have to assume that such a reaction on the part of the Jerusalem scribes is a fairly clear intimation that not merely were the miracle stories propagandist within early Christianity, but that also, during the actual ministry of Jesus, reports of his mighty deeds brought the crowds flocking to him, something that all the gospels assume, but that Mark in particular underlines by his use of the term 'hearsay' (ἀκοή, Mk 1:28,45; 5:20; 7:36; Lk 7:17).

It is usual to point to the linking of Jesus' exorcisms and healings—since these are the most commonly attested themes—with his eschatological message of the imminent in-breaking of the Kingdom of God, following the early Q saying (Mt 12:28; Lk 11:20), and to suppose that this is the context in which Jesus' miracles were perceived by those who followed him, crowds and disciples alike. Yet in view of the reservations expressed by Sanders, following a searching analysis of this linking, perhaps it is more prudent not to accept as axiomatic the apocalyptic connection in discussing the social role of Jesus' miracles, at least initially.[15] As Theissen and others have noted there is a curious absence of explicit eschatological themes in the miracle stories, thus suggesting an alternative life-setting. That may of course be due to the missionary propaganda situation in which, according to the form critics, these stories were fashioned, especially in a hellenistic environment where such an orientation would not

14. See *Jesus the Magician,* New York: Harper and Row, 1978; cf. my review in *CBQ* 41(1979) 658–61.

15. See *Jesus and Judaism,* 132–5.

have been appropriate.[16] At the same time the charge of being in league with Beelzebul had to be swiftly countered, and the fact that this was done by an appeal to the apocalyptic theme of the in-breaking of the kingdom of God, shows that this setting, with its use of signs and wonders, was a natural one for the audience.[17] This would seem to indicate that the response to the scribal vilification was early also, perhaps as early in fact as the charge itself during the actual ministry in Galilee. Without anticipating the argument of a later section, it is, perhaps, justifiable to suppose that the respone to the scribes had to come, not from the wider audiences of Jesus' miracles, but from those who were closer to him, and from whom some response might be expected.[18]

As a working hypothesis, then, we may proceed with the suggestion that the mighty deeds of Jesus had a wide popular appeal in Galilee, and that ultimately their source, motivation and purpose called for some explanation in terms of a concerted effort to discredit them. This would seem to call into question the possibility of clearly distinguishing them from oracular healings or magic, as charismatic deeds of healing, a typology that Theissen proposes.[19] That they were not obviously oracular healings in the sense of requiring a visit to a sanctuary is obvious, but the distinction between charismatic acts of healing and magical performances would seem to be very much in the eye of the beholders and dependent on the context within which they and the miracle worker sought to place the deeds in question.[20]

Perhaps an analysis of the miracle stories themselves could be of assistance in pointing to a more concrete social role than that of confirming apocalyptic expectations among Galilean

16. See Theissen, *Miracle Stories*, 281–6.

17. See Kee, *Miracles*, 146–73.

18. See Mk 2:16; Jn 12:21 e.g. as instances of the thoroughly realistic situation of questioners approaching the disciples rather than the teacher himself.

19. *Miracle Stories*, 231–46. Sanders, in *Jesus and Judaism*, 173, stops short of offering an adequate setting, while admitting that the miracles helped to gather crowds and to alert the authorities to the threat of Jesus.

20. The fact that as well as Smith's study, based for the most part on the Greek magical papyri, that of J.M. Hull, *Hellenistic Magic and the Synoptic Miracle Stories*, London: SCM, 1974, has been able to identify elements of popular magical technique and style in the Synoptic miracle stories should engender caution in making any such distinctions on 'objective' grounds.

crowds? Here Theissen's distinction between ecological (in the broad sense), class and cultural factors does provide a useful framework, even though for him it is only applicable to an analysis of the stories at a later stage of their transmission. He is prepared to accept a rural, even Galilean, setting, while claiming that the stories in their present form have travelled some distance from that milieu. Such elements as the taking of individuals outside the village away from the crowd, the possessed person being out in the countryside, the linking of stories to known geographic centres in Galilee or its environs—Naim, Cana, Capernaum, the Gadarene and Tyrian territories—all come to mind. However, it does not seem possible to link the stories to a particular class-consciousness, in terms of help for the socially deprived, as Theissen himself recognises, since in the Galilean context we meet rich and poor as beneficiaries of Jesus' healing activity.[21] Cultural boundaries are also transcended as non-Jews such as the Syro-Phoenician woman, the Gadarene demoniac and the centurion, Jairus, all experience his healing action, and there are reports of crowds coming to him from every quarter, while in other stories the healing word is spoken in Aramaic (Mk 5:41; 7:35). Such features as these point to a cross-cultural setting of Greek and Semite, but it is difficult to ignore the geographical connections with Galilee entirely, and in the light of our discussion of the social world in previous chapters there seems to be very good reason for not looking beyond them.

Earlier we demurred at Theissen's clear distinction between oracular, magical and charismatic healings, and a discussion of the treatment of illness and attitudes towards healings in Judaism may help to fill out the picture further, thus providing a more adequate social situation and interpretative framework for understanding Jesus' healing miracles. It is true that Yahweh was not thought of primarily as a healing God, and therefore, the Jerusalem cult-centre was not a healing sanctuary, such as Epidaurus, despite suggestions of an Asklepeion in Jerusalem itself.[22] Nevertheless there is

21. See *Miracle Stories*, 246–53.

22. See A. Duprez, *Jésus et les Dieux Guerisseurs*, Cahiers de la Revue Biblique 12, Paris: Gabalda, 1970.

plenty of evidence that good health was seen as one of the blessings of the covenant which the creator God had made with Israel, promising a long life in the land to those who observed its stipulations (Dt 7:15). Hence the close connection between sin and sickness, which continued into New Testament times (Sir 30:14–20; Jn 9:1f.). Such prophetic texts as Is 26:19; 29:18f.; 35:5f. promised healing of illness as one sign of messianic times, and they are applied to Jesus' ministry at an early stage of the gospel tradition (Mt 11:4f.; cf. 14:18–21). The laws concerning leprosy in Lev 11 show how the priestly point of view acknowledged this intimate connection between religious and physical conditions in terms of cultic participation. In addition the widespread belief in demons and possessions as expressive of the present evil age provided an alternative religious and mythological setting for interpreting physical malady. The presence of exorcists other than Jesus and his disciples can be documented from the gospels (Mk 9:41), and the Qumran writings as well as Josephus presume the practice of exorcisms generally (4 Q Or Nab; 1Q Gen Apoc 19:11–20.32; *J.A.* 8:46).[23] There was, then, an identifiable social role for healers/exorcists, even if their preponderance in Second Temple society may not have been as great as some have maintained (cf. Ac 19:13–19).[24] Furthermore, attempts to distinguish various forms of such activity in terms of techniques employed are, in the light of the available evidence, debatable.

Healing was not just a religious phenomenon, however, since it had definite social implications also. The cured person had the visible signs of the curse of their sinfulness removed and so could be restored to the community. Thus it is not surprising to find that side by side with a religious approach to sickness there is evidence of physicians and other forms of 'natural' healings from first-century Palestine also, symptomatic, no doubt, of hellenistic values generally in that society.

23. See D. Duling, 'Solomon, Exorcism and the Son of David', *HTR* 68(1975) 235–52; B. Chilton, 'Jesus ben David. Reflections on the Davidssohnfrage', *JSNT* 14(1982) 88–112; M. Geller, 'Jesus' Theurgic Powers: Parallels in the Talmud and Incantation Bowls', *JJS* 28(1977) 141–55.

24. See R. Kampling, 'Jesus von Nazareth. Exorzist und Lehrer', *BZ* 30(1986) 237–48, who suggests on the basis of the available evidence that while mention of possessions is frequent, exorcists are exceptional.

Luke cites the proverb 'Physician heal thyself' (4:23), which suggests a certain distrust of medics, an attitude that one might want to identify with peasant wisdom, but which apparently was not confined to the lower classes, as is clear from Pliny's strictures (Nat. Hist. 29, 1.7).[25] It comes as no great surprise that the wealthy as well as the impoverished were among Jesus' clients then. To attend physicians cost money, as the case of the woman with the issue of blood who had used up her whole livelihood, without being any better, exemplifies (Mk 5:26). Thus the urbanite, Ben Sirach, recommends a votive offering before paying a visit to the doctor, even though he does show an appreciation of their healing art (Sir 38:11f.) and Josephus tells us that the Jews used books containing cures from roots and other objects (*J.W.* 2:136; cf. Jub 10:12f.).

In the light of our description of the social organisation and the different 'worlds' represented by the village and the city, it would be natural to assume that some of these developments were more characteristic of those places touched by the urban ethos generally. However, generalisations are dangerous. Natural cures of various kinds are associated in all cultures with the countryside and the peasants' practical knowledge of the curative powers of plants and herbs. On the other hand, even the most sophisticated circles were happy to avail of the powers of religious healing throughout antiquity.[26]

This discussion, sketchy as it is, of approaches to illness and healing in first-century Palestine, helps to explain the fact that Jesus had widespread popularity in Galilee that was not confined to the lower classes, but which touched even the court circles (Mk 6:14; Lk 23:8). His role as healer transcended the boundaries of status and class, it would appear, but wherein lay its threat to the religious establishment, represented by the scribes' desire to discredit him? One study that could be seen as providing a plausible answer to this question is that of Geza Vermes, *Jesus the Jew*, (London:

25. See H. Clark Kee, *Medicine, Miracle and Magic in the Roman World*, Lecture, Boston University, 1985.

26. See H. Clark Kee, *Miracle and Magic in New Testament Times*, S.N.T.S. Monograph Series, 55, Cambridge: University Press, 1986.

Collins, 1975), comparing the miracle-working of Jesus with that of the Galilean *hasîd* Hanina ben Dosa, known to us from various rabbinic sources. There are indeed certain formal similarities between some of the stories attributed to Jesus and those ascribed to Hanina. Vermes would also include another miracle-working character, Honi, the Circle-drawer, who is never directly related to Galilee in the sources. The activity of all three, displaying Elijah-like traits, should be seen as reflecting a Galilean hasidic tradition that appealed to that 'unsophisticated religious ambiance' with its 'simple spiritual demands', and which was also inspired by 'a lively local folk-memory concerning the miraculous deeds of the prophet Elijah' (p.80). That several of the miracle stories associated with Jesus are modelled on the Elijah-Elisha cycle,[27] has long been recognised, but it was the figure of the returning Elijah that seemed to have dominated the Galilean religious scene, according to Mark, and the scribes also had dealt with that issue (Mk 9:11–13; 15:35). Elsewhere I have subjected Vermes's treatment of the Hanina traditions to a detailed criticism, indicating that his composite picture of Hanina shows scant regard for the development of the legend over several centuries.[28] In all probability the original designation was 'man of deeds' (M. Sotah 9:15), with the emphasis on his miracle-working activity coming much later, especially in the Babylonian Talmud. Furthermore, the attribution to Hanina of a mere handful of sayings of a very general nature scarcely warrants Vermes's comparison of the gospel according to Hanina with that according to Jesus.

What is most telling against the comparison, however, is the fact that it fails to explain the different treatments of the two characters by the later tradition. One can trace the process of the gradual domestication of Hanina, to the point where his deeds are made to illustrate a point of halachah of

27. See D. Bostock, 'Jesus as the New Elisha', *ET* 92(1980) 39–41; R. Brown, 'Jesus and Elisha', *Perspective*, 12(1971) 84–104; C.A. Evans, 'Luke's Use of the Elijah/Elisha Narratives and the Ethics of Election', *JBL* 106(1987) 85–111.

28. S. Freyne, 'The Charismatic' in G.W.E. Nickelsburg and J.J. Collins, ed., *Ideal Figures in Ancient Judaism*, S.B.L. Septuagint and Cognate Studies 12, Chico: Scholars Press 1980, 223–58. Cf. also, W. Scott Green, 'Palestinian Holy Men: Charismatic Leadership and Rabbinic Tradition', in *ANRW* II, 19.2, 619–47.

Rabbi Hanina. Those same sources continue unabated the vilification of Jesus, already to be found in the Beelzebul charge, as is well known.[29] This different trajectory of the Jesus and Hanina traditions within the rabbinic corpus, points backwards to a different social role for each, and however one regards the historical Hanina, the model of hasidic piety, being a threat to the Jerusalem religious establishment will scarcely by itself suffice to explain the violence of the attempt to discredit Jesus.

While Sanders is prepared to allow that Jesus' miracles created an excitement that was threatening to those who were interested in the preservation of law and order, he is reluctant to attribute any significance to them in terms of the eschatological prophet. Theissen, on the other hand, apparently ignoring the thrust of the Beelzebul charge, believes that the miracles were of no *direct* significance for Jesus' ultimate fate, since the only one that explicitly threatened Jerusalem's religious hegemony was that concerning the new temple, which he did not in fact accomplish. Rather, insofar as the miracles projected a new way of life associated with Jesus' charismatic approach, over against the existing situation represented by the temple and the holy city, they can be said to have contributed to his downfall.[30]

Neither position seems to explain the complex situation adequately in the light of the Beelzebul charge. A greater significance for the miracle-working activity seems called for than the mere disruption of law and order, even if the eschatological-sign correlation is not deemed to have been original. On the other hand, Jesus' 'new way' did not directly challenge the establishment, at least to the point of advocating the abandonment of the existing temple, as had the Essenes. His miracles were not directed against Jerusalem, as were those of the Egyptian prophet, for example, not even when the charge of destroying the temple could be laid against him, and is to be taken seriously. It seems legitimate then to look for a deeper reason than the mere suspicion of something new occurring, to explain the scribal mission to discredit him.

29. See E. Bammel, 'Christian Origins in Jewish Tradition', *NTS* 13(1966/7) 317–35.

30. See *Miracle Stories*, 245f., 258.

The performance of miracles in that or any society raises questions of the nature of divine power, how it is experienced and who controls access to it. Since Jesus' words, so far as we can ascertain, accept the legitimacy of the temple, and in view of the fact that he went there, ostensively at least, as a pilgrim, it must be acknowledged that he was giving some public recognition to the temple and what it represented. What is called for in order to explain a complex situation, therefore, is some model that can help to interpret the diffusion of divine power and access to it in the name of the God of Israel—which Jesus' miracles lay claim to—and yet explains why there is an inherent risk of real conflict with those who control that power within the existing system. In this regard Peter Brown's description of the holy man, developed from late antique religious sources, would appear to offer the possibility of elucidating both the social role of Jesus as miracle-worker and the conflict generated by those miracles, better than Theissen's outright conflictual model, which is based on an understanding of the social role of Jesus in a society deemed to have been thoroughly alienated and at total odds with the establishment, both political and religious. [31]

The suggestion is that the miracle-working activity of Jesus filled a real social need across class boundaries in Galilee. Inevitably, it was linked by some, at least, with other aspects of his ministry, presumably indeed by Jesus himself and by his disciple-companions in particular, for whom his social identity was characterised, not by that of miracle worker/magician but by that of teacher.[32] Yet given the need of healing, based on the social as well as the religious stigma of illness, the miracles were likely to have the greatest general appeal. This is the basic outline of the movement around him as depicted in all the gospels, highlighted in particular by Mark, who stresses the need to quell popular enthusiasm for his healing and other miracle-working activity. Without having to resort to the idea of a Galilee full of social turmoil, with the destitute in particular turning to a miracle worker in their plight, and lured by his 'new way', we are suggesting a

31. See P. Brown, 'The Rise and Function of the Holy Man in Late Antiquity', *JRS* 61 (1971) 80–100.

32. See Robbins, *Jesus as Teacher*, 114.

very specific social role in Galilee for Jesus as healer, within the thoroughly Jewish framework of belief that the crowds espoused, and that he himself subscribed to, not least by his going to Jerusalem at the times of pilgrimage. It is because of the general appeal of the miracles as well as their confirmatory capacity for his teaching role, that it was the scribes, rather than any other group, who sought to discredit the miracles of Jesus. We have already seen in the last chapter that priest and scribe held a delicate balance of power at the centre, the latter supporting the former's claims to a place of pre-eminence, while at the same time enjoying the special status of those who could bring about conformity to the temple among the people at large by their authoritative teachings. Should the crowds who were impressed by Jesus' mighty deeds be equally enthusiastic about his teachings and link the two together, then the temple system itself and the centrality of Jerusalem, as the seat of divine power and presence, was in danger of collapsing. The claim to destroy the temple may never have been actually uttered by the Galilean Jesus, but it was certainly implicit in his actions in Galilee, not least through his deeds of power, through which he has begun to make a real impact there. It was those deeds that needed to be discredited among the Galileans long before the temple-cleansing episode in Jerusalem spelled out in symbolic action their real significance.

Brown's model of 'the holy man' seems to fit this picture rather well. Though it lacks precise sociological definition and is drawn on the basis of a wide variety of examples from a different epoch (late antiquity) with its own social assumptions and needs, its very lack of precision is an excellent reminder of the fluidity of all social roles, as well as the fact that all ideal types are abstractions. Yet the similarities to Jesus' situation in Galilee are striking. For one thing the holy man as depicted by Brown is a product of the Syrian rather than the Egyptian scene, where the harsher landscape gave rise to a different type—the desert anchorite. In Syria, on the other hand, where the climate and terrain were physically less demanding, the holy man and his retinue lived closer to the cities, but in the countryside, attracting crowds to him, partly because of his ascetical lifestyle which provided a kind of social commentary on the prevailing ethos. Enveloped with a certain mystique, he was seen to be endowed with power, which gave his words a special authority in settling disputes while his wisdom became the arbiter of matters ethical and practical. As Brown puts it: 'his miracles are of the sort that assume that the holy man is there to play a role in society based on power....The miracle condenses and validates a situation built up by more discrete means, and the miracle story is often no more than a pointer to the many more occasions in which the holy man has already used his position in society'.

This description is not at all dissimilar to the role we are postulating for Jesus in Galilee. There the landscape, unlike that of Judea, had similar features to Syria; lower Galilee at least was densely populated, but encircled by cities, and Jesus' ascetical life-style as an itinerant preacher/healer created a definite attraction that broke down some of the social barriers within that relatively closed society, both in terms of class and culture. Yet more significantly, it helps in understanding the importance of the intimate links between his deeds and words, and the authority that people are prepared to invest in him, even in matters of private disputes about property (Lk 12:13–15). This connection is certainly not lost on the Marcan narrator, who reports that on experiencing an exorcism by Jesus, the crowd reacts with the declaration that this is a new *teaching* with authority, not like the scribes and Pharisees (Mk 1:27).

The question of authority based on access to divine power was, therefore, vital. In applying Brown's model to another situation, Jonathan Z. Smith discusses the ways in which the holy man must relate to the more institutional forms of religion, in particular to the temple.[33] As distinct from the oracular prophet who can appeal to ecstasy, or the magician who uses his techniques in a highly personalised manner, the holy man, if he is to maintain a wide popular appeal must 'keep his wits about him', walking the tight-rope of independence that still manages to show respect for the central

33. See J.Z. Smith, 'The Temple and the Magician', in W. Meeks and J. Jervell ed. *God's Christ and His People. Studies in Honour of Nils Alstrup Dahl*, Bergen: Universitetsvorlaget, 1977, 233–47.

institution, as long as it is functioning satisfactorily as a symbol system. It was only by inference, not by explicit claim, that Jesus' Galilean ministry challenged the temple authority. The presence of divine authority already laid claim to in the socially healing encounters with sinners away from the temple and its ritual, was also being applied to other human situations in a more dramatic way, but without any direct reference to Jerusalem or its temple. Yet regard for that institution—albeit within the framework of the greater importance of deeds of loving kindness in line with the prophetic critique—was preserved both in his sayings and in the symbolic going to Jerusalem on pilgrimage.

Jesus of Nazareth does not emerge primarily as an oracular prophet of doom for Jerusalem and its temple, as did Jesus, son of Hananiah, despite the striking similarity between Josephus' account of the latter and the Fourth Gospel's narrative of Jesus in Jerusalem for the feast of Tabernacles (chs. 7–8). One could, of course, suppose that his ministry took on a totally different form in its Jerusalem phase, but this would appear to be less likely on the basis of the gospel narratives and in view of the general communications between the two regions. Nevertheless, it should not be ruled out automatically. John of Gischala is an example of a Galilean whose attitudes changed dramatically on his transfer from Galilee to Jerusalem, if Josephus' account has any trustworthiness.[34] In the Galilean setting Jesus' healing and exorcising activities could function for the benefit of the Galilean populace without calling into question the integrity of their symbol system, the significance of which was so vital for keeping their social world intact, as we have seen. It was only when the implied challenge of the full ministry in Galilee was recognised for what it was, first by the scribes, but then also by the priestly aristocracy, that plans had to be made to have him removed, predictably in the Jerusalem setting, not the Galilean. To go beyond that point in deciding when precisely such decisions were taken, would be to enter the realm of speculation concerning the chronology of Jesus'

34. See U. Rappaport, 'John of Gischala: From Galilee to Jerusalem', *JJS* 33 (1982) 479–90.

ministry, about which the available information does not allow any firm conclusions. We have been more concerned with the pattern rather than the sequence of that ministry as this manifested itself and was received by different elements within Palestinian Jewish society, both in Galilee and in Jerusalem. In the light of our reading of the challenges to the central symbol of the temple, and in particular in view of the serious attempt by the Jerusalem-based scribes to discredit his deeds already in Galilee, there may be no little merit in the suggestion, based on evidence underlying the Fourth Gospel, that plans to have Jesus removed had been set in train by the Jerusalem aristocracy, priestly and lay, well before the final days.[35]

2. Jesus and the Land

The symbol of the land was, we saw, very closely related to that of the temple. On the one hand it could function as an assurance and pledge for those who already owned a share in the land, and for those who felt exploited in regard to the land it could serve as a rallying point and a challenge to bring about the egalitarian society that the Mosaic dispensation envisaged, and prophets such as Amos and Jeremiah had dreamed about. It was in the former capacity, we argued, that the symbol functioned in Galilee, in the absence of any of the organised protest movements that the notion of Israel possessing her own land had generated, unless, of course, we could classify the Jesus movement in that way. It is to this issue that we must now turn.

To begin with, even though Jesus and his followers participated in the pilgrimage to Jerusalem, and that out of respect for the existing temple and what it stood for, there is complete silence about involvment by him or his followers in

35. Cf. the articles of J.A.T. Robinson and W. Grundmann in *Jesus and the Politics of His Day*, especially 297–300 and 464–6; also E. Bammel, 'Ex illa itaque die consilium fecerunt...' in *The Trial of Jesus: Cambridge Studies in Honour of C.F.D. Moule*, ed. E. Bammel, London: SCM, 1970, The decision of the sanhedrin as reported in Jn 11:47–53 might profitably be compared with the Roman *senatus consultum ultimum*, a decree by the senate of a state of emergency which gave it extraordinary powers in a situation of national danger from 'subversive forces' within the state. Cf. M.I. Finley, *Politics in the Ancient World*, Cambridge: University Press, 1983, 3–6.

any of the temple rituals, nor do he or his followers bring offerings to the temple as fruits of the land. While we might be rightly suspicious that this silence on the issue of involvement in sacrifice and ritual was due to early Christian reflection on the death of Jesus as *the* sacrifice for sin, the silence in regard to tithing and other duties incumbent on the pious Israelite living in the land on the basis of Pentateuchal law, calls for further investigation.[36] Is this silence simply a matter of not having anything to offer because neither Jesus, nor any of his followers whose occupation is known to us, owned any land? Or is it a pointer to another, more original view with regard to the symbol of the land? It was one thing not to have any agricultural gifts to bring, and quite another to suggest that ownership of any land was distorting of the divine-human relationship. The former case was envisaged in Pentateuchal law; the latter position was a grave affront to the very constitution of Israel as a holy people and subversive of the temple/land relationship that stood at the heart of its symbolic system.

An argument from silence may be the best there is to offer on Jesus' attitude to the tithing and other agricultural offerings,[37] but we do have plenty of positive information on his attitudes towards possessions and their distorting influence on the human condition. In view of the absolutely essential role that land and agriculture played in that society, such criticism should be seen as an attack on the symbol of the land as a sign of God's absolute favour for Israel as a whole or for the individual Israelite living in the land. While Luke in particular has stressed this aspect of his teaching, it is represented in all strands of the gospel tradition, and should therefore be regarded as one of the most solidly established

36. If we agree with Jeremias and others that 1 Cor 15:3–8, is a pre-Pauline, Palestinian credal formula, then a sacrificial understanding of Jesus' death must have occurred at a very early stage indeed.

37. The second half of the 'Render to Caesar...' (Mk 12:17) saying could possibly be understood as a call for faithfulness to the obligations of temple offerings, rather than as the more usual call for total obedience to the higher divine authority represented by Jesus' preaching of the kingdom, as e.g. in G. Bornkamm, *Jesus of Nazareth*, E.T. London, SCM, 1960, 120–24. Cf. further the discussion of F.F. Bruce, 'Render to Caesar' in *Jesus and the Politics of his Day*, 249–63.

values that can be attributed to Jesus and his movement.[38]

Contrary to what some have implied, rejection of property was not something that was imposed on Jesus by force of circumstances. Certainly, none of the evangelists wants to suggest that the fact that the Son of Man had nowhere to lay his head was anything other than the result of a definite choice on his part.[39] However one translates τέκτων—carpenter or craftsman—it certainly is not an indication of a socially deprived condition, but suggests rather, in purely socio-economic terms, a degree of mobility and status.[40] Equally, fishermen and tax-collectors cannot be said to be members of the destitute classes, especially in the region of the sea of Galilee, a point that the reference to Zebedee's hired servants (μισθώτοι, Mk 1:20) makes clear. Jesus and his immediate followers were not, then, members of the landowning peasantry, great or small, but that does not identify them with the sailors or the destitute classes in Tiberias mentioned by Josephus. They were among the more economically mobile of the village culture, not the products of the urban or rural poor.

Jesus' was not a wholly original approach in that setting, however. A number of different examples of what could be described as counter-cultural life-styles can be documented. We hear of the wandering Stoic-Cynic teachers from nearby Dekapolis and in Tyre.[41] The Essenes too had apparently

38. See Fitzmyer, *The Gospel according to Luke I-IX*, 247–51; it is one of the merits of the study of L.T. Johnson, *The Literary Function of Possessions in Luke-Acts*, to have underlined the symbolic function of possessions in the Lucan account in terms of power, and to have shown how this symbolic potential is developed in regard to God's care and human trust.

39. See G. Theissen, 'Wir haben Alles verlassen (Mc X,28). Nachfolge und soziale Entwurzelung in der jüdisch-palästinischen Gesellschaft des 1 Jahrhunderts n.Chr.', *NT* 19(1976) 161–97.

40. R. Batey's effort to identify Jesus' work-place as being Sepphoris during the rebuilding of that city by Antipas is not altogether convincing, *NTS* 30(1984) 249–58. According to R. McMullen, *Roman Social Relations*, 17, carpenters were among those groups that actually organised themselves into associations in Egyptian villages, thus presupposing a degree of social importance, and on the basis of the inscriptions the designation τέκτων appears as a personal name.

41. See G. Theissen, 'Wanderradikalismus. Literatursoziologische Aspekte der Überlieferung von Wörten Jesu im Urchristentum', *ZTK* 70(1973) 245–71, with special reference to the missionary instructions to the disciples, Mk 6:7–11; Mt 10:9–14; Lk 9:3–6; 10:4–11.

made a definite option against private ownership, at least those at Qumran, and indeed saw the present condition of exile from a polluted land as the preparation for a genuine return to a sanctified land (and temple).[42] John the Baptist also had disciples who presumably adopted his ascetical life-style which presupposed no ownership of land (Mk 2:18; 6:29), and Jesus' encomium of John recorded at Mt 11:11 has the appearance of being spoken by a former disciple who found John's vision of detachment from material things a highly attractive option in that setting. On the other hand, though the later Rabbis travelled widely, many of them were large property-owners with their schools located at one centre. Consequently, we cannot infer a radical critique of the symbol of the land on the basis of life-style alone. Its significance will depend on the context within which the practice of itineracy is found, particularly in terms of God's care for his people, since the land-symbol functioned particularly to reinforce this belief.

By portraying the new value-system of Jesus in regard to property through the use of typical, yet recognisable, characters in a Galilean setting, Luke has aided us considerably in evaluating its likely impact there. Two strands may be isolated within the teaching itself. One is apocalyptic in tone, promising reversal of fortunes for those who are now excluded from possessions. The other is based rather on a wisdom-inspired view of life, which recognises the futility of riches and the foolishness of trust in what they can offer. To concentrate on the former alone means concluding that the main thrust of Jesus' teaching is consolation for the deprived, when in fact the address to the rich and the call to repentance would appear to be equally pressing, in that characters from both strata—the rich and the poor—are represented.[43] If

42. W.D. Davies, *The Gospel and the Land*, 52–4.

43. See G.W.E. Nickelsburg, 'Riches, the Rich and God's Judgment in 1 Enoch 92-105 and the Gospel according to Luke', *NTS* 25(1978) 324–44. John Drury, in *The Parables in the Gospels. History and Allegory*, London: SPCK 1984, 139–49, attributes the wisdom element to Luke's creative genius and his 'middle of time' concerns. While a plausible case can be made for Luke's development of the motif in the stories attributed to Jesus, it was certainly to be found in the Jewish ambiance of Jesus' own time, and there is no good reason to deny that he shared it. Apocalyptic and wisdom are not mutually opposed world views, as Drury himself accepts.

anything, it is the well-to-do who dominate, thereby suggesting a situation of relative affluence for Jesus' audience. The correspondence of this picture with the social world of Galilee that was reconstructed in chapter 5 is on the whole realistic, even if some intensification may be the result of Luke's own concerns and situation at the time of writing.

We have seen that the peasant Galileans were held in a double bind in relation to the demands, threats and compensations of their urban environs—the one religious (Jerusalem), the other social and economic (the surrounding hellenistic—πόλις ethos). In the latter instance the cities needed the countryside, and it in turn was dependent economically on the needs, markets and services of the cities and larger towns. To expect Galilean peasant farmers to respond with enthusiasm to a message that, if adhered to, would put them at the total mercy of urban exploitation, in the face of which they were already extremely vulnerable, was expecting the impossible in human terms (cf. Mk 10:26–31). Equally, the urban rich with a stake in the land (and that was the prime source of their wealth, we have seen), would have been alarmed by such a programme. The threatened peasant strike on the occasion of Caligula's statue being brought to Jerusalem caused consternation among the gentry, because the tribute would not have been paid and their own privileged position would have been under severe threat. What would the consequences have been if the peasantry were to respond enthusiastically to this message of radical detachment, even abandonment of property? In this light the Herodian opposition, attested for Galilee also, is entirely realistic, even if it meant joining forces with Jerusalem's religious opposition, for whom the programme had equally disastrous consequences, but for other reasons.

Ironically, it would appear that the hold of the religious aristocracy on the peasants' attitudes and values, arising from their deep-seated attachment to the cult-centre and the holy city, averted a possible major catastrophe in purely social terms, when viewed by the values of the centre. The peaceful resolution of petty squabbles, the abandonment of the desire for rank and status among the elders and the more affluent, and the rejection of the natural urge to possess more of what was in short supply, but absolutely essential for upward mobility, namely land,—these and other transformations of social relations within the village would have resulted from acceptance of Jesus' utopian position on the land. They were stifled by another and older set of religious values emanating from the Mosaic code and administered by Jerusalem for its own benefit. The peasants for the most part loyally adhered to them because they appeared to confirm the existing situation, thus making it virtually impossible for those who struggled to maintain their position within it to query its religious legitimacy. The far-reaching changes to all of life that hellenism had introduced into Galilee, were intensified under Herodian control and disrupted older patterns in the village culture. By upsetting the balance of power these changes had created a greater disparity than was tolerable within Israelite society as envisaged by the prophets, even though these were read in the synagogues on the Sabbath, as we have seen. In fact the tithing and agricultural laws helped to cloak these changes in a religious guise, and the covenant framework, of which they were an essential part, explained, also in religious terms, the impoverishment of those who could not or did not avail of the greater opportunities for social and economic improvement that might exist.

Perhaps then, it is possible to conclude that the Jesus movement was, after all, a land-based movement of social revolution, comparable in part at least to the movements of popular kingship or those of prophetic liberation examined in the previous chapter. The apocalyptic note of reversal of fortunes for poor and rich, the enthusiasm of the crowds and his exodus-style miracle in the desert leading to the popular desire to make him king (Jn 6:14f), the inscription on the cross, 'king of the Jews', and the Lucan charge that 'he subverted the people, beginning from Galilee to this place' (Lk 22:3.5)—all of these would fit into such a pattern, with its implication for an understanding of the land-symbol. The movement would have had a suitable social setting among the lower, alienated strata of the village culture, which Jesus and his movement supported, even though they did not come from that social stratum themselves.

Plausible as such a picture appears to be, there are difficulties about casting Jesus in the role of a social prophet who merely took on board the concerns of the destitute and the dispossessed. Apart from the fact that, unlike the other documented movements of protest, there was no strong political reaction to Jesus in Galilee, as has already been noted, certain other considerations would appear to make the models of prophetic liberation or popular kingship less than satisfactory for explaining his role there, at least as he saw it. In the first place the miracles, we have suggested, transcended class divisions, poor and rich alike being the beneficiaries, and concern for both their conditions is expressed in the sayings. The repeated warning about the danger of riches side by side with the apocalyptic message of reversal for the poor, is perhaps, the clearest social commentary on the situation, as seen by Jesus himself. Secondly, his ministry, at least as narrated, was cross-cultural, however much its primary focus may have been directed to the peasant ethos of Galilee. For those who were fired with the ideology of the land, its actual territorial boundaries were highly significant. Even Josephus' careful delineation of the borders of Galilee (*J.W.* 3:35–44) illustrates that point. As far as we can ascertain, Jesus shows no such awareness or concern. While this freedom can be attributed to the more relaxed political atmosphere at the time of Antipas than that which prevailed thirty years later, it is more likely to reflect his universalist vision, which included gentiles also.

The boundaries of the land were very definite reminders of Israel's separateness, and the experience at the time of the hellenistic reform led to increased sensitivity in that regard subsequently, among all strands of Second Temple Judaism.[44] In that climate the primary purpose of the symbol, God's care and concern for Israel, was in grave danger of being distorted into an ideology which generated violence, xenophobia and isolationism. These were not features of the earlier Mosaic dispensation, or the prophetic re-interpretation at an earlier period of Israel's history, and Jesus' vision seems to have been inspired by such voices, expecially that of Isaiah. Just as his healing and exorcising ministry in Galilee did not directly

44. See M. Hengel, *Judentum und Hellenismus*, 555–64.

attack the temple symbolism, but transformed its range and scope, so too his treatment of the land-symbol translated its basic meaning into a universal symbol that did not regard the confines of the land as important. In dealing with this theme of universal care images taken from the land in its primordial significance of the created universe, rather than in its capacity to symbolise Israel's special election—the birds, the trees (olive and vine), flowers and seeds—are used to probe the depths of the vision and to instil in his hearers a confidence in the message, based on their everyday experience in the land.[45] In this regard the few possible references to Israel's election in the parables are all critical of her performance rather than extolling her special election and destiny in the land.

All this is not to deny that irrespective of Jesus' intentions or vision, others were likely to interpret his words and actions in the light of their circumstances and experiences. We cannot then exclude the possibility that for some in Galilee his message and actions were taken to mean that his concerns were at once more restricted and more socially revolutionary within an apocalyptic framework of the instant reversal of fortunes. Galilean society, even among the peasants—that is, all who owned land, was not so monochromic in terms of its social constituency as to exclude such a possibility. The reactions of those who might have interpreted Jesus' words and actions in this light would naturally correspond in broad terms to other movements that can be documented from Josephus. In this connection, reactions were quite varied, according to Mark, even at the Herodian court (6:14–16; 8:27–33), and Jesus is portrayed as the teacher attempting to draw more from his special disciples than a mere acceptance of the common perception about him.[46] Nevertheless, our probing suggests that Jesus' attempt to reinterpret the symbol, land, in terms of God's universal care of all his creation did not meet with the same enthusiastic reception as did his

45. R. Tannehill, in *The Sword in his Mouth. Forceful and Imaginative Language in Synoptic Sayings*, Semeia Supplements 1, Philadelphia: Fortress Press, 1975, 60–67, has a highly suggestive discussion of some of these images.

46. According to Mk 6:33 the crowd who enthusiastically followed Jesus on the occasion of the first feeding miracle and who instigated the so-called 'revolt in the desert' (Mk 6:45; Jn 6:14f,) came from the cities, thus suggesting that it was the urban poor who were the most likely to cast Jesus in the role of popular king.

miracle-working activity in the same environment. In both instances the social situation was largely determinative of the response given—the one positive, because the miracles met a real social need, the other negative, because it was socially disruptive, even anarchic for those who had something to lose. The attitude of the peasants of Gischala, more concerned with the harvest than with a zealot-style purification of the land (*J.W.* 4:84), is surely a reliable indicator of the values of the peasantry that Jesus would have had to contend with. His lack of success is as predictable as it is understandable in social terms.

If the message met with little enthusiasm in Galilee, except for that minority who misinterpreted the basic orientation and intention, its repercussions in Jerusalem were totally predictable. A parable such as the rich fool who planned to build larger granaries for his grain produce (Lk 12:16–21) would, one must suspect, receive an unsympathetic hearing in Sepphoris, if, e.g., the recent suggestions of archaeologists about the grain silos there are proved to be correct. Those absentee Galilean landlords, at least some of whom must have been located in Jerusalem, would scarcely have missed the implications of such an attempt to devalue the land symbol, especially in the light of their preparedness to tolerate violence at the threshing floors in order to have their dues collected (*J.A.* 20:181, 206f.). As far as they were concerned temple and land were symbiotically related in terms both of symbolic functioning and social control. To challenge the centrality of the one inevitably meant debasing the value of the other. Neither could be tolerated, either by the priests who stood to lose most directly or by the scribes who sought to uphold the system by ensuring that the agricultural dues were properly discharged.

3. Jesus and the Torah

Torah, we have seen, could be variously interpreted to mean the written story of God's election of Israel, or the expressed will of God for his people. As Neusner has shown, it was only with the emergence of the Mishnah, side by side with the written Torah of Moses, as an authoritative expression of God's will for Israel, that the term came to have an all-embracing connotation of way of life.[47] Previously, during the Second Temple period the scribal class had emerged as a highly influential group of professionals, with special responsibility for exploring and interpreting the written Torah, thereby giving rise to various sectarian halachic positions, even if the doctrine of an oral torah had not yet emerged. Insofar as Jesus' understanding of the demands of temple and land differed from that which emanated from Jerusalem or was at odds with the various groups interested in developing their own interpretations, notably the Pharisees and the Essenes, he was clearly operating out of a different understanding of torah also. By highlighting the universal dimensions of Israel's call, as these had been mediated through both wisdom and apocalyptic strands of thought current in his own day, Jesus was not intent on dismantling that system in its essentials of election and call, but rather on highlighting its universal scope in a concrete way within the actual circumstances of his own life in Galilee. Others, such as the Hellenists and Paul, would provide the scriptural rationale for that stance. For Jesus himself it seems to have been a matter of praxis rather than theory.

Yet it is as teacher that he is most frequently addressed within the gospels, even though other designations, notably, those of prophet and king (annointed one) also occur (cf. Mk 8:27–30). Mark, the earliest of the gospels, though providing relatively little by way of specific teaching in contrast with deeds, still has Jesus repeatedly addressed as teacher, not just by disciples (4:38; 9:38; 10:35; 13:1), but by other 'outsiders'—the father of the epileptic boy (9:17), an unnamed person (10:17.20), Pharisees and Herodians (12:14), Sadducees (12:19), the sympathetic scribe (12:32). Furthermore, teaching is his most characteristic activity as Mark's narrator describes it (4:1; 6:6; 8:31; 9:31; 10:1; 12:35,38). The same pattern is true of the other gospels also, so that an evaluation of the role of teacher as applied to Jesus' ministry in Galilee seems called for, particularly as it may uncover something of his distinctive understanding of the torah-symbol, which had

47. J. Neusner, *Torah. From Scroll to Symbol in Formative Judaism*, Philadelphia: Fortress, 1985, especially 1–16 for a summary statement of the development.

become so identified with the teaching class in Judaism, as we have seen.

In the previous chapter we saw that while named Galilean teachers are scarce in the literary sources, the traditional place for reading and expounding torah in Judaism apart from the home, namely, the synagogue, is well attested in the Galilee of Jesus' day. This institution proved a suitable locus for scribal activity, we assumed, even if that group or their successors, the sages of rabbinic literature, did not actually control synagogue service. Among recent discussions of Jesus as teacher, the study of R. Riesner, *Jesus als Lehrer* (Tübingen: J.C.B. Mohr, 1984), seeks to identify him with the formal educational processes of teaching and learning in Judaism, building on the work of Swedish scholars H. Riesenfeld and B. Gerhardsson.[48]

Despite the fact that Riesner has assembled a massive array of facts about schools and schooling, his casting of Jesus in the role of formal teacher fails to convince for a number of reasons. It does not take account of the essentially itinerant character of Jesus' activity, which is more akin to the Cynic-Stoic model, one which also provides a framework for integrating both aspects of Jesus' activity—deeds and words. In this regard, even though Vernon Robbins's study of Jesus as teacher is concerned with the literary expression of that social role in the gospel of Mark, the actual role itself and the style of teaching belong to the larger cultural ethos of a hellenistically influenced Jewish environment, similar to that which we were able to postulate for lower Galilee.[49] Such a model captures better the basic character of Jesus' approach as shown in the gospels, combining speech and action, and calling for a response to the system he acts out as well as portrays in words and images. As Martin Hengel has commented on Gerhardsson's proposal, there is no recorded injunction to learn, but to do, in the sayings of Jesus, and more detailed study of pericopae have confirmed that, despite

48. See H. Riesenfeld, *The Gospel Tradition and its Beginnings. A Study in the Limits of Formgeschichte*, London: A.W. Mowbray, 1957; B. Gerhardsson, *Memory and Manuscript. Oral Tradition and Written Transmission in Rabbinic Judaism and Early Christianity*, Lund: C.W.K. Gleerup, 1961.

49. See Robbins, *Jesus as Teacher*, 112f., e.g.

external similarities, Jesus' style of argumentation from Scripture is not rabbinic—nor would we expect it to be![50] Despite the oral features of the recorded sayings there is no preponderance of techniques that are usually associated with Jewish schools as known to us from later sources—mnemonics, lists and the like.

Though Jesus is said to teach in the synagogues of Galilee as well as in the house, his preference appears to have been for the open air—desert places, along the sea-front, plains, on the road, hillsides, are all mentioned. While open-air learning is also known for rabbinic students, Nathanael of Cana being a possible Galilean proto-type (Jn 1:50), it is also possible to relate these situations to the wider pattern of Jesus' approach, as we have sought to plot it. Given the radical differences that clearly emerged between him and the Jerusalem scribal authorities, it is extremely unlikely that he could have continued in open confrontation with them without running the risk of jeopardising his position even further, and in that event avoidance of the synagogue must be seen as a conscious decision, corresponding to his different vision as represented by his whole ministry. In addition, abandonment of home—one of the traditional places for learning torah—was also part of Jesus' life-style for himself and his close retinue. Thus, to the extent that an explicit teaching role must be ascribed to Jesus, a new centre for learning had to be provided that was neither the home nor the synagogue, and this is the function that the permanent band of disciple-companions actually fulfils around him. If, then, we cannot accept Riesner's conclusions that the sayings tradition had its origins in a Jewish scholastic framework, there is no good reason to question an alternative type of 'school', modelled more on similar counter-cultural groups that are known to us from antiquity generally, even though the concerns were still essentially Jewish.

Jesus' differences from the scribes in the matter of torah-understanding has, up to this point, been inferred, either from opposition to his works or from the alternative style of his school and its location. Is it possible to be more specific

50. See *The Charismatic Leader and His Followers*, 42–50.

on details both of orientation towards and content of torah? Any attempt to give an adequate answer to this question highlights our lack of information on scribal teaching, other than that of various sectarian halachic interests that are known to us from later documents. As already discussed in the previous chapter, one must suppose a general acceptance of what constituted the basics—sabbath, circumcision, pilgrimage and offerings—with a greater emphasis on one or other of these elements in the different sectarian groupings. In this regard it is difficult not to assume that the later mishnaic perspective which saw Israel in essentially priestly categories in terms of its life in the village and home, was not already being developed in those circles which our sources call scribal/Pharisaic in the pre-70 period.[51]

From that point of view it seems certain that Jesus' attitude towards temple and land as expressed in his mighty deeds, his itinerant life-style and his call for the abandonment of security based on material possessions, would inevitably have clashed not just on details but in terms of a basic perspective, with several of the known groups. Inevitably it was with those who had a special interest in developing a distinctive halakah that the clash would have been most obvious and sharp. His was not the priestly point of view, and hence there was a fundamental difference with the Pharisaic perspective on what constituted God's will for Israel. From what we can infer from later sources, disagreements between various groups and individuals on matters of detail could be tolerated, provided there was no questioning of the underlying essential vision of Israel's task and destiny. This is not to deny that these differences had deep-seated social and other dimensions, and that on occasion they gave rise to bitter conflict.[52] Yet, when the Jesus-movement's point of view began to be expressed in concrete attitudes and life-style, it was seen by

51. Thus, e.g. Neusner's guarded comments in his *Judaism. The Evidence of the Mishnah*, Chicago: University Press, 70f., and more recently in *The Mishnah before 70*, Brown Judaic Studies 51, Atlanta: Scholars Press, 1987.

52. This can be most easily documented from the pre-70 period from the Qumran writings, especially, e.g., the condemnation of the 'seekers after smooth things' in 4 Q pNah 2. Later rabbinic evidence about bitter disputes between the houses of Hillel and Shammai might also be cited, and Josephus mentions tensions at least between the Pharisees and Sadducees in the matter of cultic regulations, *J.A.* 18:17.

the Pharisaic and scribal interests as the very denial of what it meant to be Israel in their terms. It was only much later that this clash of perspectives came to be openly articulated on both sides and received literary expression—on the Christian side in the gospels of Matthew and John, with their vilificatory treatment of the scribes and Pharisees, and on the Jewish side in terms of the *birkath ha-minîm* and the ongoing presentation of Yesua ha-Nozri as a deceiver and magician.[53] However clearly it is possible to recognise later factors at work on both sides that do not belong to the actual career of Jesus, it would be naïve not to presume that some inkling of the differing perspectives had emerged already in the life of Jesus and that of his earliest followers, who continued immediately after his death to implement in Palestine his radically alternative life-style and the claims that he had made for it.

If Jesus' understanding of the symbol torah was not inspired by the priestly ideal, what can be said about the positive inspiration for his position? No matter how universalist his outlook might have been when viewed by the standards of others, he lived and worked within an essentially Jewish perspective, and it is to that background that we must look for some indication of the source of his thinking and acting. The external form of his itinerant healing/teaching ministry was, we suggested, more reflective of patterns in the wider hellenistic milieu than those which can be discerned in the official strands of the Judaism of his own day. Could this background of hellenised Judaism or Jewish hellenism also provide the key to his radically different view of God's demands for Israel? Lower Galilee was sufficiently affected by the hellenisitc ethos generally for that suggestion to have been a genuine possibility, especially given his and his close companions' social mobility, and the suggestion has been made again recently in general terms.[54] However, before concluding that such was indeed the case, a number of features of Jesus' teaching need to be considered, however

53. See Freyne, 'Vilifying the Other and Defining the Self'; Bammel, 'Christian Origins'.

54. Thus e.g. Riches, *Jesus and the Transformation of Judaism*, 164f; Meyers and Strange, *Archaeology, the Rabbis and Early Christianity*, 26f.

briefly, from a decidedly Jewish perspective, in order to arrive at a more balanced and nuanced formulation of the situation.

Reference has already been made to the possibility of recapturing through the Targumic tradition something of the ways in which the Hebrew Scriptures were known and interpreted by the common people of the first century. Bruce Chilton's studies in the Isaiah Targum, are, we have seen, particularly suggestive in this regard, since in the Nazareth synagogue visit Jesus is portrayed as having actually chosen to read from Isaiah. Is Luke in fact suggesting that that prophet was the inspiration for his vision with its radically different orientation from that of the recognised teachers? Obviously, a lot more detailed work on the attributed sayings of Jesus needs to be done by Chilton and others before any definitive conclusions can be reached, yet initial results are encouraging and illuminating for our purposes. As noted, Chilton is guarded in the manner in which he frames his conclusions about the verbal and thematic links that he believes can be established between the Targum in its present state and the recorded sayings of Jesus. The argument is not that, because such similarities exist, Jesus actually quoted the Targum. In fact no such actual citation is claimed. Rather the style of Jesus' reference to Isaiah shows his clear recognition of the interpretation of the prophet known to the common people of his own day (and now transmitted to us in the later written Targum), and he drew on that in a critical fashion in order to articulate his own experience and vision of God's demands. By 'critical' Chilton means that Jesus was not using Isaiah or the targumic interpretation of that prophet to reinforce an argument by citing an authoritative source or in order to claim fulfilment of Scripture in the circumstances of his own life, but to indicate a common perception of God, whose ways he was now experiencing in a particular light which could be illustrated from the fund of religious language shared by him and his hearers.[55]

In this view it is Jesus' experience rather than a sacred text

55. See B. Chilton, *A Galilean Rabbi and His Bible. Jesus' Use of the Interpreted Scripture of His Time*, Wilmington: Glazier, 1984 148–200, especially 165–74.

as such that is the essential feature, and hence those ways of appropriating the biblical text that are known to us from his environment—midrash, pesher or targum—were not his primary concern. Life-experience rather than text was for him decisive, and this radically differentiated him from the various groupings, known and unknown to us within Judaism, who were primarily concerned with presenting an authoritative account of God's will based on the Scriptures.[56] In this freedom of expression and outlook, it would seem that the cultural experiences of lower Galilee and the mobility of his own life-style, at least to the point of not being a peasant tied to a particular plot of land, must have played a vital role since they formed an integral part of his experience and his horizons of meaning. To go beyond that point by attempting to enter Jesus' 'inner' life, or evaluate the impact of his so-called 'Jordan experience' would be to enter into the kind of speculation that was characteristic of the revisionist Christologians, and which was so tellingly criticised by Ogden. Yet this interaction between social experience and text, no matter how critically the latter is approached, shows a deep concern with the Jewish way of being religious in that culture. Isaiah too had universalist visions and utopian ideals, as well as nationalistic hopes. As a pious Jew, Jesus could appropriate the former into his own particular synthesis and yet respond to the human needs and questions that his cross-cultural experience had thrown up. Thus, a convergence of Galilean cultural experiences in the broad sense and the Jewish religious faith and expression generated, through Jesus, a radically new way that claimed allegiance to the God who was worshipped in Jerusalem and whose cult had produced a number of competing halachic traditions and interpretations. Yet, this new way was not irrevocably tied to the Jerusalem centre, even while it was still intact.

Not only did Jesus' vision generate a new movement that,

56. The approach of the framers of Mishnah who, as described by Neusner (*Judaism the Evidence of the Mishnah*, Chicago: University Press, 1981, 217–29), took their vision for Israel from Scripture but developed it quite independently of Scripture in response to their own questions, may be contrasted with Qumran Essenes, for whom Scripture and the community's special insights into its meaning are regarded as normative revelation (see Hans Aage Mink, 'The Use of Scripture in the Temple Scroll and the Status of the Scroll as Law', *SJOT* 1(1987) 20–50).

from the point of view of the Jewish teaching and learning experience, looked more hellenistic than traditionally Jewish, a fusion of these two traditions seems to have occurred in the form of some, at least, of his recorded sayings and his style of teaching, according to Robbins. Most attention has been given to his parables, because of their realism, their metaphorical and poetic character and the supposition that here, if anywhere, we can capture in a distilled, bed-rock form the very core of Jesus' vision. In this regard the fact that that core alternatively sounds like Martin Luther's theological vision or Franz Kafka's nihilism, depending on the point of view of the modern interpreter, suggests that no attempt should be made to isolate a select number of closely defined parables from the larger context of Jesus' acting and speaking and their import within his own cultural setting.[57]

There is no denying that the frequency of the parable form, not just in terms of completed stories, but of *meshalim* of various kinds, does point directly to a particular style of communication that seems to have been characteristic of Jesus' approach generally. John Drury's recent study, *The Parables in the Gospels. History and Allegory* may be an overreaction to some of the more extravagant claims that have been made for Jesus the parabler, in that he ignores any concern with the historical Jesus altogether, suggesting that the gospel texts are the only appropriate context for interpreting the parables.[58] Yet there is no denying that Drury has done parable studies a genuine service by first of all broadening the base of discussion to include all the *meshalim* in Jesus' repertoire, and by pointing to the wider use of the genre within the literary tradition of Second Temple Judaism, in both its wisdom and apocalyptic strands.[59]

It is possible to identify the use of parables in both strands of Jesus' teaching, in the service, on the one hand, of his

57. W. Beardslee has illustrated this aspect of modern parable study in a most illuminating way in his article, 'Parable Interpretation and the World Disclosed by Parable', already referred to, ch.1 n.19.

58. Mary Ann Tolbert's study, *Perspectives on the Parables. An Approach to Multiple Interpretations*, Philadelphia: Fortress Press, 1979, discusses the contexts in which a parable can be interpreted and the applicability of various criteria in deciding between different readings, which is both helpful and pertinent to an assessment of Drury's claims.

59. See *Parables in the Gospels*, 7–38.

eschatological urgency, and on the other as an aid to his new vision of God's will that breaks with existing expressions. One dimension of the parables that has not received adequate attention, however, is the artistry with which scriptural allusions or images and realistic situations have been interwoven into stories which challenge, provoke and call for a deeper appropriation of the biblical understanding of God and his ways, because of their elusiveness. Here again we can share Chilton's view of Jesus' critical appropriation of the Scriptures occurring in a new and creative manner that combines biblical images with thoroughly realistic everyday experiences drawn from the commercial, social and political life of Galilee.[60]

There are some specific issues of torah-observance that emerge in the attributed sayings of Jesus which take on a new colouring when judged by the Galilean social experience. Given the fact that several of the issues are framed in terms of a controversy story, and, therefore, are judged form critically to have been shaped by early Christian disputes, it should first of all be made clear what is *not* in dispute between him and those who are reputed to have challenged his teaching on specific issues. In terms of our claims about Galilean Jewish affiliations and Jesus' overall attitudes, it is surely significant in the light of subsequent disputes in early Christianity that nowhere in the New Testament is Jesus said to have pronounced on circumcision or spoken against it. Equally, as we have seen, he does not speak against tithing or the other agricultural offerings, and is never accused of having done so. Indeed, his response on the question of paying taxes to Caesar could, we saw, be interpreted to mean that he supported the idea of taxes for the temple also (Mk 12:17). There were differing opinions on what constituted violation of the Sabbath, and it is within that framework, rather than any undermining of the institution itself, that the various reported disputes are to be interpreted. Equally, handwashing and dietary laws were matters of sectarian halachah, not issues that determined one's essential Jewishness in religious terms in the period, and in the Galilean setting we

60. Hengel's study, 'Das Gleichnis von den bösen Weingärtnern', is a good illustration of how this combination could be achieved.

have postulated a Pharisaic fringe among those who dwelt in the larger towns and the cities, not among the peasantry. It was not then on these specifics that the radical newness of Jesus' teaching was likely to have emerged clearly for a Galilean audience.

In dealing with the question, 'Did Jesus break the law?', Sanders discusses the saying 'Let the dead bury their dead'. Here, at least, would appear to be a radical break with what could be regarded as one of the essential points of Jewish piety, respect for the dead. In this instance it is based on the demands of the Mosaic command, 'Honour your father and mother'—the radical nature of which, Martin Hengel's study has so convincingly illustrated.[61] Sanders attempts to soften the impact of Jesus' statement somewhat by suggesting that it was directed only to those who actually followed him, and was not intended for all. [62] However, it could be questioned whether the saying should be evaluated in terms of being a violation of the Mosaic dispensation on the part of Jesus. Rather, its real impact is better measured against the radical break that Jesus intended with the value-system of village life generally, which was, we saw, so tied up with matters of kinship. Disregard for these values in the sacred matter of respect for the dead, was just as radical as the attitudes towards possessions and land already examined—an attack on the prevailing way of life and its social configuration in Jewish Galilee.

Thus, in judging the impact of Jesus as teacher from the point of view of specific issues, it would seem that he cannot be properly understood so long as the question is posed in terms of his leniency or otherwise on specific questions. There is a hyperbolic quality of his various specific ethical instructions, which Robert Tannehill has called 'focal instances of intensification'.[63] These seek to shock the hearer into a new way of action which makes an essential break with moral categories based on a judgment of whether or not certain actions may be deemed permissible in terms of the demands of halachah. In this regard it is noteworthy that in

61. See *The Charismatic Leader*, 8–16.
62. See *Jesus and Judaism*, 252–55.
63. See *The Sword in His Mouth*, 72f., 82.

the one instance in which Jesus is said to have become involved in an issue which was in dispute among various halachists—that of the reasons for divorce—he responded by employing his critical approach to Scripture already discussed, thereby undercutting the current debate altogether. By juxtaposing one text of Scripture (Gen 1:27) with another (Dt 24:1.3), in order to challenge the assumptions of the latter, he was able to present a very different vision to the prevailing one of how family relations, and by implication, those in society generally, should be regulated.

In order to bring some further precision to this issue of Jesus and the torah, it may be helpful to introduce a comparative approach, not on specific issues, but on expectations among Jews generally in regard to torah. Such an approach is usually adopted in relation to the gospel portraits of Jesus on the assumption that it was only in the light of early Christian experience that a proper evaluation of Jesus and his claims was initiated. But this is an unwarranted assumption. The gospels presume that a lively discussion had already taken place during the public ministry, precisely in terms of possible biblical antecedents, and presumably those who were challenged by him required some interpretative framework within which to understand his claims, just as those who sought to vilify him had done.

It is worth noting that Jesus is never accused of being a false teacher, either in Galilee or in Jerusalem, even though warnings against such were a feature of his own instructions for disciples. This may be because his opponents on halachic matters did not come from the apocalyptic circles in which such warnings were a feature. More probably it is because the accusation of being in league with Beelzebul struck at his broad-based popular appeal, rather than his acceptance as a teacher among the intimate band of disciple-companions. On the other hand a wide spectrum of teaching types can be documented from Judaism of the period, laying claim to special authoritative instruction, ranging from the teachers who form the chain of tradition that reaches back to Moses at Sinai (*Aboth*), through the inspired scribe whose knowledge comes both from study and divine inspiration (*Ben Sirach*) to the eschatological prophet like Moses whose task it will be to reveal all the secrets of torah and explain its puzzling features at the end of days (Teacher of Righteousness).[64] What is particularly interesting about all these models is that they combine an appeal to an authoritative source with the inclusion of additional material within the scope and range of torah acquired through study, be it the sayings of the wise (*Aboth*), the knowledge of parables (Sir 39:1–3) or the special rules of the Qumran elect (1 QS 4:8f.). Thus, while the principle of torah as God's will for Israel is maintained, its specific content is determined by the real experience of the group in question. It should also be noted that as we move along the three points of this grid (which could easily be extended) the emphasis on direct divine communication increases, with less stress on the role of the human agency in attaining to wisdom.

Applying this grid to Jesus as torah-teacher as we have described his activity in this regard, it can be seen that while his primary field of reference is the Jewish scriptures, he veers towards that end of the spectrum which emphasises his own personal authority as teacher rather than to that which stresses the role of teacher as revealer of hidden mysteries, except that in the case of Jesus there is no mention of study, a fact noted in the admittedly highly polemical setting of Jn 7:15.

The value of this comparison is not that it demonstrates that he readily fits into any one of these categories, but that it helps to highlight the differences within this broad framework. Unlike the sages in *Aboth* he does not see himself within a chain of tradition; his reference to Israel's past, through the use of its literary heritage, is more oblique and highly personal, as we have seen, and his words are deemed to be authoritative in their own right. Like Ben Sirach, he is presented by the evangelists as an expounder of parables and oracles (Mk 4:1–2,33f.; 7:6f.; Sir 39:1–3) and he also claims the spirit of wisdom (Mt 11:25–7; Sir 39: 5–7), but his wisdom is not identified, either with the book of the covenant of the Most High or the wisdom of the ancients (Sir 24:22;

64. See G.W.E. Nickelsburg, 'Revealed Wisdom as a Criterion for Inclusion and Exclusion: From Jewish Sectarianism to Early Christianity', in '*To See Ourselves as Others See Us*', 73-92, which gives an excellent overview of the various expressions from the Second Temple literature.

39:3). Jesus' wisdom has both folk and gnomic, as well as aphoristic qualities, which are rooted in human experience, and often presume life in the countryside as their social matrix, though collected in court circles.[65] Finally, while the eschatological content of Jesus' teaching cannot be expunged entirely, thus prompting a comparison with the teacher from Qumran, the absence of a heightened sectarian mentality in his followers suggests that for him the apocalyptic colouring and content of his vision was tempered to a considerable degree by a this-world, wisdom perspective.

Social role, content and style all contribute to a very distinctive picture of Jesus as teacher within the Galilean Jewish setting. The ideal type of the sage with the Torah scroll does not, however, capture the reality of Jesus as teacher very well, despite the fact that that is the most frequent appelation for him in the gospels. Jesus' appeal to the Scriptures in answer to his questioners is assumed in several gospel stories (Mk 10:19f; 12:26,29–31). Yet his familiarity with the Targumic tradition and its more flexible approach to the written text shows that he was no literalist, but aligns him rather with an understanding of God's word which requires application to human life and experience. Important as this conclusion is for an appreciation of his approach to the torah-symbol, it seems that we can go even further still. While Jesus remains firmly anchored to the biblical story in its essential outline and demands, his approach would seem to assign a far greater role to social and personal experiences than did any of the contemporary types of teaching that are known to us, or indeed than did any of the distinctively Jewish hopes about an end-time teacher of torah that we can document. The range of human life, both in terms of form and content that is represented in the First Book of Enoch, in its present, admittedly composite, form is perhaps the closest parallel from within the Jewish setting to Jesus' range. Yet it is his personal authority and conviction, rather than the authority

65. Cf. L. Perdue, 'The Wisdom Sayings of Jesus', *Forum* 2,3, 3–35, with a complete bibliography, giving a recent excellent survey and classification of Jesus' wisdom sayings. He lists the following as belonging to the category of folk wisdom in the synoptic tradition: Mt 5:14, 6:22 (= Lk 11:34); 6:24 (= Lk 16:13); 6:34; 10:10 (= Lk 10:7; 1 Cor 9:14; 1 Tim 5:18); 10:16; 12:33 (= Lk 6:44); Mt 12:34; Lk 4:23; Lk 5:39.

of the seer with a visionary experience that ultimately characterises Jesus as teacher, thereby defying any attempt to isolate his teaching from his life-style and his mighty deeds. Thus the model of the holy man, already proposed, rather than any of the recognised teaching types in Judaism, remains the most useful social type to describe Jesus the teacher in the Galilean setting, especially in view of the various levels of authority which such figures could claim, not just for their words but for their deeds as well.

Conclusion. This examination of the Jesus-traditions—his deeds *and* his words—in search of basic attitudes towards temple, land and torah, has shown, we believe, the essential role that Galilee played in shaping his overall attitude and vision. While it is true that any shift of emphasis in regard to one of those symbols inevitably meant a change of focus on all three, thereby giving rise to a new Judaism, as Neusner has suggested, the Galilean setting had a real influence on Jesus' appropriation of all three symbols. His was an interlocking approach with a decidedly universalist outlook, and it would be impossible to decide which was the more fundamental of the three as far as his point of view was concerned. Together they generated a new vision that not merely supported a separate identity for his group within a shared Jewish inheritance with other groups, but was soon to give rise to an alternative system that would break the mould of that inheritance as this was generally understood in the first century.

It was the Galilean distance from, yet attachment to, the temple that made it possible for him to operate within the framework of a shared Judaism, as a holy man whose deeds filled a genuine social need, but which also contained an implied threat to the central role of the temple and its personnel as the locus of divine presence and power. It was the Galilean peasant ethos, with its dominant value-system based on attachment to the land and the consequent acceptance of a narrow outlook on life, even within the village confines, that was directly challenged by the universalising of the symbol of the land in terms of God's care for all. Finally, it was the tensions within the Galilean peasant life, caught between the opposing poles of a hellenistic city-ethos and a particularistic Jewish centre, that formed an integral part of Jesus' human and social experience and challenged him personally to adopt a critical yet appreciative stance in regard to his religious inheritance. He was thereby prompted to formulate on his own authority a new understanding of God's will that was deeply inspired by that received tradition, yet could include insights of human wisdom also, even as these had been expressed within the peasant ethos itself. In the process he articulated through very concrete examples a radical view of the demands of God's call, if one was to share in the blessings of the new age that he proclaimed as present.

How was this radical alternative received in Galilee? At the outset it was suggested that this is one of the questions which has to be tackled by the historian of Jesus, but it presents itself most acutely for anyone attempting to write that history in social rather than religious categories. Our approach has been that in first-century Galilee these two dimensions were inextricably bound together, however useful it may be to separate them for analytical purposes. It has been possible to suggest, on the basis of both the evidence and the social needs, a wide popular appeal for Jesus' miracles of healing and exorcism, which thus attracted crowds to him, and gained the attention of the well off as well as the deprived. The social gospel of detachment from possessions, on the other hand, met with a very mixed reception, it would seem, if the condemnation of some of the more prosperous centres of his ministry is any yardstick. Yet the message did resonate with the poor, whose presence in the Galilean setting, as well as everywhere else in antiquity, it would be foolhardy to deny. The contention has been, however, that these did not form the bulk of the population, and were to be found drifting to the cities rather than in the countryside. Insofar as the Herodian affluence was an obvious and clear reminder to them of their position of social inequality, as it certainly was later at Tiberias, according to *Life*, there is little difficulty in understanding their desire to cast Jesus in the role of popular king in contrast to the Herodian tyrant. Yet the failure of such a strategy and its lack of impact on the populace at large is best attested by the absence of any move against him by the political authorities, something that was a feature of all instances of popular aspirants to kingship known to us.

As a teacher, Jesus is represented in the gospels as having operated a two-tiered system, with different audiences for different occasions and settings and two different styles—one for the crowds and the other for a small band of companion-disciples. It is difficult to decide how far that picture is the product of later ecclesial tensions and patterns of organisation, since redaction criticism has certainly been able to uncover different concerns of different evangelists in that regard also.[66] Yet, on the basis of our analysis of the social world, there does seem to be a strong possibility that the pattern in its basic outline has genuine historical roots. The contents of Jesus' teaching corresponded with both its style and his own critical stance in regard to the prevailing attitudes and assumptions. Given the preponderance of warnings to the rich and the admonitions on the dangers of riches, it seems safe to assume that Jesus' audiences comprised as many of the relatively affluent as of the destitute in that society. There may be a hint of a more permanent teaching location at Capernaum or Cana, but in all the gospels the constant pattern is that of an itinerant ministry, accompanied by a small band of disciple-companions. It is to these, we have suggested, that the teaching of Jesus was primarily directed, and it is in this 'school' that his words began to be transmitted and reflected upon.

Since the outcome in Jerusalem does not suggest a large band of Galileans as part of that permanent retinue, the more likely assumption must be that this band was always a fairly limited group, rather than the opposite, namely that he had a large band of permanent followers who subsequently became disillusioned. Theissen speaks of sympathisers in the local communities, since all could not possibly have undertaken the radical life-style envisaged in the teaching.[67] While this is indeed a fair assumption, based on the instructions that were issued to the disciples-become-missionaries, yet the frequent

66. Cf. in particular the articles by P. Minear: 'The Disciples and the Crowd in the Gospel of Matthew', in *Gospel Studies in Honour of S.E. Johnson*, ed. M. Sheppard jr. and E.C. Hobbs, ATR Supplement Series III, 1974, 28–44; 'Audience Criticism and Markan Ecclesiology', in *Neues Testament und Geschichte. Festschrift Oscar Cullmann*, Tübingen: J.C.B. Mohr, 1972, 79–90.

67. See *Sociology of Early Palestinian Christianity*, 17–23.

warnings about rejection and persecution as well as the relatively few traces of a Galilean Christianity in our later sources strongly suggest that such sympathisers, in the sense of those who were committed to his new way to the point of being willing to abandon the pattern of their Jewish practice (pilgrimage, offerings and the like), were in a definite minority, both during Jesus' life-time and immediately after his death. The example of the Galilean, James, who represented a more conservative point of view on the question of the relationship of the old and the new, than did his brother, Jesus, or for that matter, the leader of the Twelve, Peter (Gal 2:1–10), should warn against assuming that entry into, or sympathy with the new movement centred on Jesus, was an easy option, either on religious or on social grounds, for Galilean Jews.

At several points in the preceding discussion eschatological and/or apocalyptic ideas surfaced, but we did not choose to pursue these for several reasons. The symbol βασιλεία τοῦ θεοῦ was undoubtedly central to Jesus' own religious vision, and for those Jews whose religious faith found expression in the concrete symbols of temple, land and torah, it was also the master symbol, of which these others were the concrete embodiments.[68] As Israel's king Yahweh was enthroned in the Jerusalem temple, the land of Israel was his property, which Israel held in trust for him, and his will was expressed in the written torah, irrespective of the different interpretations and the need to produce an oral torah alongside the written one. Most approaches to the historical Jesus view his kingdom-understanding as central and determinative of everything else about his ministry—teaching, miracles, call to discipleship. However, such an approach has its inherent dangers in that an implicit Christology can determine the way

68. It is one of the values of Norman Perrin's last work, *Jesus and the Language of the Kingdom*, Philadelphia: Fortress, 1976, that he challenged the prevailing view of the kingdom in the preaching of Jesus as a *concept*, arguing instead that it should be regarded as a *symbol*. In an as yet unpublished paper, 'Where is the Kingdom?', delivered to the British and Irish Theological Society in 1985, I attempted to develop Perrin's insight comparatively, by reviewing the different ways in which the symbol was appropriated in different segments of Judaism and Early Christianity, suggesting that it had a social rather than a temporal significance. Cf. further along the same lines, M. Borg, 'A Temperate Case for a Non-Eschatological Jesus', *Forum*, 2,3, 81–103.

in which the recoverable historical data about Jesus are interpreted and made to cohere. Since our explicit concern was to explore the meaning of Galilee for Jesus' self-understanding, the focus intentionally was on the way in which the Jewish religious tradition was appropriated in that particular social setting with a view to evaluating its impact on Jesus' career. It seemed better to approach that tradition through its concrete, tangible expressions rather than through the more mythological symbolism of Yahweh's kingship. In adopting this approach, we are being faithful to our initial starting-point, since all the gospel writers, while setting the story of Jesus within the more inclusive story of the kingdom, do not allow that background to take over to the point of destroying, the realistic, 'historical' character of their respective narratives.

Yet there are those scholars, such as Lohmeyer, who claimed that Galilee was the home of apocalyptic expectation, often combining such assertions with other stereotypes about the region, such as its revolutionary character, its lack of concern with torah and its impoverished social conditions. Hopefully, all these views have been challenged to the point that they can no longer be regarded as tenable on the basis of the discussion in the previous chapters. Yet, in view of the fact that social scientists now associate the apocalyptic mentality with conditions of relative, rather than absolute deprivation, there is perhaps a new case to be made for an apocalyptic mood in Galilee.[69] Could it be that the Galileans, enjoying a situation of relative affluence but excluded from power, while contributing handsomely by the payment of their dues to the maintenance of the existing power-structure, had been able to reconstruct an alternative symbolic system that was centred on themselves rather than on the Jerusalem priestly and scribal aristocracies? We have seen that there would appear to have been some end-time speculation centred on the return of the northern-based prophet, Elijah, and that *I Enoch* and *The*

69. J. Gager, *Kingdom and Community. The Social World of Early Christianity*, Englewood Cliffs, N.J., Prentice Hall, 1975. 22–27, basing himself on the anthropological studies of S. Talmon and D. Aberle in *Reader in Comparative Religion: An Anthropological Approach*, edts. W. Lesa and E. Vogt, New York, Harper and Row, 1965, 522–537 and 537–41.

Testament of Levi locate certain visions that were critical of Jerusalem and its priesthood in Upper Galilee. Suggestive as both examples are in providing a backdrop for Jesus' ministry in Galilee, we are too poorly informed on how apocalyptic ideas might have found expression among country people to have any confidence in claiming a widely-based apocalyptic mood in Galilee. It is to the literate groups such as the Essenes and the Pharisees, both originating, it seems, in the *hasîdîm* of Maccabean times, as well as to the scribes who taught about Elijah, that we must attribute the continuance of apocalyptic speculation and its literary expression, and Galilee, we saw, did not provide the proper social basis for such movements, at least on any large scale that would have been popular with the masses.

Ultimately, it is the Jesus movement itself that provides the best examples of a Galilean-based movement of apocalyptic inspiration, and as we have seen, it was less than successful with the masses, even though it filled a genuine social need, and in one aspect at least, offered a form of re-organisation that might have been expected to have wide appeal in Galilee. The Twelve, symbolic of the restored Israel and its tribal leaders, and acting as its judges, were Galileans, not Judeans, and, like Jesus himself, their position was not due to any inherited office of family or lineage.[70] This particular image of 'restoration eschatology', with its appeal to the pre-Mosaic and pre-Davidic constitution of Israel might have been expected to have a particular resonance in the north, in view of the history of the northern tribes and the still lively speculation as to their fate in first-century apocalyptic literature. Yet, if our analysis is correct, the group, or its leader, did not fire the Galileans at large with the belief that the new age had in fact dawned. True to the peasant point of view

70. The most thorough study of the background to the selection of the Twelve in terms of the ongoing Jewish tradition in its various forms from the LXX to later rabbinic commentaries, is that of W. Horbury, 'The Twelve and the Phylarchs', *NTS* 32(1986) 503–27. His concluding remarks are highly pertinent to the point we are developing here: 'Further, the choice of the Twelve suggests a distinctive mentality. Jesus thereby attached himself to an archaic, non-synedrial and eschatologically charged constitutional model... Contemporary interpretation of the phylarchs suggests that a mind that could summon up the Twelve worked on lines that were uncongenial to 'the rulers and elders and scribes in Jerusalem' (Ac 4:5).

everywhere, they remained innately suspicious of the locals made good, a pattern we see repeated at the time of the first revolt when it was the Jerusalemite, Josephus, rather than the native John of Gischala, who was accepted as leader, and who was able to implement a system of courts throughout the province without any demur on the part of the Galileans.

Our examination of the way in which the system of temple, land and torah had been re-interpreted by Jesus, can help to explain why not even the claim of being about to inaugurate the new age could sever the attachment of the Galileans to these symbols as they were administered by the priestly and scribal aristocracies of rank and power. The symbol 'kingdom' was itself polyvalent and, like all symbols drawn from the realm of human affairs rather than nature, had its specific referents determined by prevailing cultural and social assumptions. In first-century Judaism its range of associations included the roles of law-giver, judge, warrior, benefactor, upholder of the moral order as chastiser of the ungodly, all-holy one, creator, lord of the universe. These aspects are not of course exclusive of each other, and many of them are found in association in the different groups known to us and their philosophies. In attempting to attribute a new and, as it transpired, revolutionary meaning to this Kingdom symbol, Jesus was faced with a delicate hermeneutical task, given all the popular associations and prevailing moods. The absence of any regal or courtly images, as well as the removal of almost all militaristic overtones and associations of domination or power over others, were subversive of the expectations generally associated with the symbol, especially within apocalyptic circles where it had been developed in association with the A.N.E. divine-warrior combat myth. Jesus had transformed it into an image of service through association with his own career, to the point that not even his close disciple-companions understood its implications. A new kingdom-praxis was articulated that was both novel and subversive of the value-system that the accepted symbols enjoined in the name of God's authoritative rule over Israel. Despite the fact that the majority of Galileans did not accept the new understanding or badly misjudged its intentions, Galilee emerged not just as a remembered homeland but as a symbol of that newness for the few Galileans who continued to grapple with the meaning of their experiences after the project initiated by Jesus appeared to have ended in total failure. The narratives of Jesus the Galilean that have been left to us in the gospel portraits of his career there are an eloquent testimony to just how radical and transforming that experience had, after all, proved to be.

EPILOGUE

Galilee, Jesus and the Gospels

FOR Mark, Galilee is the place of definitive disclosure of the meaning of Jesus as God's agent of salvation. Matthew is at pains to show that the region can indeed receive a messianic visitation and that God's holy mountain of eschatological hope can be located there. Luke portrays it as a place of beginnings, some of whose residents were privileged to be witnesses of the divine visitation occurring in Jesus and were destined subsequently to initiate a mission to the end of the earth. John's Galileans are among those who receive Jesus, as distinct from the Jews who reject him, and hence his narrative also ends with a final commissioning scene in Galilee.

Thus, in all the versions of the story of Jesus which have come down to us, Galilee is charged with a highly positive symbolism in terms of the proclamation of the early church concerning God's saving action in Jesus. As such, it stands over against Jerusalem, the holy city, whose central role for Jewish hopes is recognised, but which tragically remained unfulfilled because of the rejection of Jesus. The actual destruction of the temple by the Romans in the year 70 CE stands between the writers of the gospel narratives and the events being narrated, and this traumatic event for Jews and Christians is woven into their story in the form of prophetic or parabolic utterances that would soon be realised. Thus the rejection of Jesus by Jerusalem and Jerusalem's rejection by God are two poles of the axis around which the narratives revolve.

The present study has been concerned to uncover the dimensions of this faith-story in all their rich diversity and tragic irony, while at the same time enquiring about the ways in which actual historical experiences within a Galilean setting might lie at the root of later reflection. Our investigations suggest that there are, indeed, interesting correspondences between the contours of the story of Jesus as narrated and what could plausibly be said of his own and his movement's impact in a Galilean setting. Indeed, not only do the broad outlines correspond, but at several points significant details stand up to vigorous critical examination in terms of their historical likelihood. That broad conclusion, based as it is on the literary and theological creativity that has generated our gospels, poses interesting questions about the role of those narratives within early Christian self-definition, and the intentions of those who produced them. At the same time it stands as a challenge to those who study the gospels to recognise the importance of a variety of approaches to documents which are themselves highly polyvalent in their conception, production and intention.

Yet our study has not merely been an attempt to justify a particular methodological approach to the gospels, but an exploration of the meaning of the symbol Galilee in relation to Jesus and his movement. The kerygmatic portrayals point the way back to the historical reality, but this in turn enlightens the faith proclamation. The complex set of social and religious tensions within which Galilean life was lived in the first century was indeed fertile soil for the emergence of an alternative view of Jewish faith and practice; on the one hand this was deeply attached to and respectful of the central symbols of that faith, and yet, on the other hand it was constantly being drawn to break out of a narrow definition of the meaning of those symbols and to recognise their universal importance in religious terms. That this re-defining within a particular social setting would eventually lead to a very different vision in which elements of the old would be brought together to create a new system, may have been perceived only dimly by those Galileans who first encountered Jesus, but it must have been perceptible in some blurred fashion even during the Galilean ministry. By the time the gospels came to be written it had come clearly into focus. God's presence had been completely de-centred for the followers of Jesus and the system of observances that a localised understanding of that presence had sanctioned was for them thoroughly destabilised.

It is possible to point to an intermediate stage between Jesus and the final gospel narratives as the articulation of this vision within the New Testament itself. The hellenist, Stephen, spoke openly against the temple and the law, arguing from the Scriptures, according to Luke, that the Almighty did not dwell in temples made with hands, and that God's election was not confined to the land of Israel. While one can recognise the 'Lucan' character of this speech, both in terms of style and content, it would be unwise to dismiss its sentiments as being merely the product of much later circumstances, without also acknowledging Luke's historical intention in relating the whole Stephen episode. What, if any, contacts did the hellenists have with the original Galilean experience? What, if any, mission to Galilee took place after Stephen's death, and how has it left its mark on the narratives about Galilee which we have been discussing? These are difficult questions that must largely go unanswered in the absence of any positive information beyond the very brief notice of Acts 9:31. Yet, the sense of rejection and persecution reflected in some, at least, of the sayings preserved in the Q source, as well as the lack of evidence for a widespread Galilean Chrisitianity in the second century, point to the fact that such a mission, if, in fact, it did take place, was no more successful than was that of Jesus with the Galilean masses. In that sense at least there was continuity between the pre- and post-Easter experiences, however the continuities of the personnel involved are regarded.

Our study has recognised in passing, at certain points, this intermediate phase in the development of the story of Jesus the Galilean, but it has not been possible to address formally the question of tracing the stages of such a development within the context of the present discussion. The aim was to investigate the possible correlation of the narratives about Jesus in Galilee with the shape of his actual ministry there, as this could be critically reconstructed in the light of the prevailing social and religious world. Yet in the Stephen episode as well as in the Q-community's experience, we can recognise important stepping-stones along the winding path that leads from the Galilean Jesus and his vision to the story about him as narrated by the different evangelists.

Insofar as all those narratives use Galilee as a symbol of the periphery becoming the new, non-localised centre of divine presence, and portray a Galilean charismatic and his retinue replacing the established religious leaders of Judaism, there is a highly paradoxical, even comic, character to the story. The pilgrim from Galilee subverts the place of pilgrimage even as he goes there; his journey becomes the new way that replaces the torah-symbol for those who follow him; their journey is to lead them, not to the centre where their Jewish faith has told them God can be encountered, but to bear witness to a new mode of encounter outside the land. Thus, the religious implications of the narratives of Jesus' career bear a striking resemblance to the paradoxical, comic kerygma of the folly of the cross confounding the wisdom of this world. The two statements, the one in narrative form, the other in kerygmatic proclamation, have a similar pattern and intent. It was, perhaps, this correspondence, rather than any nostalgic, 'biographical' memories from the past, which ensured that genuine reminiscences of Jesus' career in Galilee, in its social role and its religious claims, continued to play a significant part in the expression of early Christian belief and identity. If Christian faith is to maintain its distinctive identity today, the historical as well as the kerygmatic intentions of those narratives must continue to be retrieved.

Bibliography

Applebaum, S., 'Hellenistic Cities of Judea and its Vicinity', B. Levick, ed., *The Ancient Historian and his Materials. Essays in Honour of C.E. Stevens*, Farnborough, 1975, 59–73.

Applebaum, S., 'Jewish Urban Communities and Greek Influences', *Scripta Classica Israelitica*, 5(1979) 158–77.

Applebaum, S., 'Judea as a Roman Province. The Countryside as a Political and Economic Factor'. *ANRW* II, 8, 355–96.

Ashton, J., 'The Identity and Function of the 'ΙΟΥΔΑΙΟΙ in the Fourth Gospel', *NT* 27(1985) 40–75.

Avery-Peck, A., *Mishnah's Division of Agriculture. A History and Theology of Seder Zeraim*, Brown Judaic Series 79, Chico: Scholars Press, 1985.

Avi-Yonah, M., 'The Foundation of Tiberias', *IEJ* 1(1950) 160–69.

Bachmann, M., *Jerusalem und der Tempel: Die geographisch-theologischen Elemente in der lukanischen Sicht des jüdischen Kultzentrums*, BWANT 109; Stuttgart: Kohlhammer, 1980.

Bagatti, B., 'Caphernaum, la ville de Pierre', *La Monde de la Bible* 27 (1983) 8–16.

Bammel, E., 'Christian Origins in Jewish Tradition', *NTS* 13(1967) 317–35.

Bammel, E., (editor and contributor), *The Trial of Jesus. Cambridge Studies in Honour of C.F.D. Moule*, London: SCM 1970.

Bammel, E. & Moule, C.F.D., ed., *Jesus and the Politics of his Day,* Cambridge: University Press, 1984.

Barker, M., 'Some Reflections on the Enoch Myth', *JSOT* 15(1980) 7–29.

Barrett, C.K., 'Saint John: Social Historian', *PIBA* 10(1986) 26–39.

Bassler, J., 'The Galileans: A Neglected Factor in Johannine Research', *CBQ* 43 (1981) 243–57.

Batey, R., 'Is not this the Carpenter?', NTS 30(1984) 249–58.

Bauer, W., 'Jesus der Galiläer', in G. Strecker, ed., *Aufsätze und Kleine Schriften*, Tübingen 1907, 91–108.

Baumgarten, J., 'The Essene Avoidance of Oil and the Laws of Purity', *RQ* 6(1967) 184–92.

Beardslee, W., 'Parable Interpretation and World Disclosed by Parable', *Perspectives in Religious Studies* 3 (1976) 123–39.

Best, E., 'The Role of the Disciples in Mark', *NTS* 23 (1976) 377–401.

Betz, O., 'Probleme des Prozesses Jesu', *ANRW* II, 25.1, 565–647.

Biran, A., 'To the God who is in Dan', in A. Biran ed. *Temples and High Places in Biblical Times,* Jerusalem: Nelson Glueck School of Biblical Archaeology, 1981, 142–51.

Blomberg, C.L., 'The Law in Luke-Acts', *JSNT* 22(1984) 53–80.

Boff, L., *Jesus Christ Liberator. A Critical Christology for Our Times,* E.T. New York: Orbis Press, 1978.

Bokser, B.M., 'Wonder-Working and the Rabbinic Tradition: The Case of Hanina ben Dosa', *JSJ* 16(1985) 42–92.

Boobyer, G., 'Galilee and Galileans in St. Mark's Gospel', *BJRL* 35(1953) 334–48.

Booth, W., *The Rhetoric of Fiction*, Chicago: University Press, 1961.

Booth, W., *A Rhetoric of Irony*, Chicago: University Press, 1974.

Borg, M., 'A Temperate Case for a Non-Eschatological Jesus', *Forum* 2,3, 81–103.

Bornkamm, G., *Jesus of Nazareth*, E.T., London: SCM. 1960.

Bornkamm, G., 'The Stilling of the Storm in Matthew', in G. Bornkamm, G. Barth and H.J. Held, *Tradition and Interpretation in Matthew*, London: SCM, 1963, 52–7.

Bösen, D.W., *Galiläa als Lebenstraum und Wirkungsfeld Jesu*, Freiburg im Breisgau: Herder, 1985.

Bostock, D., 'Jesus as the New Elisha', *ET* 92(1980) 39–41.

Boucher, M., *The Mysterious Parable. A Literary Study*, CBQMS 6, Washington D.C.: The Catholic Biblical Association of America, 1977.

Brandon, S.F.G., *Jesus and the Zealots*, Manchester: University Press, 1967.

Brodie, L.T., 'Towards Unraveling Luke's Use of the Old Testament: Lk 7:11–17 as an *Imitatio* of 1 Kgs 17:17–24', *NTS* 32(1986) 247–67.

Brooten, B., *Women Leaders in Ancient Synagogues*, Brown Judaic Series 36, Chico: Scholars Press, 1982.

Brown, P., 'The Rise and Function of the Holy Man in Late Antiquity', *JRS* 61(1971) 80–100.

Brown, R.E., 'Jesus and Elisha', *Perspectives* 12(1971) 84–104.

Brown, R.E., *The Gospel according to John*, 2 vols., Anchor Bible 29 and 29A, New York: Doubleday, 1966 and 1968.

Brown, R.E., *The Community of the Beloved Disciple*, London: Geoffrey Chapman, 1979.
Bruce, F.F., 'Render to Caesar', in Bammel/Moule, ed., *Jesus and the Politics of His Day*, 249–63.
Burridge, K., *New Heaven, New Earth*, New York: Schocken, 1961.

Carney, T.F., *The Shape of the Past. Models and Antiquity*, Lawrence, Kansas: Coronado Press, 1975.
Chatman, S., *Story and Discourse. Narrative Structure in Fiction and Film*, Ithaca and London: Cornell University Press, 1978.
Chilton, B., *God in Strength: Jesus' Announcement of the Kingdom*, Freistadt: Plöchl, 1979.
Chilton, B., 'Announcement in Nazara', in R.T. France and D. Wenham, ed., *Gospel Perspectives*, II, Sheffield: JSOT Press, 1982.
Chilton, B., 'Jesus ben David. Reflections on the Davidssohnfrage', *JSNT* 14(1982) 88–112.
Chilton, B., *A Galilean Rabbi and his Bible. Jesus' Use of the Interpreted Scripture of his Time*, Wilmington: Glazier, 1984.
Coggins, R.J., *Samaritans and Jews. The Origins of Samaritanism Reconsidered*, Oxford: Blackwell, 1975.
Cohen, S., *Josephus in Galilee and Rome. His Vita and Development as an Historian*, Leiden: Brill, 1979.
Conzelmann, H., *The Theology of Luke*, E.T. London: Faber, 1960.
Cook, M., *Mark's Treatment of the Jewish Leaders*, Leiden: Brill, 1978.
Cope, L., *Matthew. A Scribe Trained for the Kingdom of Heaven*, CBQMS 5, Washington D.C.: The Catholic Biblical Association of America, 1975.
Corbo, V., 'Resti della sinagoga del primo secolo a Cafarnao' in G.C. Bottini, ed., *Studia Hierosylimitana* III, Jerusalem, 1982, 313–57.
Cross, F.M., *Canaanite Myth and Hebrew Epic*, Cambridge, Mass: Harvard University Press, 1973.
Crossan, J.D., *In Parables*, New York: Harper and Row, 1975.
Crossan, J.D., (editor and contributor), *Semeia* 4, *Paul Ricoeur on Biblical Hermeneutics*, Missoula: Scholars Press, 1975.
Crossan, J.D., *In Fragments*, New York: Harper and Row, 1983.
Cullmann, O., *The Johannine Circle*, E.T. London: SCM 1976.
Culpepper, A., *The Anatomy of the Fourth Gospel. A Study in Literary Design*, Philadelphia: Fortress Press, 1983.

Danker, F., *Luke*, Proclamation Commentaries, Philadelphia: Fortress Press, 1976.

Davies, P., 'The Ideology of the Temple in the Damascus Document', *JJS* 33(1982) 287–301.

Davies, W.D., *The Gospel and the Land. Early Christianity and Jewish Territorial Doctrine*, Berkley: University of California Press, 1974.

Demaux, A., 'L'hypocrisie des Pharisiens et le dessein de Dieu: Analyse de Lc XIII 31–33, in F. Neirynck, ed., *L'Évangile de Luc. Problèmes Litteraires et Théologiques*, Louvain: Peeters Press, 1983, 244–85.

Dodd, C.H., *The Interpretation of the Fourth Gospel*, Cambridge: University Press, 1953.

Donahue, J.R., *Are You the Christ? The Trial Narrative in the Gospel of Mark*, SBL Dissertation Series 10, Missoula: Society of Biblical Literature, 1973.

Donahue, J.R., 'Tax-Collectors and Sinners. An Attempt at an Identification', *CBQ* 33(1971) 39–61.

Donahue, J.R., 'Jesus as the Parable of God in the Gospel of Mark', *Interpretation* 32(1978) 369–86.

Donaldson, T., *Jesus on the Mountain. A Study of Matthean Theology*, Sheffield: JSOT Press, 1985.

Downing, G., 'Freedom from the Law in Luke-Acts', *JSNT* 26 (1986) 49–52.

Drury, J., *The Parables in the Gospels. History and Allegory*, London: SPCK, 1984.

Dufour, X.L., 'Les Évangiles Synoptiques', in A. Robert and A. Feuillet, ed., *Introduction à la Bible*, Tournai: Desclée, 1959, 144–336.

Duling, D., 'Solomon, Exorcism and the Son of David', *HTR* 68(1975) 235–52.

Dunn, J.G., 'Let John be John', in P. Stuhlmacher, ed. *Das Evangelium und die Evangelien*, *WUNT* 28, Tübingen: J.C.B. Mohr, 1983, 309–40.

Dupont, J., *Teologia della Chiesa negli Atti degli Apostoli*, Bologna: Edizioni Dehoniane, 1984.

Duprez, A., *Jésus et les Dieux Guerisseurs*, Cahiers de la Revue Biblique 12, Paris: Gabalda, 1970.

Elliot, J., *Home for the Homeless, A Sociological Exegesis of I Peter. Its Situation and Strategy*, Philadelphia: Fortress Press, 1981.

Elliot, J., 'Social-Scientific Criticism of the New Testament: More on Methods and Models', *Semeia* 32(1986) 1–33.

Evans, C.A., 'Luke's Use of the Elijah/Elisha Narratives and the Ethics of Election', *JBL* 106(1987) 85–111.

Finley, M.I., *Politics in the Ancient World*, Cambridge: University Press, 1983.

Fitzmyer, J., *The Gospel according to Luke*, 2 vols. Anchor Bible, 28 and 28A, New York: Doubleday, 1981 and 1985.

Fleddermann, H., 'A Warning about Scribes', *CBQ* 44(1982), 52–68.

Flusser, D., 'Paganism in Palestine', in Safrai/Stern, ed., *Compendia* 2, 1065–100.

Fortna, R.T., 'Source and Redaction in the Fourth Gospel's Portrayal of Jesus' Signs', *JBL* 89(1970) 151–66.

Fortna, R.T., 'Theological Use of Locale in the Fourth Gospel', *ATR* Supplements 3, 1974.

Fowler, R., *Loaves and Fishes. The Function of the Feeding Stories in the Gospel of Mark*, Chico: Scholars Press, 1981.

Fowler, R., 'Who is the Reader in Reader-Response Criticism?', *Semeia* 31(1985) 5–26.

Fowler, R., 'Reading Matthew, Reading Mark: Observing the First Steps toward Meaning-as-Reference in the Synoptic Gospels', in K. Richards, ed., *SBL Seminar Papers*, Atlanta: Scholars Press 1986, 1–16.

Freyne, S., *The Twelve: Disciples and Apostles. An Introduction to the Theology of the First Three Gospels*, London: Sheed and W ard. 1968.

Freyne, S., *Galilee from Alexander the Great to Hadrian. A Study of Second Temple Judaism*, Wilmington: Glazier/Notre Dame Univ ersity Press, 1980.

Freyne , S., 'The Galileans in the Light of Josephus' *Vita*', *NTS* 26(1980) 397–413.

Freyne, S., 'The Disciples in Mark and the *maskîlîm* in Daniel. A Comparison', *JSNT* 16(1982) 7–23.

Freyne, S., 'Vilifying the Other and Defining the Self. Matthew's and John's Anti-Judaism in Focus', in Neusner/Frerichs, ed., '*To See Ourselves as Others See Us*', 117-44.

Freyne, S., 'Our Preoccupation with History. Problems and Prospects', *PIBA* 9(1985) 1–19.

Freyne, S., 'Galilee-Jerusalem Relations in the Light of Josephus' *Life*, *NTS* 33(1987) 600–609.

Freyne, S., 'Bandits in Galilee. A Contribution to the Study of Social Conditions in First-Century Palestine', in Neusner *et al.* ed., *The Social World of Formative Christianity and Judaism. Essays in Tribute of Howard Clark Kee*, Philadelphia: Fortress Press, 1988, 50–69.

Freyne, S., 'The Charismatic' in G.W.E. Nickelsburg and J.J. Collins, ed., *Ideal Figures in Ancient Judaism*, S.B.L. Septuagint and Cognate Studies 12, Chico: Scholars Press 1980, 223–58.

Fuks, G., 'The Jews of Hellenistic and Roman Scythopolis', *JJS* 33(1982) 407–16.

Gager, J., *Kingdom and Community. The Social World of Early Christianity*, Englewood Cliffs, N.J.: Prentice Hall, 1975.

Garland, D., *The Intention of Matthew 23*, Leiden: Brill 1979.

Garnsey, P., 'Peasants in Ancient Roman Society', *JPS* 2(1975) 222-35.

Geertz, C., *The Interpretation of Cultures*, New York: Basic Books, 1973.

Geller, M., 'Jesus' Theurgic Powers: Parallels in the Talmud and the Incantation Bowls', *JJS* 28(1977) 141–55.

Gerhardsson, B., *Memory and Manuscript. Oral Tradition and Written Transmission in Rabbinic Judaism and Early Christianity*, Lund: C.W.K. Gleerup, 1961.

Gerhardsson, B., *The Origins of the Gospel Traditions*, E.T. London: SCM 1979.

Green, W. Scott, 'Palestinian Holy Men: Charismatic Leadership and Rabbinic Tradition', *ANRW* II, 19.2, 619–647.

Green, W. Scott, ed., *Approaches to Ancient Judaism, Vol. 5 Studies in Judaism in its Greco-Roman Context*, Brown Judaic Studies 32, Atlanta: Scholars Press, 1985.

Goodman, M., *State and Society in Roman Galilee A.D. 132–212*, Totowa N.J.: Rowman and Allenheld, 1983.

Goodman, M., Review of H.A. Harris, *Greek Athletics and the Jews*, Cardiff: University of Wales Press, *JJS* 28(1977) 206f.

Goodman, M., 'The First Jewish Revolt: Social Conflict and the Problem of Debt', *JJS* 33(1982) 417–26.

Grundmann, W., *Jesus der Galiläer und das Judentum*, Leipzig, 1941.

Guttman, S., 'The Synagogue at Gamla', in L. Levine ed., *Ancient Synagogues Revealed*, 30–34.

Hanson, R., *Tyrian Influences in Upper Galilee*, Cambridge, Mass.: ASOR Monographs, 1980.

Harvey, A.E., *Jesus and the Constraints of History*, London: Duckworth, 1982.

Hengel, M., *Die Zeloten*, 2nd edn, AGSU 1, Leiden: Brill, 1976.

Hengel, M., *Judentum und Hellenismus, Studien zu ihrer Begegnung unter besonderer Berücksichtigung Palästinas bis zur Mitte des 2 Jh's vor Chr.*, 2nd edn, *WUNT* 10, Tübingen: J.C.B. Mohr, 1973.

Hengel, M., 'Das Gleicnis von den bösen Weingärtnern, Mc 12:1–12, im Lichte des Zenonpapyri und der rabbinischen Gleichnisse', *ZNW* 59(1968) 1–39.

Hengel, M., *The Charismatic Leader and his Followers*, E.T. Edinburgh: T. and T. Clark, 1981.

Hengel, M., *Rabbinische Legende und frühpharisäische Geschichte. Schimeon ben Schetach und die achtzig Hexen von Askalon*. Heidelberg: Carl Winter Universitätsverlag. 1984.

Hengel, M., *Studies in the Gospel of Mark*, E.T. London: SCM, 1985.

Hengel, M., 'Jakobus der Herrenbruder—der erste Päpst?', in E. Grässer and O. Merk ed., *Glaube und Eschatologie. Festschrift für W.G. Kummel zum 80. Geburtstag*, Tübingen: J.C.B. Mohr, 1985, 71–104.

Hengel, M., Charlesworth J., & Mendels, D., 'The Polemical Character of 'On Kingship' in the Temple Scroll. An Attempt at Dating 11 Q Temple', *JJS* 37 (1986) 28–38.

Hobsbawn, E., 'Peasants and Politics', *JPS* 1(1974) 3–23.

Hobsbawn, E., *Bandits*, 3rd rev. edn, New York: Pantheon Books, 1981.

Hoehner, H., *Herod Antipas*, *SNTS* Monograph Series 17, Cambridge: University Press, 1972.

Hoffmann, L., *The Canonization of the Synagogue Service*, Notre Dame: University Press, 1979.

Hollenbach, P., 'Social Aspects of John the Baptiser's Preaching Mission in the Context of Palestinian Judaism', *ANRW* II, 19. 1, 850–75.

Hooker, M., 'Christology and Methodology', *NTS* 7(1971) 480–88.

Horbury, W., 'The Twelve and the Phylarchs', *NTS* 32(1986) 503–27.

Horsley, R., 'Josephus and the Bandits', *JSJ* 10(1979) 37–63.

Horsley, R., 'Ancient Jewish Banditry and the Revolt against Rome', *CBQ* 43(1981) 409–32.

Horsley, R., 'Popular Messianic Movements around the Time of Jesus', *CBQ* 46(1984) 475–95.

Horsley, R., 'Like One of the Prophets of Old', Two Types of Popular Prophets at the Time of Jesus', *CBQ* 47(1985) 435–63.

Horsley,R., 'Popular Prophetic Movements at the Time of Jesus. Their Principal Features and Social Origins', *JSNT* 26(1986) 3–27.

Horsley, R., 'Menahem in Jerusalem. A Brief Messianic Episode among the *Sicarii*—Not "Zealot Messianism"', *NT* 27(1985) 334–48.

Horsley, R., 'Ethics and Exegesis: 'Love your Enemies' and the Doctrine of Non-Violence', *JAAR* 54(1985) 3–31.

Horsley, R., 'High Priests and Politics in Roman Palestine', *JSJ* 17(1986) 23–55.

Horsley, R., 'The Zealots. Their Origin, Relationship and Importance in the Jewish Revolt', *NT* 18(1986) 159–92.

Horsley, R., & Hanson, J.S., *Bandits, Prophets, and Messiahs. Popular Movements at the Time of Jesus*, New York: Winston Press (A Seabury Book), 1985.

Hull, J., *Hellenistic Magic and the Synoptic Miracle Stories*, London: SCM 1976.

Isenberg, S., 'Power through Temple and Torah in Greco-Roman Palestine', in J. Neusner ed. *Christianity, Judaism and Other Greco-Roman Cults*, Leiden: Brill 1975, 24–53.

Jeanrond, W., *Text and Interpretation as Categories of Theological Thinking*, E.T. Dublin: Gill and Macmillan, 1988.

Jeremias, J., *Jerusalem at the Time of Jesus*, E.T. London: SCM 1969.

Jervell, J., *Luke and the People of God. A New Look at Luke-Acts*, Minneapolis: Augsburg Publishing House, 1972.

Johnson, L.T., *The Literary Function of Possessions in Luke-Acts*, *SBL* Dissertation Series 39, Missoula: Scholars Press 1977.

Jones, A.M.H., 'The Urbanisation of Palestine', *JRS* 21(1933) 265–75.

Juel, D., *Messiah and Temple. The Trial of Jesus in the Gospel of Mark*, *SBL* Dissertation Series 31, Missoula: Scholars Press, 1977.

Kampling, R., 'Jesus von Nazareth. Exorzist und Lehrer', BZ 30(1986) 237–48.

Kee, H. Clark, *Community of the New Age. Studies in Mark's Gospel*, Philadelphia: Westminster Press, 1977.

Kee, H. Clark, *Miracle in the Early Christian World. A Study in Socio-historical Method*, New Haven and London: Yale University Press, 1983.

Kee, H. Clark, 'Medicine. Miracle and Magic', Boston: University Lecture, 1985.

Kelber, W., *The Kingdom in Mark. A New Time and a New Place*, Philadelphia: Fortress Press, 1974.

Kelber, W., *The Oral and Written Gospel*, Philadelphia: Fortress Press.

Kingsbury, J., *Matthew: Structure, Christology, Kingdom*, Philadelphia: Fortress Press, 1975.

Kingsbury, J., *Matthew as Story*, Philadelphia: Fortress Press, 1986.

Kingsbury, J., 'The Developing Conflict between Jesus and the Jewish Leaders in Matthew', *CBQ*. 49(1987) 57–73.

Kippenberg, H., *Religion und Klassenbildung im Antiken Judäa*, Göttingen: Vandenhoeck und Ruprecht, 1978.

Klauck, H.J., 'Der erzälerische Rolle der Jünger im Markusevangeliums', *NT* 24(1982) 1–27.

Klein, G., *Die Zwölf Apostel. Ursprung und Gehalt einer Idee, FRLANT* 77, Göttingen: Vandenhoeck und Ruprecht, 1961.

Klein, S., *Galiläa vor der Makkabäerzeit bis 67*, Berlin, 1928.

Klijn, A.F.J., 'Jerome's Quotations from a Nazarean Interpretation of Isaiah', *RScR* 60 (1972) 241–52.

Kolenkow, A.B., 'The Relationship between Miracle and Prophecy in the Greco-Roman World', *ANRW* II, 23. 2, 1470–1506.

Kraabel, A.T., 'New Evidence of the Samaritan Diaspora has been found on Delos', *BA* 47(1984) 44–6.

Kreissig, H., *Die Sozialen Zusammenhänge des Judaischen Krieges*, Berlin, 1970.

Landau, Y.H., 'A Greek Inscription found near Hefzibah', *IEJ* 16(1966) 56–70.

Lang, B., 'The Social Organisation of Peasant Poverty in Biblical Israel', in id. ed., *Anthropological Approaches to the Old Testament*, London: SPCK, 1975, 83–99.

Lang, F., 'Über Sidon mittens ins Gebiet der Dekapolis. Geographie und Theologie in Markus 7:31', *ZDPV* 94(1978) 145–59.

Levenson, J., *Sinai and Zion*, New York: Winston Press, 1985.

Levine, L., 'R. Simeon ben Yohai and the Purification of Tiberias', *HUCA* 49(1974) 143–85.

Levine, L., ed., *Ancient Synagogues Revealed*, Jerusalem: Israel Exploration Society, 1981.

Levine, L., 'The Second Temple Synagogue: The Formative Years', in id. ed., *The Synagogue in Late Antiquity*, Philadelphia: ASOR Publications, 1986.

Lifshitz, B., 'Scythopolis. L'histoire, les institutions et les cultes de la ville a l'époque hellenistique et impériale', *ANRW* II, 8, 262–94.

Lightfoot, R.H., 'A Consideration of Three Markan Passages', in *In Memoriam E. Lohmeyer*, Stuttgart, 1951, 111–15.

Lightstone, J., 'Yose the Galilean in Mishnah-Tosefta and the History of Early Rabbinic Judaism', *JJS* 31(1980) 37–45.

Loffreda, S., 'Ceramica ellenistico-Romana nel sottosuole della singagoga di Cafarnao' in G.C. Bottini, ed., *Studia Hierosylimitana* III, Jerusalem, 1982, 273–312.
Lohmeyer, E., *Galiläa und Jerusalem*, *FRLANT* 34, Göttingen: Vandenhoeck und Ruprecht, 1936.
Lowe, M., 'Who were the *IYDAIOI*?', *NT* 18(1976) 101–30.
Luz, U., 'The Disciples in the Gospel according to Matthew', in G. Stanton, ed., *The Interpretation of Matthew*, London: SPCK, 1986, 98–128.

McKnight, E., *The Reader and the Bible*, Philadelphia: Fortress Press, 1986.
McLean Harper, G., 'Village Administration in the Roman Province of Syria', Yale Cl. St. 1(1928) 105-68.
McMullen, R., *Roman Social Relations, 50 B.C. to A.D. 284*, New Haven and London: Yale University Press.
McNamara, M., *Targum and Testament*, Shannon: Irish University Press, 1972.
McNamara, M., 'The Spoken Aramaic of First Century Palestine', *PIBA* 2(1977) 95–138.
McNamara, M., *Palestinian Judaism and the New Testament*, Wilmington: Glazier, 1983.
Maddox, R., *The Purpose of Luke-Acts*, Edinburgh: T. and T. Clark, reprint 1985.
Malina, B., 'Miracle or Magic', *RSR* 11(1985) 35–9.
Martyn, J.L., *History and Theology in the Fourth Gospel*, rev. edn, Nashville: Abingdon, 1979.
Marxsen, W., *Der Evangelist Markus. Studien zur Redaktionsgeschichte des Evangeliums*, *FRLANT* 67, Göttingen: Vandenhoeck and Ruprecht, 1956.
Meeks, W., 'Galilee and Judea in the Fourth Gospel', *JBL* 85(1966) 159–69.
Meeks, W., *The First Urban Christians*, New Haven and London: Yale Universty, Press, 1984.
Meier, J., 'John the Baptist in the Gospel of Matthew', *JBL* 99 (1980) 383–405.
Meier, J., *The Vision of Matthew. Christ, Church and Morality in the First Gospel*, New York: Paulist Press, 1979.
Metzger, B., *A Textual Commentary on the Greek New Testament*, London/New York: United Bible Societies, 1977.
Meyer, B., *The Aims of Jesus*, London: SCM, 1979.
Meyers. E., 'Galilean Regionalism as a Factor in Historical Reconstruction', *BASOR* 221(1976) 95–101.
Meyers. E., 'The Cultural Setting of Galilee: The Case of Regionalism and Early Judaism', *ANRW* II, 19.1, 686–702.

Meyers, E., 'Sepphoris, Ornament of All Galilee', *BA* 49(1986) 4–19.

Meyers, E., 'Galilean Regionalism: A Reappraisal', in W. Scott Green, ed., *Approaches to Ancient Judaism*, vol. 5, *Studies in Judaism and its Greco-Roman Context*, Brown Judaic Series 32, Atlanta: Scholars Press, 1985.

Meyers, E., Strange, J. & Groh, D., 'The Meiron Excavation Project: Archaeological Survey in Galilee and the Golan', *BASOR* 230(1978) 1–24.

Meyers, E., Strange, J. & Groh, D., *Archaeology, The Rabbis and Early Christianity*, London: SCM 1981.

Meyers, E., Strange, J. & Meyers, C., 'Preliminary Report on the 1977 and 1978 Seasons at Gush Halav (el—Jish), *BASOR* 233(1979) 33–58.

Meyers, E., Strange, J. & Meyers, C., 'Preliminary Report on the 1980 Excavations at en-Nabratein, Israel', *BASOR* 224(1981) 1–25.

Meyers, E., Strange, J. & Meyers, C., 'Second Preliminary Report on en-Nabratein, Israel', *BASOR* 246(1982) 35–54.

Meyers, E., Kraabel, T. & Strange, J., *Ancient Synagogue Excavations at Khirbet Shema'. Upper Galilee, 1970–72*, Annual of the American School of Oriental Research 42, Durham, NC: Duke University, 1976.

Meyers, E., Netzer, E., Meyers, C.L., 'Artistry in Stone. The Mosaics of Ancient Sepphoris', *BA* 50 (1987) 223–31.

Miller, S., *Studies in the History and Traditions of Sepphoris*, Leiden: Brill, 1984.

Minear, P., 'Audience Criticism and Markan Ecclesiology', in *Neues Testament und Geschichte. Festschrift O. Cullmann*. Tübingen: J.C.B. Mohr, 1972, 79–90.

Minear, P., 'Jesus' Audiences according to Luke', *NT* 16(1974) 81–109.

Mink, Hans Aage, 'The Use of Scripture in the Temple Scroll and the Status of the Scroll as Law', *SJOT*1 (1987) 20–50.

Mink, Hans Aage, 'The Disciples and the Crowd in the Gospel of Matthew', ATR Supplement Series 3 (1974) 28–44.

Moessner, D., 'Luke 9:1–50: Luke's Preview of the Journey of the Prophet like Moses of Deuteronomy', *JBL* 102(1983) 574–605.

Moore, S., 'Narrative Homiletics: Lucan Rhetoric and the Making of the Reader', unpublished Ph.D dissertation, Trinity College, Dublin, 1985.

Moxnes, H., 'Luke and the Pharisees', unpublished MS, Oslo, 1987.

Mussies, G., 'Greek in Palestine and the Diaspora', in *Compendia*, 2, (1976) 1040–64.

Mussner, F., 'Gab es eine Galiläische Krise?', in P. Hoffmann, N. Brox, W. Pesch, ed., *Orientierung an Jesus. Zur Theologie der Synoptiker, Für Joseph Schmidt*, Freiburg: Herder, 1973, 238–52.

Murphy-O'Connor, J., 'The Damascus Document Revisited', in K. Richards, ed., *SBL Seminar Papers*, Atlanta: Scholars Press 1986, 369–83.

Murray, R., 'Jews, Hebrews, Christians: Some needed Distinctions', *NT* 24(1982) 194–208.

Murray, R., 'Disaffected Judaism and Early Christianity', in J. Neusner and E. Frerichs, ed., *To See Ourselves as Others See Us*, 263–81.

Neusner, J., *Development of a Legend. Studies in the Traditions concerning Yohanan ben Zakkai*, Leiden: Brill, 1970.

Neusner, J., 'Studies in the *Taqqanoth* of Yavneh', *HTR* 63(1970) 183–98.

Neusner, J., *A History of the Mishnaic Law of Women*, Part Three, Leiden: Brill, 1980.

Neusner, J., *Judaism. The Evidence of the Mishnah*, Chicago: University Press, 1981.

Neusner, J., 'Galilee in the Time of Hillel: A Review', in *Formative Judaism. Religious, Literary and Historical Studies*, Brown Judaic Studies 37, Chico: Scholars Press, 1982.

Neusner, J., *Judaism in Society, the Evidence of Yerushalmi. Towards the Natural History of a Religion*, Chicago: University Press, 1983.

Neusner, J., *Messiah in Context. Israel's History and Destiny in Formative Judaism*, Philadelphia: Fortress Press, 1984.

Neusner, J., *Major Trends in Formative Judaism*, Third Series: *The Three Stages in the Formation of Judaism*, Brown Judaic Studies 99, Chico: Scholars Press 1985.

Neusner, J., *Judaism in the Beginning of Christianity*, London: SPCK, 1985.

Neusner, J., *Torah. From Scroll to Symbol in Formative Judaism*, Philadelphia: Fortress Press 1985.

Neusner, J., 'The History of a Biography. Yohanan ben Zakkai in the Canonical Literature of Formative Judaism', in *Formative Judaism. Religious, Historical and Literary Studies*, 5th Series, Brown Judaic Studies 91, Chico: Scholars Press, 1985, 79–96.

Neusner, J., 'Three Pictures of the Pharisees. A Reprise', ibid. 51–78.

Neusner, J., 'The Experience of the City in Late Antique Judaism', in W. Scott Green, ed., *Approaches to Ancient Judaism*, vol. 5, Atlanta: Scholars Press, 1985, 37–52.

Neusner, J., *The Mishnah before 70*, Brown Judaic Studies 51, Atlanta: Scholars Press, 1987.

Neusner, J., ed., *Christianity, Judaism and Other Greco-Roman Cults. Studies for Morton Smith at Sixty*, Four Parts, Leiden: Brill, 1975

Neusner, J. & Frerichs, E., ed., *'To See Ourselves as Others See Us'. Jews, Christians, Others in Antiquity*, Brown Studies in the Humanities, Chico: Scholars Press, 1985.

Neusner, J., Borgen, P., Frerichs, E., & Horsley, R. ed., *The Social World of Formative Judaism. Essays in Tribute of Howard Clark Kee*, Philadelphia: Fortress Press, 1988.

Neyrey, J., 'The Idea of Purity in Mark's Gospel', *Semeia* 35(1986) 91–127.

Nickelsburg, G.W.E., 'Riches, the Rich and God's Judgment in 1 Enoch 92–105 and the Gospel according to Luke', *NTS* 25(1978) 324–44.

Nickelsburg, G.W.E., 'Enoch, Levi and Peter: Recipients of Revelation in Upper Galilee', *JBL* 100(1981) 575–600.

Nickelsburg, G.W.E., 'Revealed Wisdom as a Criterion for Inclusion and Exclusion: From Jewish Sectarianism to Early Christianity', in J. Neusner and E. Frerichs, ed., *'To See Ourselves as Others See Us'*, 73–92.

Nickelsburg, G.W.E., 'I Enoch and Qumran Origins', in K. Richards, ed., *SBL Seminar Papers*, Atlanta: Scholars Press, 1986, 341–60.

O' Fearghail, F., 'A Study of the Role of Lk 1:1–4:44 in the Composition of Luke's Two-Volume Work', unpublished doctoral dissertation, P.I.B., Rome 1987.

O' Fearghail, F., 'Israel in Luke-Acts', *PIBA* 12(1988).

Ogden, S., *The Point of Christology*, London: SCM, 1982.

Olsen, B., *Structure and Meaning in the Fourth Gospel: A Text-Linguistic Analysis of John 2:1–11 and 4:1–42*, Lund: C.W.K. Gleerup, 1974.

Oppenheimer, A., *The Am Ha-Aretz. A Study of the Social History of the Jewish People in the Hellenistic-Roman Period*, Leiden: Brill, 1977.

O' Toole, R., 'Luke's Message in 9:1–50', *CBQ* 49(1987) 74–89.

Pancaro, S., 'The Church and Israel in St. John's Gospel', *NTS* 21(1975) 386–405.

Pancaro, S., *The Law in the Fourth Gospel*, Leiden: Brill, 1975.

Perdue, L., 'The Wisdom Sayings of Jesus', *Forum* 2, 3, 3–35.

Perrin, N., *What is Redaction Criticism?*, Philadelphia: Fortress Press, 1969.

Perrin, N., *Jesus and the Language of the Kingdom. Symbol and Metaphor in New Testament Interpretation*, Philadelphia: Fortress Press, 1976.

Petersen, N., *Literary Criticism for New Testament Critics*, Philadelphia: Fortress Press, 1978.

Petersen, N., 'Point of View in Mark's Narrative', *Semeia* 12(1978) 97–121.

Pixner, B., 'Searching for the New Testament Site of Bethsaida', BA 48(1985) 207–16.

Potterie, I. de la, 'Les deux noms de Jérusalem dans l'Évangile de Luc', RSR 69(1981) 59–70.

Pryor, J.W., 'John 4:44 and the *patris* of Jesus', *CBQ* 49(1987) 254–63.

Pummer, R., "Argarizin; A Criterion for Samaritan Provenance', *JSJ* 18(1987) 18–25.

Rabin, C., 'Hebrew and Aramaic in the First Century', in *Compendia*, 2, 1007–39.

Rappaport, U., 'Jewish-Pagan Relations and the Revolt against Rome in 66–70 c.e.', in *The Jerusalem Cathedra*, 2, ed. L. Levine, Jerusalem, 1981, 81–95.

Rappaport U., 'John of Gischala: From Galilee to Jerusalem', *JJS* 33(1982) 479–90.

Rappaport, U., 'John of Gischala in Galilee', in L. Levine, ed., *The Jerusalem Cathedra*, 3, Jerusalem, 1983, 46–57.

Rhoads, D., *Israel in Revolution, 6–74 c.e. A Political History based on the Writings of Josephus*, Philadelphia: Fortress, 1976.

Rhoads, D. & Michie, D., *Mark as Story. An Introduction to the Narrative of a Gospel*, Philadelphia: Fortress Press, 1982.

Riches, J., *Jesus and the Transformation of Judaism*, London: Darton, Longman and Todd, 1980.

Riches, J., 'Works and Words of Jesus the Jew', *Heythrop Journal* 17(1986) 53–62.

Ricoeur, P., *Hermeneutics and the Human Sciences*, E.T. Cambridge: University Press, 1981.

Riesenfeld, H., *The Gospel Tradition and its Beginnings. A Study in the Limits of Formgeschichte*, London: A.W. Mowbray, 1957.

Riesner, R., *Jesus als Lehrer. Eine Untersuchung zum Ursprung der Evangelien-Überlieferung*, WUNT 2 Reihe, 7, Tübingen: J.C.B. Mohr, 1981.

Rimmon-Kenan, S., *Narrative Fiction: Contemporary Poetics*, London and New York: Methuen, 1983.

Rivkin, E., 'The Internal City: Judaism and Urbanisation', *JSSR* 5(1966) 225–40.

Rivkin, E., *What Crucified Jesus?*, London: SCM 1984.

Robbins, V.K., *Jesus as Teacher. A Socio-Rhetorical Interpretation of Mark*, Philadelphia: Fortress Press, 1984.

Robinson, J.A.T., 'His Witness is True: A Test of the Johannine Claim', in E. Bammel and C.F.D. Moule, ed., *Jesus and the Politics of his Day*, 453–76.

Robinson, J.M., *The Problem of History in Mark*, London: SCM, 1957.

Roth, C., 'The Debate on the Loyal Sacrifices', *HTR* 53(1960) 93–7.

Safrai, S., *Die Wahlfahrt im Zeitalter des zweitens Tempels*, Neukirchen-Vlyun: Neukirchener Verlag, 1981.

Safrai, S. & Stern, M., *Compendia Rerum Judaicarum ad Novum Testamentum. The Jewish People in the First Century*, vol. 1 Assen: van Gorcum, 1974, and vol. 2 Philadelphia: Fortress Press, 1978.

Sanders, E.P., *Jesus and Judaism*, London: SCM 1985.

Sanders, J., *The Jews in Luke-Acts*, London: SCM, 1986.

Sanders, J.A., 'From Is 61 to Lk 4', in J. Neusner, ed., *Christianity, Judaism and Other Greco-Roman Cults*, Part One, Leiden: Brill, 1975, 75–106.

Sanders, Jack T., *Ben Sira and Demotic Wisdom*, SBLMS 28, Chico: Scholars Press, 1983.

Schillebeeckx, E., *Jesus. An Experiment in Christology*, E.T. New York: Seabury, 1979.

Schillebeeckx, E., *The Christ. The Experience of Jesus Christ as Lord*, E.T. New York: Seabury, 1982.

Schnackenburg, R., *The Gospel according to John*, 3 vols. E.T. London: Burns Oates, 1980–82.

Schwank, B., 'Neue Funde in Nabatäerstädten und ihre Bedeutung für die Neutestamentliche Exegese', *NTS* 29(1983) 429–35.

Scholes, R. & Kellogg, R., *The Nature of Narrative*, New York: Oxford University Press, 1966.

Schwartz, D., 'Josephus and Nicolaus on the Pharisees', *JSJ* 14(1983) 157–71.

Schwartz, D., 'The Three Temples of 4Q Florilegium', RQ 10 (1979) 83–91.

Schürmann, H., *Das Lukasevangelium*, 2 vols. HTKNT 3, 1 and 2, Freiburg: Herder, 1969.

Schürer, E. Vermes, G. & Miller F., *The History of the Jewish People in the Age of Jesus Christ*, 4 vols, Edinburgh: T. and T. Clark, 1973–85.

Scott, B. Brandon, *Jesus, Symbol-Maker of the Kingdom*, Philadelphia: Fortress Press, 1981.

Scott, B. Brandon, 'Essaying the Rock: the Authenticity of the Jesus Parable Tradition', *Forum*, 2, 1(1986) 3–53.

Segundo, J. L., *The Historical Jesus of the Synoptics*, E.T. New York: Orbis, 1985.

Shanin, T., 'The Nature and Logic of Peasant Economies', *JPS* 1(1974) 186–204.

Sherwin-White, A.N., *Roman Society and Roman Law in the New Testament*, Oxford: University Press, 1963.

Smallwood, M., 'High Priests and Politics in Roman Palestine', *JTS* 13(1962) 17-37.

Smith, J., 'The Social Description of Early Christianity', *RSR* 1 (1975) 19–25.

Smith, J., 'The Temple and the Magician', in W. Meeks and J. Jervell, ed., *God's Christ and his People. Studies in Honour of Nils Alstrup Dahl*, Bergen: Universitetsvorlaget, 1977, 233–47.

Smith, M., 'On the Wine God in Palestine. Gen. 18, Jn 2 and Achilles Tatius', in *Salo M. Baron Jubilee Volume*, Jerusalem 1975, English Section, 815–29.

Smith, M., *Jesus the Magician*, New York: Harper and Row, 1978.

Sobrino. J., *Christology at the Crossroads*, E.T. New York: Orbis, 1978.

Stemberger, G., 'Galilee—Land of Salvation?', in W.D. Davies, *The Gospel and the Land*, Berkley, 1974, Appendix 1V, 409–38.

Stendahl, K., 'Quis et Unde? An Analysis of Matthew 1–2', in G. Stanton, ed., *The interpretation of Matthew*, London: SPCK, 1983, 56–66.

Stock, K., *Boten aus dem Mit-Ihm-Sein. Das Verhältnis zwischen Jesus und den Zwölf nach Markus*, Analecta Biblica 70, Rome: P.I.B. Press, 1975.

Strange, J., 'Archaelogy and the Religion of Judaism in Palestine', in *ANRW* II,19.1, 646–85.

Strange J., 'The Capernaum and Herodium Publications. A Review Article', *BASOR* 226(1977) 65–73.

Strange, J. & Longstaff, T., 'Sepphoris (Sippori) 1983, Notes and News', and 'Sepphoris (Sippori)—Survey 1984', *IEJ* 34(1984) 51–2 and 269–70.

Strange, J. & Sharks, H., 'Synagogue where Jesus Preached found at Capernaum', *BAR* 9(1983)24–31.

Struthers Malbon, E., 'Galilee and Jerusalem: History and Literature in Marcan Interpretation', *CBQ* 44(1982) 242–55.

Struthers Malbon, E., 'The Jesus of Mark and the Sea of Galilee', *JBL* 103(1984) 363–73.

Struthers Malbon, E., 'Fallible Followers: Women and Men in the Gospel of Mark', *Semeia* 27(1984) 29–48.

Struthers Malbon, E., 'Τῇ οἰκία αὐτοῦ: Mark 2:15 in context', *NTS* 31(1985) 282–92.

Struthers Malbon, E., 'Disciples/Crowds/Whoever: Marcan Char acters and Readers', *NT* 28(1986) 104–30.

Tannehill, R., *The Sword of his Mouth*, *Semeia* Supplements 1, Missoula: Scholars Press 1975.

Tannehill, R., 'The Disciples in Mark. The Function of a Narrative Role', *JR* 57(1977) 134–57.

Tannehill, R., 'The Gospel of Mark as Narrative Christology', *Semeia* 16(1979) 57–95.

Tannehill, R., 'Israel in Luke-Acts. A Tragic Story', *JBL* 104(1985) 69–85.

Tannehill, R., *The Narrative Unity of Luke-Acts*, vol.1, Philadelphia: Fortress Press, 1986.

Teixidor, J., *The Pagan God. Popular Religion in the Greco-Roman Near East*, N. Jersey: Princeton University Press, 1977.

Theissen, G., 'Wanderradikalismus. Literatursoziologische Aspekte der Überlieferung von Worten Jesu im Urchristentum', *ZTK* 70(1973) 245–71.

Theissen, G., 'Die Tempelweissagung Jesu. Prophetie im Spannungsfeld zwischen Temple und Land', *TZ* 32(1976) 144–58.

Theissen, G., 'Wir haben alles verlassen' (Mk 10:28). Nachfolge und soziale Entwurzelung in der jüdisch-palästinischen Gesellschaft des 1 Jahrhunderts n. Ch.', *NT* 19(1977) 161–96.

Theissen, G., *Sociology of Early Palestinian Christianity*, E.T. Philadelphia: Fortress Press, 1977.

Theissen, G., *The Miracle Stories in the Early Christian Tradition*, E.T. Edinburgh: T. and T. Clark, 1983.

Theissen, G., *Studien zur Soziologie des Urchristentums*, 2nd edn Tübingen: J.C.B. Mohr, 1983.

Theissen, G., *The Shadow of the Galilean*, 1987.

Tolbert, M.A., *Perspective on the Parables. An Approach to Multiple Interpretations*, Philadelphia: Fortress Press 1979.

Tracy, D., *The Analogical Imagination. Christian Theology and the Culture of Pluralism*, London: SCM, 1981.

Trilling, W., *Das Wahre Israel. Studien zur Theologie des Matthäusevangeliums*, 3rd edn *SANT* 10, Munich, 1964.

Tuckett, C., ed., *The Messianic Secret*, London: SPCK, 1984.

Turner, V., *Image and Pilgrimage in Christian Culture. Anthropological Perspectives*, Oxford: Blackwell, 1978.

Tzaferis, V., 'New Archaeological Evidence on Ancient Capernaum', *BA* 48(1985) 207–16.

Vale, R., 'Literary Sources in Archaeological Description. The Case of Galilee, Galilees and Galilean', *JSJ* 18(1987) 210–28.

Vermes, G., *Jesus the Jew*, London: Collins, 1975.

Vermes, G., *Jesus and the World of Judaism*, London: SCM, 1983.

Völkel, M., 'Der Anfang Jesu in Galiläa. Bemerkungen zum Gebrauch und zur Funktion Galiläas in den Lukanischen Schriften', *ZNW* 64(1973) 222–32.

Von Rad, G., *Theology of the Old Testament*, 2 vols. E.T. London: Oliver and Boyd, 1965.

Von Tilborg, S., *The Sermon on the Mount as an Ideological Intervention*, Assen: van Gorcum, 1986.

Von Wahlde, U.C., 'The Johannine "Jews": A Critical Survey', *NTS* 28(1982) 33–60.

Weeden, T., 'The Heresy that necessitated Mark's Gospel', *ZNW* 59(1968) 145–68.

Weinberg, G.D., 'Hellenistic Glass from Tel Anafa in Upper Galilee', *Journal of Glass Studies* 12(1970) 17–27.

Weinert, F.D., 'Luke, the Temple and Jesus' Saying about Luke's Abandoned House (Lk 13:34–35)', *CBQ* 44(1982) 68–76.

Wengst, K., *Bedrängte Gemeinde und verherrlichter Christus. Der historische Ort des Johannesevangelium als Schlüssel zu seiner Interpretation*, Neukirchen-Vluyn: Neukirchener Verlag, 1983.

Wilder, A., *Jesus Parables and the War on Myths. Essays on Imagination in the Scriptures*, London: SPCK 1982.

Wilson, S., *The Law in Luke-Acts*, SNTS Monographs, Cambridge: University Press, 1983.

Wright, N.T., 'Constraints and the Jesus of History', *SJT* 39(1986) 189–210.

Yadin, Y., *The Temple Scroll*, E.T. 3 vols., Jerusalem: Israel Exploration Society, 1984.

Yoder, J., *The Politics of Jesus*, Grand Rapids: Eerdmans, 1972.

Young, N.H., 'Jesus and the Sinners: Some Queries', *JSNT* 19 (1983) 73–5.

Zeitlin, S., 'Who were the Galileans? New Light on Josephus' Activity in Galilee', *JQR* 64(1974) 189–203.

Ziesler, J., 'Luke and the Pharisees', *NTS* 25(1979) 146–57.

Zimmerli, W., 'The Land in the Pre-Exilic and Early Post-Exilic Prophets' in *Understanding the Word. Essays in Honor of B.W. Anderson*, ed. J.T. Butler, E.W. Conrad, B.C. Ollenburger, Sheffield: JSOT Press 1985, 247–64.

Index Of Ancient Sources

Subject and Name Index